Working and Living
AUSTRALIA

Contents

Author's acknowledgements

Special thanks to Don Ambrose for his invaluable assistance and to Elizabeth and John de Angelis for all they did, and to Angela Shirras for her constant support. Thanks too to Martin Gilbert for providing very useful additional research on a range of topics, particularly crime. Iain MacIntyre deserves a credit for his expert advice with dangerous creatures. Ginny Farrugia was a great help with health and safety and Ruth McGeough provided real practical help. Dave Healy was incredibly diligent with additional information, while Mark Maidment should be thanked for his hospitality.

About the author

Jane Egginton is an award-winning travel writer and photographer who has been writing and editing guide books for more than 15 years. A member of the British Guild of Travel Writers, she produces glossy, highly illustrated coffee-table books and comprehensive, fact-filled publications, as well as destination articles for international and national magazines and newspapers. Jane has travelled extensively throughout the world, writing about everything from adventure travel in Central America to country walking in Britain for publishers such as Reader's Digest, Insight, Berlitz, Thomas Cook and the AA. She has a tendency to stay near the sea, whether circumnavigating India by rail, visiting Britain's seaside resorts, flying around Brazil's coastline or Caribbean island-hopping.

Jane has lived and worked in Australia and dreams of swapping her small north London flat for her sister's four-bedroom house with Balinese deck by the beach in Sydney. Although she originally planned to buy a ramshackle property on Croatia's Adriatic Coast, she plumped instead for a purpose-built apartment on Bulgaria's Black Sea, which proved easier to rent out. Jane is author of *Buying a Property in Eastern Europe*, also published by Cadogan.

Conceived and produced for Cadogan Guides by
Navigator Guides Ltd, The Old Post Office, Swanton Novers, Melton Constable, Norfolk, NR24 2AJ
info@navigatorguides.com
www.navigatorguides.com

Cadogan Guides
2nd Floor
233 High Holborn
London WC1V 7DN
info@cadoganguides.co.uk
www.cadoganguides.com

The Globe Pequot Press
246 Goose Lane, PO Box 480, Guilford,
Connecticut 06437–0480

Cover design: Sarah Rianhard-Gardner
Cover photographs: © Jane Egginton and © Brand X Pictures/Alamy
Colour essay photographs © Jane Egginton
Series editor: Linda McQueen
Editor: Susannah Wight
Proofreader: Patricia Briggs
Indexing: Isobel McLean

Printed in Finland by WS Bookwell Oy

A catalogue record for this book is available from the British Library
ISBN 1-86011-204-8

The author and publishers have made every effort to ensure the accuracy of the information in this book at the time of going to press. However, they cannot accept any responsibility for any loss, injury or inconvenience resulting from the use of information contained in this guide.

Please help us to keep this guide up to date. We have done our best to ensure that the information in it is correct at the time of going to press. But places are constantly changing, and rules and regulations fluctuate. We would be delighted to receive any comments concerning existing entries or omissions. Authors of the best letters will receive a copy of the Cadogan Guide of their choice.

Introduction

This book is about the reality, not the hype, of working and living in Australia. It takes a very human approach to helping you make both the decision to move and the move itself: the author has interviewed numerous experts in everything from immigration to pet transportation, and distilled the experiences of many British people who have taken the plunge. It looks at the big issues, taking you through the immigration maze and the political system, as well as helping you with the little things, such as what sports to watch on television and where to buy Marmite and Angel Delight. It answers all-important questions such as 'Are Australians really as relaxed as we think they are?' and 'What do locals call an off-licence?'

The first chapter, **Getting to Know Australia**, introduces you to the country, telling its history from the Ice Age to the 21st century, whetting your appetite with descriptions of the food and wine, and describing the weather, geography and dangerous creatures that live there. The next chapter, **Profiles of the Regions**, takes you on a tour of the country to help you decide where you might want to settle. **Australia Today** looks at contemporary life, politics, family and women, the media, art and culture, and internal issues. Chapter 4, **First Steps**, examines why you might want to move to Australia and gives you all the information you need about how to get there, advising you on how to pick your flight and airline and even on how to avoid jetlag. Chapter 5, **Red Tape**, while not light reading, is a crucial chapter, because without cutting through it, and securing yourself a visa, you will not be able either to live or to work in Australia.

The largest chapter, **Living in Australia**, guides you on how to find a home, whether renting or buying, and advises you about the intricacies of home utilities. Here we tell you where you can watch *Coronation Street* or your favourite American sitcom, and how to bring your cat to Australia safely from the other side of the world. This chapter also covers social services and retirement, education, study and sport. **Working in Australia** aims to assist you with gaining employment and inspire you with business ideas, informing you about subjects as diverse as business etiquette and volunteering. Finally, the **References** chapter contains essential facts, as well as advice about what books to read and films to watch, and details on subjects from festivals to rainfall.

Getting to Know Australia

Natives call Australia the 'lucky country' and they were not the first to think so. Aboriginal people, the first settlers, believe their land was created in the 'Dreamtime' and have a spiritual connection with it that is at the heart of their very being. D. H. Lawrence wrote, 'Australia's like an open door with the blue beyond... You just walk out of the world and into Australia,' and when Charles Darwin visited Hobart, Tasmania, aboard the *Beagle* in 1836, he declared, 'If I was obliged to emigrate I should certainly prefer this place.'

Of course, the English have a long history of migration to Australia, although the first shiploads could have been more willing arrivals. Despite the familiarities of the language and culture, and a history closely entwined with the English, Australia is at the same time undeniably foreign. The old joke about two countries divided by a common language rings as true here as it does of America. Situated quite literally on the other side of the world, the country has a tropical climate and unique wildlife, although cities like Melbourne can feel positively English. Australia has abundant fruits of the land and sea, which have spawned both bush tucker and food and wine with a world-class reputation.

History

Aboriginal People

Australia's original inhabitants, whose origins date back to the Ice Age, have the longest continuous cultural history in the world. There is much that is not known about this time in prehistory, but most experts agree that the first Aborigines arrived by sea from Indonesia about 70,000 years ago. Historically, their biological isolation made them far removed from all other people in the world, while their ability to adapt to the unforgiving Australian landscape only increased their cultural isolation. Today, there are around 400,000 Aboriginal people living in the country – one of the least understood people in the world.

Dreamtime

The beginning of the world is known as 'Dreamtime' or 'the Dreaming' by Aboriginal people. They believe that during this period their ancestors came from beneath the earth to become different elements of nature, such as animals, plants, rivers, mountains and sky. They completed journeys on an epic scale and, as they travelled, they 'sang' life into the landscape, creating 'song-lines'. As they did this, the spirit ancestors awarded custody of the land to different groups, along with distinct language, culture and laws.

The Dreamtime is not just a creation myth for the Aboriginal people, but has a sacred resonance for them today. They talk of 'jiva' or 'guruwari', a seed power found in the earth, and believe that every meaningful activity, event or life process leaves behind a vibrational residue in the earth. According to Aboriginal belief, the land's features – its mountains, rocks, riverbeds and waterholes – were formed by these unseen vibrations, so that nature's creations are spiritual footprints of the metaphysical beings whose actions created our world.

Although we tend to think of Aborigines as one homogenous group, communities across the country consist of very distinct groups, with unique languages, traditions and lifestyles. Aboriginal people were supremely expert in adapting to their environments, with 'territories' ranging from lush woodland areas to harsh desert surroundings. Different groups needed to develop different skills and build a unique body of knowledge about their particular territories. There are more than 200 languages spoken, making Aboriginal Australia one of the most linguistically diverse areas on the planet, so that within just tens of miles you could pass through an area with languages more different than Russian is from Hindi.

Land and identity are inseparable for Aboriginal people. The ownership of land and sea is passed down the generations from the community's elders. It is deeply sacred and involves caring for the physical environment and the ancestors who live there. Through a system of 'managers', who usually have a connection to the land through their mothers, and 'owners', who generally are linked by their fathers, both a practical and spiritual form of caretaking occurs, although these obligations are not documented in any way. The environment is not just economic, but social and spiritual. Particularly in the north, there is a sense of the land as a living being which, like a person, as well as providing and giving energy, needs nurturing.

Timeline of Aboriginal History from 1800

1804 Settlers in Tasmania are authorised to shoot Aboriginal people.

1810 Aboriginal people are moved to 'missions', in practice to be used as slaves and taught a European way of life. The government introduces a policy of absorbing Aborigines into the white population in the hope that their reproduction can be controlled.

1824 There is increased conflict between European settlers and Aboriginal people, and over 100 Aboriginal people are massacred at Bathurst, New South Wales.

1830 With the establishment of colonies, Aboriginal people in Tasmania are forced off their land and settled on Flinders Island, where many die due to terrible living conditions.

1834 In Western Australia a large number of Aboriginal people are killed.

1837 British Parliament reports that genocide is occurring in the Antipodes. It recommends the appointment of a protector of Aborigines, which sets in motion the involvement of the Catholic Church in missionary work and the establishment of schools for Aboriginal children. Two hundred Aboriginal people are killed in New South Wales.

1838 A massacre of Aboriginal people in New South Wales is the first in Australian history where the offenders are punished by law.

1840 An entire Aboriginal community is killed at Long Lagoon.

1841 A massacre of Aboriginal people occurs at Rufus River with 30 dead.

1847 Police are brought to Queensland to kill Aboriginal people and open up the land for settlement.

1858 The non-Aboriginal population reaches one million.

1868 150 Aboriginal people are killed resisting arrest in the Kimberley.

1869 The Victorian Board for the Protection of Aborigines is established, giving the right to order the removal of any child to a reformatory or industrial school. Later, similar legislation is passed in other colonies: New South Wales (1883), Queensland (1897), Western Australia (1905) and South Australia (1911).

1876 The last surviving tribal Tasmanian Aborigine dies in Hobart.

1884 A massacre of Aboriginal people takes place on the McKinlay River, Northern Territory.

1897 The Queensland Aboriginal Protection and Restriction of the Sale of Opium Act allows for the removal of Aboriginal people on to land reserves. This means that Aboriginal people are confined to reserves and banned from towns and every aspect of life is controlled, including the right to marry, guardianship of children, the right to work outside reserves, and management of assets.

1901 Aboriginal people are denied citizenship and indigenous people are not included in any census, excluding them from civil liberties.

1911 The South Australian Aborigines Act makes the Chief Protector the legal guardian of every Aboriginal and 'half-caste' child under 21, with control over the child's place of residence. The Northern Territory Aboriginals Ordinance makes the Chief Protector the legal guardian of every Aboriginal and 'half-caste' child under 18.

1914 Aboriginal people serve in the First World War, despite the Defence Act 1909, which prohibits any person not of 'substantially European' origin from serving. Aboriginal soldiers are among Australian troops at Gallipoli.

1915 The New South Wales Aborigines Protection Board is empowered to remove Aboriginal children. Similar policies allowing the removal of Aboriginal children apply in other states and these practices continue right up to the 1970s. Over one-third of Aboriginal children are forcibly taken from their parents to provide household servants and stockmen for non-Aboriginal society.

1920 The Aboriginal population is estimated to be at its lowest, at between 60,000 and 70,000.

1926 Following the killing of a European in Dala, Western Australia, 11 Aboriginal people are murdered in police custody; no prosecutions follow.

1927 A federal law for family endowment excludes Aboriginal people and instead payments go to the Aborigines Protection Board. Aboriginal people are denied maternity allowance and old age pension. Aboriginal people are banned from central Perth until 1948.

1928 A massacre takes place in Coniston, Northern Territory, in which settlers and police admit to shooting over 30 Aboriginal people after a white dingo trapper is killed.

1934 Under the Aborigines Act, Aboriginal people can apply to 'cease being Aboriginal' and have access to the same rights as 'whites'.

1937 The first Commonwealth and State conference on 'native welfare' adopts 'assimilation' as the national policy, which results in the destruction of Aboriginal identity and culture, justification of dispossession and the removal of Aboriginal children from their communities. At the same time, segregationist practices continue until the 1960s with separate sections in theatres; hospitals with separate wards; hotels refusing drinks; and schools refusing enrolment to Aboriginal children.

1939–45 Although not recognised as citizens, Aboriginal people serve in the Second World War.

1940 Discrimination against Aboriginal people begins to raise community disquiet. South Australian Premier Playford requests Commonwealth Government to pay maternity benefits along with the old age pension to Aboriginal people.

1943 An Exemption Certificate is introduced, which means that certain Aboriginal people are entitled to vote, drink alcohol and move freely.

1945 Aboriginal workers on stations in the Pilbara, Western Australia, go on strike for better wages and conditions; the strike lasts until 1949.

1951 Aboriginal assimilation – Federal Government convenes the Australian Conference for Native Welfare, which officially adopts a policy of 'assimilation' for Aboriginal people. 'Assimilation means, in practical terms, that it is expected that all persons of Aboriginal birth or mixed blood in Australia will live like white Australians do.'

1960 Aboriginal people become eligible for social service benefits.

1961 A Conference of Native Welfare Ministers agrees to strategies to assist the assimilation of Aboriginal people. These include the removal of discriminatory legislation and restrictive practices, the incorporation of Aboriginal people into the economy through welfare measures and education and training, and the education of non-Aboriginal Australians about Aboriginal culture and history. After the conference, all states and territories amend their legislation. The conference marks the beginning of modern land rights movement and widespread awakening by non-Aboriginal Australians to claims for justice by Aboriginal and Torres Strait Islander people.

1962 Aboriginal people finally get the vote.

1963 Yirrkala Aboriginal people from Arnhem Land, Northern Territory, protest to the Commonwealth Government about part of their reserve land being given over for mining.

1965 The 'Freedom Ride' is led into northwestern New South Wales. It demonstrates the extent of discrimination against Aboriginal people in country towns, including refusal of service and segregation. As a result, the Australian Labour Party drops the White Australia policy from its party platform.

1966 South Australia passes the Aboriginal Lands Trust Bill and the Prohibition of Discrimination Bill, the first state act prohibiting discrimination on grounds of race, colour or country of origin.

1967 A referendum on Aboriginal Rights results in 90 per cent of the Australian population voting to give the Commonwealth power to legislate for Aboriginal and Torres Strait Islander people and to include them in the Census.

1968 The Commonwealth Government establishes the Office of Aboriginal Affairs.

1970 Limited land-lease rights are given to Aboriginal people on Northern Territory reserves.

1971 The United Nations holds an International Year for Action to Combat Racism, and the Aboriginal flag is flown for the first time in Victoria Square, Adelaide. The first Aboriginal person is elected to Federal Parliament.

1972 A policy of self-determination for Aboriginal people is adopted by Federal Government, which means they have the right to cultural and linguistic maintenance and management of natural resources on Aboriginal land.

1973 The census numbers the national Indigenous population at 160,000.

1976 The Aboriginal Land Rights Act is passed, transferring reserve land to Aboriginal ownership.

1978 The Aboriginal Development Commission is established and the Northern Territory Aboriginal Sacred Sites Ordinance is passed, instituting prosecution for trespass and desecration of Aboriginal sites.

1980 A dispute at Noonkanbah, Western Australia, over drilling on sacred sites draws national and international attention to Aboriginal rights.

1981 The South Australian Pitjantjajara Land Rights Act is passed, the first such State Act.

1984 The 'Goondiwindi riot' between Aboriginal and non-Aboriginal residents of Goondiwindi on the New South Wales and Queensland border leads to public acknowledgment of poor living standards and low socio-economic expectations of Aboriginal people in the area. Tens of thousands of Aboriginal and Torres Strait Islander people and their supporters march through the streets of Sydney on Australia Day, 26 January, to celebrate their survival, during national bicentennial celebrations.

1991 The *Report of the Royal Commission into Aboriginal Deaths in Custody* is tabled in Federal Parliament, detailing the lives and deaths of 99 Aboriginal people who died in gaol; 45 were people who were separated from their families as children. As a result, Federal Government begins to address disparity in living conditions between Aboriginal and non-Aboriginal Australians. The Council for Aboriginal Reconciliation is set up by the Commonwealth Government to foster better understanding between Indigenous people and the wider Australian community.

1993 In the 'Redfern Park speech', Prime Minister Keating launches Australian celebration of the International Year of the World's Indigenous Peoples by accepting responsibility for past mistreatment of Aboriginal people and calling for reconciliation. The Native Title Act recognises the native title rights of Indigenous Australians who have maintained a 'continuing connection' with their land and waters.

1994 The Native Title Tribunal is established to hear land claims. A Federal election results in a second Aboriginal person being elected to Federal Parliament.

Aboriginal People in Australia Today

By the end of the 19th century most Aboriginal people had been made part of white communities, causing death for many from exposure to European diseases. Incredibly, it was only in 1967 that Aboriginal people were granted full citizenship rights. It wasn't until the 1970s that the country's original settlers began to be heard and in 1976 The Aboriginal Land Rights Act was passed, recognising tribal connections with certain territories. A landmark case was brought in 1992 when the land rights of the country's indigenous people were

Boomerangs that Don't Come Back

The classic comic Aussie icon was invented by the Aboriginal people as a very powerful weapon, although it was also found in ancient Egypt and Eastern Europe. 10–30-inch pieces of wood were taken from the roots of the Mulga or Black Wattle trees, which already had the right shape, and shaped into a curve. By throwing the boomerang hard – and these ones did not come back – Aborigines could decapitate a small animal such as a baby kangaroo at long range. Larger and heavier fighting versions were called killer boomerangs, and could cause serious injury during tribal warfare.

There were other uses, too. Boomerangs were used to cut grass to create ceremonial sites, and even for digging up earth to make ovens. In ceremonies, two boomerangs were clapped together to make a rhythm alongside the didgeridoo; these kind were usually decorated, imitations of which can be found in tourist gift shops all over the country. The boomerangs that came back – created by making them flat on one side and convex on the other – were used in sport. Thrown overhand, they would circle in the air before landing at the feet of the thrower.

recognised. Eddie Koiki Mabo of the Torres Strait Islands maintained he had a right to his traditional land, and the court overruled the original law that no one owned the land before the Europeans arrived. As a result, Aboriginal people were given increased welfare benefits and wages, and greater autonomy.

The last mass-killing of Aboriginal people was in 1926 after a European-Australian was reportedly killed by an Aborigine, prompting a local policeman to collect a gang of people to kill the local tribe. Ill-treatment of Aboriginal people continues today. In December 2004, newspapers reported yet another death in custody of an Aboriginal man, and in February of that year there were major race riots in Sydney, sparked by the death of an Aboriginal teenager.

The story of the modern-day Aborigine is a tragic one. Essentially dislocated from their homeland, which has much greater significance than just land ownership, they have effectively lost their will to live. Stripped of their knowledge, their values alien to the modern world and their self-respect, many have turned to drink. Many are unemployed, with health inferior to that of people in the developing world, and they are the poorest group in the country.

The Lost Generation

An especially tragic part of the Aboriginal history in Australia involves the government programme that took Aboriginal children, particularly those of mixed race, without their parents' consent and gave them to white families. The thinking behind this was that it would assimilate the children into mainstream culture. While many of them received an education they wouldn't otherwise have had, and a material comfort they would not have experienced, this programme destroyed families. Many parents had no idea where their children were and those who did were not allowed to make contact with them. There was no enquiry about the practice until 1996, when the government report *Bringing Them Home* acknowledged that between 1910 and the 1970s as many as 30 per cent of children were taken from their family homes by force, creating a 'Lost Generation'. The Australian government has recently instituted National Sorry Day to make a formal apology for this practice.

Aboriginal Art and Culture

Art, like everything else in Aboriginal culture, is inextricably linked with the land. 'Culture is the land; take that away and you take away our reason for existence. We are dancing, singing, and painting for the land. We are celebrating the land. Removed from our lands, we are literally removed from ourselves,' says one Aborigine. Originally, traditional art was sacred and seen only by those with the proper knowledge during ceremonial practices, but in recent years it has begun to be created for the public. It may take the form of carvings on rock or bark, sculptures in wood or painting on head-dresses, but it almost always draws on the 'Dreamtime' as inspiration.

Music is traditionally played at significant events, such as battles, to bring the rains or to heal. It is an organic process that is passed on through the generations and very much a communal event. Aboriginal musical tradition varies greatly between the different communities but broadly falls into one of three types. Ceremonial music is reserved for the initiated and is separate for women, men and children; semi-sacred music is performed during the initiation of boys; and songs for entertainment are the only form of music that can be carried out by anyone and crosses over between tribes.

Europeans

Convicts

Most of the convicts brought over from England were incredibly poor and illiterate and suffered terrible conditions and social injustices. There were a significant number from a variety of other backgrounds, including Indian, West Indian, Chinese and French. Most were young, the average age being just 26, and many were children. It didn't take long for a class system to establish itself among the convicts, with those born of convicts branded 'currency' while the offspring of officials were called 'sterling'. Released convicts set up a class of 'emancipists', which was scorned by soldiers and the free population; Australia's first police force was a band of 12 of the most well-behaved ex-prisoners.

Rations were strict in the early days, and many convicts starved. A typical day's food would consist of: breakfast – a roll and a bowl of watery porridge; lunch – a roll with dried meat; dinner – a roll and possibly a cup of tea.

Waltzing Matilda

Much more famous than the Australian national anthem (which was 'God save the Queen [King]' until 1984 when it became 'Advance Australia Fair') is the song that tells the tale of thousands of Australians who roamed the outback during the Depression looking for jobs. These 'swagmen' were so called because they carried their few belongings on their back in a bag or 'swag', along with their 'matilda', or bedroll. In the words of the song, a swagman camps by a 'billabong', a water hole, and boils up his 'billy', or pan of water, under the shade of a 'coolibah', a kind of gum tree. He catches a sheep, or 'jumbuck', and hides it in his 'tuckerbag', or food bag.

Once a jolly swagman camped by a billabong,
Under the shade of a coolibah tree;
And he sang as he watched and waited till his billy boiled,
You'll come a-waltzing Matilda with me!

Waltzing Matilda, Waltzing Matilda,
You'll come a-waltzing Matilda with me,
And he sang as he watched and waited till his billy boiled,
You'll come a-waltzing Matilda with me!

Down came a jumbuck to drink at that billabong,
Up jumped the swagman and grabbed him with glee,
And he shoved that jumbuck into his tuckerbag,
You'll come a-waltzing Matilda with me!

Waltzing Matilda, Waltzing Matilda,
You'll come a-waltzing Matilda with me,
And he sang as he watched and waited till his billy boiled,
You'll come a-waltzing Matilda with me!

'Terra Australis Incognita'

Captain Cook was not the first person to 'discover' Australia. The Aboriginal people had established a close relationship with their country over the tens of thousands of years they had lived there. By the time Cook arrived, the west and the north had already been mapped by the Dutch, Spanish and Portuguese explorers who had landed on the shores. However, Cook was the first to stumble across the East Coast's Botany Bay in his ship the *Endeavour*, and on 22 August 1700, in Queensland, he claimed the whole of the east coast for King George III.

In 1787 the first fleet of eleven ships, with around 800 convicts and supplies for two years, was sent out as a way of easing overcrowding in Britain's prisons, and colonisation began, a system that continued until 1853. Free settlers followed and Aboriginal people were forced off their land to make way for mining or farming, and materials were sent out to England where the industrial revolution was taking place.

Australians commemorate the founding of the new Australian nation with celebrations throughout the country on 26 January each year. For the indigenous population, though, it is a day of protest and mourning, as it marks the desecration of their history.

The Australian Gold Rush

Early gold discoveries in Australia around 1844 were initially kept quiet, for fear that a gold rush would plunge the largely convict population into chaos and lawlessness. However, just four years later, the rush to search for gold in California depleted the new colony's small population and forced the authorities to think differently about Australian gold. In 1851 Edward Hargraves'

Key Dates in Australian History

70,000 BC Aboriginal people are thought to have emigrated to Australia from other countries.
42,000 BC Aboriginal engravings in South Australia date back to this time.
35,000 BC Aboriginal people are believed to have reached Tasmania.
1300 Marco Polo talks of a great unexplored southern land.
1616 Dirk Hartog, a Dutch explorer, sails to Western Australia.
1770 Captain James Cook lands on the east coast of Australia and claims it for Britain.
1804 Hobart Town is established in Tasmania.
1851 The gold rush begins in New South Wales.
1868 The last convicts are transported to Australia.
1873 Ayers Rock is seen by Europeans.
1901 The Commonwealth of Australia is born.
1914–18 Australian troops fight in the First World War.
1927 The first Federal Parliament is held in Canberra.
1932 Opening of the Sydney Harbour Bridge.
1939–45 Australian troops fight in Second World War.
1956 Melbourne hosts the Olympics.
1965 Australian troops sent to the Vietnam War.
1971 Neville Bonner becomes the first Aboriginal person to become a member of parliament.
1973 The opening of the Sydney Opera House.
1983 Australia wins the America's Cup.
1988 Bicentenary and the opening of the new Parliament House in Canberra.
2000 Sydney hosts the Olympics.
2002 UN criticises holding asylum-seekers in detention camps until visa applications processed.
2002 88 citizens killed in a bombing in Bali, Indonesia.

discovery of gold in New South Wales marked the beginning of the Australian gold rush. Towns appeared overnight, vanishing just as quickly when gold was found somewhere else. When deposits of gold were large, permanent settlements developed, as in the case of Kalgoorlie, Coolgardie and Ballarat. The largest nugget found was the 'Welcome Stranger', weighing an amazing 78.4 kilograms and worth the equivalent of about 50 years' salary for most people.

Notions of Nationhood

Although in the early 1900s Australians had a strong sense of pride about their country, many of them at this time were ambivalent about the idea of Australian nationhood. Aligning themselves closely with Britain and its empire, they fought with Britain in the Boer War and then in the Second World War. However, during the Second World War, when America protected the country from the Japanese, Australia shifted its allegiance and went on to support the USA in the Korean and Vietnam wars.

The Bush Legend

Despite the fact that until the 1960s most immigrants arrived in Australia by ship, and the ocean has a huge influence on everyday life in island Australia, the outback has an enormous resonance in the Australian psyche. Those people who first went out into the interior were true pioneers, smallholders who had farms or sheep and who struggled against the elements with practically no assistance from anyone, and who shunned any kind of authority. The 'Bush legend' may be just that, but it continues to have an undeniable force today.

Federation

One of the triggers of the push for an Australian Federation was the 1890s depression, which highlighted the inefficiencies of the six colonies and the need to unite them under one federal government. Other factors were a perceived need for a common immigration policy, fear of France and Germany, which were expanding into the region, and the desire for a national army and navy. The Federation Movement was led by New South Wales Premier, Sir Henry Parkes. It led to the adoption by the British government of an act to constitute the Commonwealth of Australia in 1900, with Queen Victoria giving her assent. When the act came into effect in 1901, the states joined together and the Commonwealth of Australia was created. After the Second World War the government embarked on a programme of immigration (*see* below), in which more than five million Europeans went to live in Australia.

Melbourne became the temporary seat of government while a purpose-designed capital city, Canberra, was built. The future King George V opened the

Rebel Without a Cause?

For many, the notorious criminal Ned Kelly embodies the spirit of the Bush Legend. Born in 1854 in Victoria, when his ex-convict father died, Kelly became the chief wage-earner at the age of 12. He formed his now infamous gang in the bush in 1878, eventually killing three policemen and taking a town's population hostage in the local pub. Kelly donned his home-made armour and when the police opened fire they killed the gang, but Kelly managed to escape, only returning to rescue his brother. The police shot at his legs and captured him, and he was hanged in 1880 at Melbourne Gaol at the age of just 25, speaking his last words, 'Such is life.'

Ned Kelly's life has inspired writers, film-makers and artists since the first book on the Kelly gang was printed in 1879. *The Story of the Kelly Gang*, filmed in Melbourne in 1906, could well be the world's first feature film. A radio play broadcast in 1942 was a big success, there was a ballet in the 1950s, and in 1970 Mick Jagger starred in a film version of Kelly's life, which was shot in New South Wales. Well over 100 years after his death, most Australians have a strong opinion about Ned Kelly and will tell you he was either a murderer without morals, or a free-spirited rebel who represents all that is good about Australia. What is certain is that Kelly was an incredibly powerful and colourful character. And his legacy lives on. In 2000 a poll showed that more than 90 per cent of the population believed that he didn't get a fair trial. In the same year, Peter Carey's Booker prize-winning novel *True History of the Kelly Gang* was published, and Kelly was even portrayed in the Olympics ceremony in Sydney.

first parliament on 9 May 1901, and the first session took place in Canberra in 1927. It wasn't until 1942 that Australia became officially autonomous, and only in 1986 that the Australia Act removed the last remnants of British legal authority.

During the First World War more than 60, 000 Australians lost their lives at Gallipoli, on the Turkish coast in France, the highest death toll per capita of any Allied country. Every year, on 25 April, Australians pay tribute to those who died on ANZAC (Australian and New Zealand Army Corps) day.

Immigration

Shortly after the Second World War, Australia began an important immigration programme. The reasoning was that, having only just managed to escape a Japanese invasion, Australia must 'populate or perish'. Over two million people emigrated to Australia from Europe during the 20 years after the end of the war, with large numbers from Greece, Italy and Yugoslavia, and later Turkey and Lebanon.

Republicanism

Australian republicanism had been important in the 1890s, but became much less significant after the First World War. When Queen Elizabeth II completed a hugely successful tour in 1954, monarchism reached its peak. Talk of a republic surfaced again in the 1970s and then in the 1990s when prime minister Paul Keating declared in 1993 that he would introduce an Australian federal republic by 2001. Although the majority of polls showed that most Australians wanted a republic, the result of a referendum in 1999 surprised the world when the proposal was rejected. The result may have been because of prime minister John Howard's monarchist stance, and was more likely because the wording of the proposal talked of an indirectly elected president, which a large number of radicals were not in favour of.

Climate, Geography and Wildlife

Australia is both the world's largest island and its smallest continent. Approaching the size of the whole of Europe, it is a country of extreme diversity. Fringing its enormous coast are sunny cities, with thousands of offshore islands, while in the interior is the vast, flat expanse of the red outback. In the north are pockets of dense, lush rainforest and the great spine of the Great Barrier Reef.

The Great Dividing Range does just that, running down the east of the continent, separating the urban centres of the east coast from the desert interior.

Time Zones

Australia is ahead of Greenwich Mean Time (GMT) by the number of hours shown in this table:

	Australian Summer Time (hours ahead of GMT)	Australian Winter Time (hours ahead of GMT)
Adelaide	+10.5	+8.5
Brisbane	+10	+9
Canberra	+11	+9
Darwin	+10.5	+8.5
Hobart	+11	+9
Melbourne	+11	+9
Perth	+8	+7
Sydney	+11	+9

Climate

Australia is divided into six states and two territories: Western Australia (WA), Northern Territory (NT), South Australia (SA), Queensland (Q), New South Wales (NSW), Australian Capital Territory (ACT), Victoria and Tasmania. The sheer size of the country means that there are huge variations in weather, so that it can easily be 30°C (86°F) in Darwin in the north, and 5°C (41°F) in Tasmania.

In general, though, the weather is divided along the Tropic of Capricorn so that the northernmost states have the hottest climates, while Victoria and Tasmania can get so cold as to have snow. Much of the land is arid, with very low rainfall (less than 600mm a year, compared with an average of 450mm).

The interior of the country is desert, so it is hot and dry with cold nights. And of course in the southern hemisphere, in the land 'down under', the seasons are reversed. So, summer begins in December and runs through to February, while winter is from June to August. In the north of Australia the country becomes

The Down Side of Life Down Under

When you are enduring yet another seemingly endless, cold, grey winter in England, the searing heat of Australia can appear like a heavenly vision. Bear in mind though that being on holiday in tropical temperatures is very different from living and working in them. When lying by a pool or on a beach relaxing, temperatures of over 38°C (100°F) can be lapped up. But if you have to get on a train and work in a city office, albeit air-conditioned, the same temperatures can soon feel like hell. Heat and humidity can be incredibly draining and as soon as you get to Australia you may find yourself complaining about the weather again. While Christmas on the beach can seem appealing, some expatriates say it doesn't feel like Christmas at all, and because the sun always sets relatively early, others lament the loss of long summer nights.

Also, don't make the mistake of thinking that all weather in Australia is either good or the same. The state of Victoria with its city of Melbourne, for example, is notorious for having weather like England – generally bad and highly changeable. A Sydney taxi driver told of how he spent two years living in Melbourne but in the end had to move back to his own city because of the lack of sun. Then there are the rains in the north of the country, which regularly flood the tropical landscape, making roads impassable for weeks on end.

Yes, outdoor life is big in Australia, but playing tennis or doing other outdoor sports in the open air can be impractical in searing heat. Soaring skin cancer rates prompted the government to launch a massive and highly successful 'Slip, slop, slap' campaign more than 20 years ago, advising people to slip on a shirt, slop on some sun cream and slap on a hat. With a great hole in the ozone above the country, the sun can be a killer and most locals wear factor 15+ sunscreen and try to avoid it.

tropical, with just two seasons – wet from December to March, and dry between May and September. On the west coast, a sea breeze affectionately called 'the doctor' cools things down in summer.

Some of the more extreme weather phenomena in the world take place in Australia, which is particularly prone to bushfires, droughts and floods, as well as tropical cyclones. In the tropical north there is a distinct monsoon season.

For more information on the weather, see the **Bureau of Meteorology** website, **www.bom.gov.au**, or contact **Weather by Phone** on t 1900 926 113.

See **References**, pp.223–4, for climate tables.

Wildlife

Much of the flora and fauna in Australia is unique, created when the country separated itself from the ancient continent of Gondwanaland. National symbols are kangaroos, wallabies, wombats and koalas, all of which are marsupials like half of all Australian mammals. Monotremes are the other main group. These are egg-laying mammals, which are believed to have been formed when reptiles evolved into mammals. The dingo is the country's wild dog, made famous internationally by those 'a dingo ate my baby' stories. It was thought to have been introduced to the country in the Ice Age by Aboriginal people who entered from Southeast Asia.

Beneath the sea are an enormous number of tropical fish, humpback whales, dolphins and dugongs, and the largest reef in the world, the Great Barrier Reef. This forms a World Heritage Site, and there are 14 others in the country. Sadly, while the Aboriginal people had a deep relationship with the land which respected and caused little damage to the environment, Europeans brought damage and destruction.

An A–Z of Australian Species

Despite the impact of European settlement (in the last 200 years over half the mammals that have become extinct in the world have been Australian), the country is still home to over a million species of plants, animals and micro-organisms, twice as many as Europe and North America combined. Many of the species are unique to the country, and in terms of biodiversity Australia is hugely important, contributing 7 per cent of the world's species.

There are several species of **bandicoot** in Australia, and, although they can be seen during the day, they are mostly nocturnal creatures. About the same size as a rat, the bandicoot dines on small insects and plants. The southern brown bandicoot is found in eastern and western Australia. The eastern barred bandicoot is now critically endangered on the mainland, though in Tasmania they are more common.

The **dingo** is has been Australia's wild dog for thousands of years. Thought to have been introduced to mainland Australia by Aboriginal people for companionship and hunting, dingos inhabited most parts of mainland Australia, where they replaced what came to be known as the Tasmanian devil. The dingo doesn't bark like domestic dogs, but makes a distinctive howling sound. They are most active at sunrise, sunset and night; they rest during the day. Dingos eat mice, rabbits, rats and possums, although they can also attack livestock when hungry.

The **emu** is Australia's largest bird, growing to a height of almost 2m (7ft). It has a thick, lush plumage and long thin legs. The female lays from six to twelve eggs, although the male is the one who hatches the eggs and looks after the young. The emu cannot fly, but roams wild from the dusty inlands to the wet southern coast. Its diet is mainly insects, nuts and grains. Emu farming was legalised in 1970, and it is a growth industry. The birds are principally farmed for their meat (which is low in cholesterol and fat), for their high-quality leather (used in clothing and accessories), and for their oil (used as a liniment rub). Emu oil has a reputation largely derived from its traditional use over hundreds of years by Australian Aboriginal people.

The **frilled lizard** lives in the bush of eastern and northern Australia, and was depicted on the now defunct two-cent coin. The lizard's 'frill' is a flap of skin, which lies in folds round its shoulders and neck. When threatened, it will open its mouth wide to activate its frill and scare off predators, but the frilled lizard would rather avoid trouble. If approached, it will quickly move to the opposite side of the tree trunk it is perched on, and will continue to move round to stay out of view. If it has to run, it can do so very quickly, upright on its hind legs.

The **galah** can be found throughout Australia, although this noisy, colourful bird prefers open plains and savannah woodland to extreme desert or rainforest. Galahs are very sociable birds, spending most of the year in flocks that can number up to several hundred birds.

The **goanna** lizard lives in various parts of Australia and can grow to 2m (7ft) in length. The perentie goanna, in central Australia, is the largest lizard in Australia. Although many goannas are herbivores, perentie goannas are meat-eaters. They have even been known to kill kangaroos, and have been seen to catch seagulls by hiding under vehicles until the birds come close enough to be ambushed.

Perhaps the best known of all Australian animals is the **kangaroo**. There are over 60 different species of kangaroo and their close relatives, most of which are found only in Australia. Most are nocturnal but some are active in the early morning and late afternoon. The larger species, whose males are typically more than 2m (7ft) tall, tend to shelter beneath trees and in caves, but the cat-sized tree kangaroo usually keeps to the treetops, coming to ground only between trees too far apart to jump. Kangaroos are herbivorous, and have only two natural predators – dingoes and humans. Aboriginal people have hunted kangaroos for tens of thousands of years, for both the meat and the skins. When Europeans arrived in Australia, in the late 18th century, they too hunted kangaroos for survival. Today, legislation throughout Australia protects kangaroos, with severe penalties for cruelty and inhumane treatment. Nonetheless, the most abundant species (the red kangaroo, eastern grey kangaroo and western grey kangaroo) are commercially harvested under government licence, and kangaroo meat and skins are exported all over the world.

Although its scientific name, *phascolarctos cinereus*, means 'ash grey pouched bear', the **koala** is not a bear, nor is it related to bears. A relative of kangaroos and wombats, it makes its home high in the branches of eucalyptus gum trees in eastern Australia. The koala is an important part of Aboriginal culture and features in many of their myths. One such myth first records the koala's existence, telling of the pact the Kulin people made with the koalas, by which they promised to treat the animals with respect if they would stop taking the Kulin's water and give them good advice when asked (the eucalyptus leaf is high in water content and so koalas drink relatively little). Dreamtime myth also ascribes to koalas the ability to disappear at will. Indeed, although European settlers first arrived in 1788, it was 10 years before John Price recorded the first sighting of a koala, and a further three before one was captured. As late as the 1930s, koalas were hunted for their pelts, but public revulsion at the killing of this harmless animal forced state governments to declare the koala a protected species. However, the biggest threat facing wild koala populations today is the decimation of their habitat. Since the white settlement of Australia, approximately 80 per cent of the koala's habitat has been destroyed. Of the remaining 20 per cent almost none is protected and most occurs on privately owned land. It is reckoned that only around 100,000 koalas remain in Australia, compared with the many millions that used to inhabit the country.

The **kookaburra**, or laughing jackass, *Dacelo gigas*, is a large and noisy bird found in the Australian bush. Although a member of the kingfisher family, the kookaburra does not eat fish but dines mainly on large insects and small reptiles and amphibians. A maximum of 47cm (18in) in length, and with a 10cm (4in) bill, the kookaburra is larger than most kingfishers, but its brown and tan plumage is drab by the standards of the family. Their loud cries, which resemble human laughter and are typically chorused at dawn and dusk, are one of the characteristic sounds of the Australian bush.

A truly unique Australian animal, the **platypus** has a duck-bill, short legs with webbed feet and a beaver-like tail, and belongs to the monotreme family. Males grow to an average of 50cm (20in) with about one-fifth of their length made up of tail. Platypuses live among Australia's eastern waterways, and spend most of their time in the water, though the females build nesting burrows on the riverbanks. Their main sources of food are small crustaceans, as well as tadpoles and worms. A protected species, like the koala, the platypus is nevertheless under threat as its natural habitat is eroded and increasingly damaged by pollution, damming and drainage.

The **possum** can be found in many parts of the Australian bush, but they have also adapted well to living in proximity to humans. Accomplished scavengers, like the common ringtail possum and the nocturnal common brushtail possum, they are often seen in suburban gardens. About the size of a cat, the common ringtail possum is grey with white patches behind the eyes and on the belly, and orange-brown tinges on the tail and limbs. Its long prehensile tail has a white tip and it uses it like a fifth limb to climb and jump between connecting branches, fences and powerlines. This possum is known to eat it own faecal pellets, in order to extract the maximum amount of nutrients. The sugar glider is a species of possum that can 'fly' from tree to tree, thanks to a membrane that connects its front and back legs.

Just as the dingo is Australia's dog, the **quoll** is its cat. It grows to about the size of a domestic cat, and spends most of its time in trees. Various species include the eastern quoll, the northern quoll, the spotted-tailed quoll and the western quoll. Eastern quolls are solitary creatures, hunting and scavenging mostly at night. During the day they will sleep in underground burrows. The spotted-tailed quoll has smaller eyes and ears but is no less accomplished when it comes to hunting. They compete for food with the Tasmanian devil, and have even been seen to chase one away from its catch.

Despite its name, the **Tasmanian devil** is a solitary and shy nocturnal animal. But early European settlers who beheld its spine-tingling cry, black coat and ferocious-looking teeth christened it the 'devil'. It once inhabited the Australian mainland, but disappeared thousands of years ago, possibly overtaken by the dingos that were brought into the country by Aboriginal people. Tasmanian devils eat a range of small birds and mammals, either as carrion or prey. They have also been known to eat reptiles, amphibians and insects. They have a black coat, with a small bear-shaped head, and can grow to about 60cm (2ft) long. The famous open-mouthed screech that so terrified the early settlers is less an aggressive act, and more a bluff in the face of fear on the devil's part. But for over a century they were trapped and poisoned, and it looked as though they were doomed to extinction like the Tasmanian tiger. Finally, in 1941 the devil was protected by law and the population has since gradually increased until today the Tasmanian devil is plentiful and safe.

There are around 25 different species of **wallaby** in Australia. Closely related to the kangaroo, wallabies are generally smaller and with distinctive dentition. Many species have been exterminated, and many (such as the yellow-footed rock wallaby) are on the verge of extinction. The wallaby is an inquisitive creature and has become notorious for raiding backpacks and picnic baskets. All young wallabies box and wrestle with each other, but as they start to mature the females give up this pursuit, leaving males to spar with one another. Usually this is just a form of recreation, but in the breeding season it becomes the manner of establishing dominance.

The **wedge-tailed eagle** is Australia's largest bird of prey. It has dark feathers with a yellow beak, and a 'wedge'-shaped tail. Its 2m (7ft) wingspan allows it to fly at great heights (sometimes up to 2,000m) and swoop down on prey. Before 1970, tens of thousands of wedge-tailed eagles were poisoned or shot in Queensland and Western Australia, as farmers suspected them of killing lambs. Today, it is the most abundant of the world's large eagles, though habitat loss is still a risk.

With its ungainly gait and hefty bulk, it is something of a surprise that the **wombat** will often wander for over two miles in one night searching for food. Looking rather like a beaver without a tail, it can grow up to 1.3m (4ft) in length and weigh up to 30kg. Of the three species of wombat found in Australia, the common wombat is the most abundant, found in many parts of the southeast of the country. The southern hairy-nosed wombat is less common. It is found throughout South Australia and in western Victoria and western West Australia. The northern hairy-nosed wombat is the rarest of the three. Until recently presumed extinct in New South Wales, it is now listed as endangered. In Queensland, only 113 wombats live in one small protected area, making it the most endangered mammal in the state.

Dangerous Creatures

Despite its press, few of Australia's creatures are likely to kill you. Although there are poisonous spiders and snakes, man-eating sharks and crocodiles, stinging insects and jellyfish, the chances of your being poisoned or attacked are very low. In fact, you are statistically more likely to be killed by a wombat or a kangaroo in a road accident. However, the **flies** can drive you crazy, getting in your food and in your mouth so that when you are in the outback you can actually understand the reason for those ridiculous corked hats. The bizarre platypus, which has a duck-bill, otter's tail, webbed feet, and lays eggs, has venomous barbs attached to its hind legs.

There are around 2,000 species of **spiders**, some of which are poisonous, but few people die from their bites. The funnel-web, red-back and white-tail are the three most dangerous spiders. They can be found anywhere – in the home, on the beach or in the bush – and a bite from any of them demands immediate medical attention. Red-back spiders are a relative of the black widow and take their name from the orange and red stripe on their upper abdomen. Although red-backs love to bite, only the female is dangerous (it can make victims very ill and even kill), and because the jaws are so small, a lot of bites have no effect.

Australia is home to eight of the 10 most dangerous **snakes** in the world. If you do get bitten, try to remember what the snake looked like so that the most appropriate medical attention can be given to you.

The sea can be a dangerous place in Australia. The **box jellyfish** – also sometimes called a sea wasp – causes more deaths in Australia than snakes, sharks and salt-water crocodiles put together. It is found in the north and northeast of the country along the Great Barrier Reef, and toxins in its tentacles, which can be several feet long, produce the effect of an electric shock so strong that the victim usually ends up screaming. Depending on where the person has been attacked, cardio-respiratory functions may stop within three minutes, making mouth-to-mouth resuscitation and first aid essential to keep the victim alive. It's important that you stay with the victim, and send someone to phone for or get an ambulance.

Salt-water **crocodiles** live in the waters of the north of the country. Sometimes up to seven metres long, these ugly creatures love meat, including humans. Living in rivers and beaches, they sleep and swim on the bottom of the water, which makes them difficult to see.

The **scorpion fish** has long spines that contain enough poison to kill. Although they live all over Australia, they prefer coral reefs. Its relative, the stonefish, inhabits river mouths and rocks throughout the country and is just as dangerous. The **stonefish** sits on the seabed, appearing to be a rock, and has venomous barbs sticking out of its back.

Sharks are all over the coast, but are less likely to attack than any of the other creatures mentioned. The **Portuguese Man-of-War** (usually called a blue bottle by Australians) is another stinging jellyfish, and much more common than the box jellyfish or sea wasp. A sting will give you a sharp pain, but it is not as deadly as that of the sea wasp.

Food and Drink

A History of Eating

English people who have never travelled to Australia might be forgiven for thinking that Australians start their day with an English breakfast and a cup of tea. But in the urban centres, at least, the first meal of the day is likely to be an expertly made cappuccino and a buttery croissant or a fresh fruit yoghurt drink. In the outback of course, it's a whole different story, where you would be hard pushed to find anything other than steak, egg and chips, or a gravy-soaked pie.

In fact, pies are a staple and eaten all over the country, from truckers in the northern territory right through to wealthy urbanites in Sydney tucking into a gourmet version at the legendary Harry de Wheels. Australians love their meat

Food Finder

Don't assume that just because Australians speak English, you will necessarily understand what they are saying. There are a number of words that are different, particularly when it comes to food and drink:

amber nectar/fluid beer
Anzac biscuits biscuits made with coconut and golden syrup
bag of fruit rhyming slang for a man's suit
Balmain bugs small crayfish
barbie barbecue
bickie biscuit
bottle-shop off-licence
bring a plate bring a dish, for instance, to a barbecue at someone's house
B.Y.O bring-your-own alcohol; there is usually a small corkage charge
chips crisps
chook chicken
damper unleavened bread baked in the ashes of a fire
deli food shop
eggplant aubergine
entrée starter
esky drinks cooler
flat white cappuccino with less froth
floater meat pie in soupy peas or gravy

and it's usually good and cheap. Barbecues are part of everyday life, either at home, on the beach or in a local park, and are as much about fresh fish and giant prawns as steak and sausages.

In many ways, the story of Australian cooking can be traced through its history. When Australia was settled by the British 200 or so years ago, the industrial revolution had already taken hold and the country did not have the chance to develop its own cuisine. The original settlers were so unaware of the riches around them that many actually starved while waiting for ration ships to arrive. At that time, the influence was largely Anglo-Saxon, rather than being informed by what was naturally available.

Largely isolated from the rest of the world, Australians were shocked when in the 1950s the first wave of Italians arrived and hung their fresh pasta on clothes lines in their backyards. Today, Australian cuisine is so deeply informed by the Italian way that it can be difficult to know where one ends and the other begins. In homes and restaurants all over Australia, olive oil is used for frying when once only lard would do.

After the Second World War, other southern Europeans, such as Spaniards and Greeks came along with the Italians, intensifying the Mediterranean influence.

frankfurts frankfurters
grog general name for alcohol
hot chips chips (used to distinguish from crisps; not used in restaurants)
icy pole ice lolly
lamingtons small sponge cakes with chocolate and coconut
lolly sweet
middy a medium-sized (9oz) glass of beer; used in New South Wales and
   Western Australia
muddie a mud crab
Moreton Bay bugs shellfish (not insects)
pavlova dessert with meringue, cream and fruit
pawpaws papayas
pikelets small pancakes
sanger sandwich; also *sango*
schooner large glass of beer (15oz)
shallots spring onions
snag sausage
stubby small bottle of beer
tinnie a can of beer
tucker food
vintage mature wine
yabby freshwater crayfish
zucchini courgettes

When Asian immigrants began to arrive in the late 1970s, they brought woks
and cooking styles from home and locals woke up to the fact that Australia is on
Asia's doorstep, not the UK's. Once again the face of Australian cooking was
dramatically changed and today 'Modern Australian' food is as much about the
east – Thailand, Vietnam, Japan, Korea and China – as it is the west.

Modern Australian

It is possibly this ability to adapt so readily to outside influences, along with its
natural abundance of foodstuffs, that means that Sydney now rivals New York
and London as one of the food capitals of the world.

Australian food is typically described as 'fusion', but the combining of ingredients from different countries is done seamlessly and with confidence.
Australian chefs are equally at ease cooking ocean trout with wasabi, or emu
with bush-tomato, as they are Cantonese stir-frying a kangaroo steak, with
hardly a backward glance towards Europe.

'Modern Australian' is a result of a combination of a relaxed attitude – people
really do just 'throw a shrimp on the barbie' – wonderfully fresh ingredients and

the influence of so many cultures. Australians loathe pretension, so even in the most upmarket restaurants the emphasis is on high-quality ingredients and friendly service, with usually just two or three key elements in a dish.

Local Produce

A restaurant's claim that the emphasis is on 'good, fresh, local produce' is a cliché in some countries in the world, but in Australia it happens to be true. And with the raw ingredients available, it makes sense. The sheer size of the country is such that almost anything can be grown, and animal and plant life thrives in the Australian climate. The waters are home to some of the best and biggest fish and seafood in the world, and the land nurtures spring onions the size of leeks, and lemons that look more like grapefruit.

Sugar cane is grown in the tropical heat of northern Queensland, while the cooler conditions in the south churn out high-quality dairy products, including Australian-style French brie and Italian gorgonzola. The trees produce plump, exotic fruits and, thanks to its climatic diversity, the country nurtures the whole range, from blackberries to lychees. Rich pasture land creates succulent, free-range beef and milk-fed lamb; gourmet foods such as prosciutto and cold-pressed olive oil are produced here and Australia even manages to export rice to Japan.

Unlike in the UK or many other parts of the world Australia imports relatively little produce, which means food is eaten according to the season and is pretty much always fresh. Natives can enjoy apples from the cool climate of Tasmania alongside papayas from the tropics of Queensland. Strawberries and asparagus are available in spring, while summer is the time for mangoes. Although many foods are available countrywide, as in Italy and France, there are distinct regional specialities when it comes to Australian produce:

- **New South Wales: rock oysters, milk-fed lamb, Balmain bugs** (*see* p.24)
- **Victoria: Gippsland beef, corn-fed chicken, Meredith lamb**
- **South Australia: Coffin Bay scallops, olive oil**
- **Queensland: mangoes, papaya, Moreton Bay bugs** (*see* p.25), **mudcrabs**
- **Northern Territory: Barramundi fish, crocodile, Mangrove Jack fish**
- **Tasmania: salmon, oysters, trout**

However, some English expats complain that even in a food capital like Sydney, the supermarkets are restricted to Woolworth's and the like, and there is not a Sainsbury's, let alone a Waitrose in sight. There are hardly any good-quality, pre-packaged meals to be had off the supermarket shelf; the philosophy is that if you want a decent meal, you should make it yourself.

Fast Food Australian-style

Australians have successfully adopted the Asian dining concept of food halls, where a number of food sellers can be found under one roof. The food is usually Asian (for instance, Vietnamese, Malaysian or Thai), although sandwiches and salads can normally be had and typically there will often be a Turkish or a Lebanese food stall in there somewhere. City workers on a lunch break are more likely to pick up a box of sushi or chilli for a couple of quid as a sandwich.

Fish and seafood are heavily featured. Australia fish and chips invariably blow the English version out of the water, with fresher-than-fresh fillets in light, often beer batter served with light, non-greasy golden chips.

The advantages of food halls are many: the food is cheap, it can be eaten in air-conditioned comfort and each diner can eat a different meal if they choose. Most shopping centres and inner cities boast a food hall, which are very popular with office workers, shoppers, families and tourists alike.

Bush Tucker

Bush tucker describes any food – including herbs, fruits, vegetables, animals, birds and insects – that is native to Australia. When the Aboriginal people lived off the land 50,000 years ago, it was the only food there was. The original Australians ground seeds to make flour for bread called 'damper', and ate a kind of insect larva called 'witchetty grub' as a delicacy.

Ancient Australian Foods

wattle seed dry-roasted, ground and used for their nutty, coffee-like flavour

lemon myrtle leaves and stems of rainforest tree with intense citrus flavour and aroma

lurrajong seeds roasted and ground, they make a nutritious, dark flour

macadamia nuts and oil the first of Australia's indigenous plants to be used commercially

warrigal greens used as a spinach substitute by Captain Cook in 1770

illawarra plums exotic dark berries

Bunya nuts large nuts from the Bunya pine tree

lemon aspen small lemon-like fruits that grow in the rainforest

pepper leaves spicy leaves from a large shrub used as pepper

wild limes small fruits similar to limes, with a grapefruit flavour

native cranberries (or *muntries*) small, sweet, textured berries

Kakadu plum a tart, green plum packed with vitamin C

wild rosella flowers bright red petals from the hibiscus family with a sharp berry-like flavour

bush tomatoes small, strong-tasting berries that grow in the desert

Because Aboriginal people knew the land so intimately they were skilled in making the best use of the scant resources there were. Honeypot ants were used as a sugar source and insects were used not only as food, but as medicine and as part of spiritual practices. The bush cockroach was used as a local anaesthetic, and the green tea ant as a drink and headache cure. Sadly, the lack of understanding about the Aboriginal culture meant that for many years these types of practices were ridiculed.

Although for many it still has only novelty value, acclaimed chefs on the lookout for 'new' tastes have began to recognise this unique and exciting type of cuisine. They now use Australian fruits in jams, serve native nuts in pies and have put dishes like meat with ground kurrajong flowers and quandong (wild peach) ice cream on their menus. Today kangaroo steaks grace the tables of some of the smartest restaurants, and emu is reared commercially in Australia as a high-class source of protein.

World-class Wine

In 2004 it was revealed, to the horror of French producers, that six out of the top 10 wines sold in the UK are Australian, and Aussie bottles now account for around half of the middle market in Britain, where wines are sold for around £5 a bottle.

In the mid-1990s that would have seemed like an Antipodean pipe dream. At that time 25 million cases sold in the UK were French, while just 3.5 million were Australian. Many thought that our eagerness to down good-value Aussie bottles would be short-lived and we would return to the solid tradition of French classics. We now drink about the same quantity of French as Australian wines in Britain.

Just as with the country's cuisine, the success of Australian wines is in the ability to adapt, to not be hampered by tradition and to take a thoroughly modern approach. Australian wine marketing is completely of the 21st century.

Top Ten Best-selling Wines in the UK, 2004

1	Hardy's	Australia
2	Blossom Hill	USA
3	Jacob's Creek	Australia
4	E&J Gallo	USA
5	Stowell's	Various
6	Kumala	South Africa
7	Lindeman's	Australia
8	Banrock Station	Australia
9	Rosemount	Australia
10	Wolf Blass	Australia

A Wonderful Wine Tour

Most of the major grapes – Semillon, Shiraz and Chardonnay – are suitable for growing in the climate and the soil of the Hunter Valley. Situated in New South Wales, about two hours north of Sydney, the valley is the site for popular one- or two-day wine tours from the city. As so many of the wineries are concentrated, the area invites itself for touring and some of them are close enough to each other to reach on foot. The cellar doors of the wineries are open for wine sampling and many of them also have vineyards, which can be toured to learn about the whole wine-making process. In addition restaurants are often attached so you can enjoy some fine Australian food with your local wine.

It is also informed by the Australian psyche, which is essentially no-nonsense, with a strong resistance to any kind of pretension. It seems that we have taken to Aussie wines because they are good, user-friendly and available at a reasonable price.

A key factor is that the labelling is consumer-led; Australia was the first country to brand its wines according to its variety of grape – Merlot, Shiraz and so on – rather than its place of origin, which was much more meaningful to a customer trying to pick out a bottle from a shelf. Research has shown that the easy to remember anglicised brands of the New World wines are more appealing to many people than the complex maze of foreign vineyards and châteaux. French wine producers have a particular problem: the industry is divided into hundreds of mostly small châteaux, while Australia essentially has just three major companies – Fosters, Southcorp and Hardy.

Locals have long been aware of the quality of their wines, enjoying home-produced Cabernet Sauvignons and high-quality sparkling wines, but it wasn't until the 1980s that the bottles began to be exported in any real numbers. And it was only in 1993 that the Geographical Indications (GI) was created, which followed the broad principles of European appellations (to protect wine quality), but without its tight controls over the actual wine-making process.

More than a hundred varieties of grape are grown in Australia. The key wine-producing regions are New South Wales, Victoria and Southern Australia, followed by Western Australia, Tasmania and Queensland. English consumers are most likely to be familiar with names from Southern Australia, most of which are created for early consumption.

A pioneering spirit has been sweeping the industry, which has resulted in a much wider range of wine grape varieties being used. They could be classified as the classic whites – Chardonnay, Semillon, Riesling and Sauvignon Blanc – and the classic reds, which tend to be as bold and upfront as Aussies themselves – Cabernet Sauvignon, Pinot Noir, Merlot, Shiraz (the Australian version of French Syrah) and Grenache, all of which are French. And Australians love to mix their wines, so that a Cabernet Sauvignon might be blended with a Shiraz, or a Semillon combined with a Chardonnay.

Sparkling wines, which include even reds, are amazingly good and reasonably priced. Although legally they cannot be called champagne, they are made using the traditional champagne grapes of Chardonnay, Pinot Noir and Pinot Meunier, and the quality is such that Moët and Chandon has now established itself in Victoria's Yarra Valley in Victoria.

The Australian wines we are used to seeing at home retail for around the same price in Australia, which is relatively expensive for locals. Wine boxes, called casks in Australia, are widely available and a real bargain, and there is no shame in turning up with one at a good B.Y.O. restaurant. The other good news is that, like France, Australia holds back its best bottles for itself and doesn't export them.

Barossa has been described by some as the Napa of Australia (although it is only half the size), because both regions produce some of their country's best wines. At one time, most of the grapes from Barossa were used in fortified wines until red table wines gained popularity. When white wines became the favourite choice, the red grapes were largely redundant and the government introduced a shocking plan, which involved paying growers to pull up some of these age-old vines. Thankfully some refused and traditional Barossa Shiraz is still here today.

The Amber Nectar

It's no secret that Australians love their beer. One joke runs that a seven-course meal in Australia is a pie and a six-pack. But you might be surprised to learn that they drink less per capita than the British, Czechs, Germans, Irish and Belgians, and the increasing popularity of wine and other drinks has caused beer consumption to fall.

The two Foster brothers, Ralph and William, were the first to come up with the idea of selling cold beer in Australia in 1888. Until lager arrived, the national brews were ales and stouts conditioned in the cask or bottle. The most well-known beers in Australia are now lagers, which are made lighter and cheaper with cane sugar, rather than rice, as in America, or maize, as in Britain.

The great Aussie drink is a 'tinnie' (can) of beer, which some seem to drink as if it were water. It is crucial that the beer is as cold as possible and the further you go into the interior – where the hotter it is – the more extreme the obsession becomes, so that by the time you get to Alice Springs you are given an iced can from the fridge in a 'stubby holder' so the heat from your hands doesn't warm your drink; in Darwin the beer is served in an ice bucket. Most brands have about 4.8 per cent alcohol but 'light' beers are widely available, with less than 3 per cent alcohol.

A word of warning: don't criticise an Australian beer unless comparing it to another kind of Australian beer. Fosters is the brand most internationally

How to Order a Beer

- In New South Wales a **middie** (285ml) is roughly half a pint, and a **schooner** (425ml) a pint.
- In Victoria they drink only **pots** (285ml).
- Tasmanian bars serve **tens** (285ml) and **pints** (425ml).
- Queenslanders drink **pots** (285ml) and **schooners.**
- In South Australia, ask for a **pony** (142ml), a **butcher** (200ml), a **schooner** (285ml) or a **pint** (425ml).
- Measures in Western Australia are a **bobby** (200ml), a **glass** (285ml) or a **pot** (425 ml).
- And in the Northern Territory a **six** is 200ml, a **seven** 285ml and a **handle** 425ml.

known and actually the third most available beer in the world, sold in over 130 countries. But most Australians would never touch the stuff, tending to prefer beers produced in their own state.

One of the most popular beers is Victoria Bitter – which is actually a lager and known as 'VB' – ask for it by its full name and your barman is likely to fall on the floor laughing. Logically enough, this is most commonly drunk in Melbourne and the state of Victoria, although some say this is one of the worst kinds of Australian beers and too weak to drink. If the rumours are true, actor Russell Crowe flies cases of Victoria Bitter into the film set wherever in the world he is working.

In New South Wales, Tooheys (new or old) is the local brew while XXXX (Four-ex) is the beer of choice up in Queensland. It has been drunk there since 1924, but is still hard to find outside the state border. Coopers and West End are brewed in South Australia, although Coopers has found its way to the East Coast. In Western Australia, they drink Swan Lager and Emu bitter, and in the Northern Territory NT Lager.

There's no such thing as a pint (except in Tasmania) or a half in Australian bars, and to make matters even more confusing there are enormous variations between the states when it comes to ordering the size of your beer. If in doubt, just ask for your preferred brew and let the bar person prompt you on the measure.

Other Drinks

Coffee is big in Australia, due mainly to the large Italian population, which dates back more than 50 years. Café society is an integral part of life and natives can get their caffeine fix any way they like it – 'skinny' or with soya milk, New York style, a more traditional 'flat white', which is a cappuccino with less froth, or a 'long black', which is as it sounds.

'Smoothies' are big, too – made with fresh fruit and either milk or yoghurt. Local spirits come down to port and brandy and the export on these is not big. The northern state of Queensland, where sugar cane grows, produces two nationally popular rums – sweet Bundaberg and traditional Beenleigh.

Profiles of the Regions

Choosing where to live in a country the size of a continent is no easy task. That said, the bottom right-hand corner from Brisbane on the east coast all the way down to Adelaide in the south, represents just 5 per cent of Australia's land mass, but is home to over 80 per cent of the population. And within what has been dubbed the 'Boomerang Coast', the vast majority of Brits pick Sydney or Melbourne as their home. Once you go inland there is little but harsh desert with rocky outcrops and dry salt lakes. In wonderful contrast, the coast – particularly in the east – is one of the most stunning in the world.

The main appeal of the country is that, while England is a small, over-crowded island, Australia is a large, mostly empty one. When making the decision on where to make your home, take into account that distances are huge; driving from Sydney to the next major city of Melbourne is like driving from London to Scotland. Many Australians think nothing of doing such a trip just for a party, however, and in the remote areas of the country some locals will travel for three hours to get a takeaway!

Most people gravitate to cities because this is where the work is, and the cities in Australia are some of the least expensive anywhere. The cost of living in Melbourne, Adelaide, Brisbane and Perth is less than half that of the world's most expensive cities, yet they are all ranked in the world's top 30 for quality of life. In a country as vast as Australia, it is not surprising that there is a certain of amount of, let's say, healthy rivalry. Melbourne and Sydney compete with each other as the chief city in the country, while everyone outside of Canberra makes fun of the man-made capital with little character, and Queenslanders are said by those outside the state to be 'banana-benders'.

Building Styles

House styles are very different from those in the UK. When the first settlers came, the standard was to build houses on a quarter of an acre of land, but subsequently this was reduced to half that size. Even though you will find Victorian architecture in the major cities, which is rather incongruous with the country's vast open spaces, later designs tend towards large ranch-style houses with lots of rooms and big land plots. Typical of Australia are 'federation' buildings, which are colonial-style with attractive lacy ironwork balconies, but there are a number of regional differences. Sydney has many 19th-century terraced houses originally built as basic accommodation for workers, many of them with small gardens and pretty iron balconies; yet houses in Queensland are often built on stilts to provide ventilation in the searing heat. Some foreign visitors find it hard to come to terms with the fact that many homes come without central heating even though it can get cold, particularly in the south.

New South Wales

Sydney

Australia's most populated state is also the most visited by its tourists. Sydney is indisputably the country's most visually appealing city; it also happens to be the oldest and most cosmopolitan. To anyone familiar with London, it has an almost small-town feel; it's easy to walk around the compact centre, the sea is never far away and the residents seem laid-back and friendly. To the rest of Australia, however, it is a busy, even stressed-out place, and Melbourne residents in particular describe it as shallow and showy.

The city's waterfront is nothing short of spectacular, and it never fails to dazzle, no matter how many times you have visited or how long you have lived there. In terms of sheer beauty and beaches, Sydney is up there in the top three cities in the world, alongside Rio de Janeiro and Cape Town. While die-hard Londoners bemoan the lack of grit and energy, confirmed Sydneysiders embrace the easy lifestyle and the fact that their city is everything that England's capital isn't.

Sydney is a huge city and seven times the size of Paris. It is made up of a staggering 400 'suburbs', the most remote being around 60 miles from the centre. At its physical and psychological heart is **The Rocks**. This charming district, which includes the twin icons of the Harbour Bridge and Circular Quay, is where the first convicts arrived, and this history is echoed in its historic alleyways and colonial buildings. The Rocks border the CBD – **Central Business District** – which is made up of a manageable collection of skyscrapers and remnants of some of the country's oldest buildings.

Sydney's most desirable neighbourhoods are, predictably, close to the centre and its beautiful beaches. Homes in **Double Bay** (nicknamed 'Double Pay' because of the price of property), **Point Piper** and **Vaucluse** are the most expensive in the whole country, and with reason. East of here, **Bondi Beach** is something of an English enclave. The beach from which the suburb takes its name is one of the most famous in the world, yet it has a faded grandeur reminiscent of some of England's traditional seaside resorts. This was the site of the world's first lifesaving club in 1906 and where dangerous rip tides still spit out unwary bathers. Surfers, posers and families all flock here on summer days.

The inner east also attracts English migrants. **Paddington, Darlinghurst** and **King's Cross** are decidedly urban, with attractive terraced houses and lively nightlife. King's Cross is still, after all these years, the red-light district of the city where street-walking prostitutes are not an uncommon sight, yet for some its bars and clubs make up for its seedy image. Darlinghurst is the epicentre of the gay community, where the Mardi Gras continues to draw up to 500,000 revellers of all persuasions each year.

Hotels Making History

Sydney has a wonderful variety of hotels which have all made history in their own right, and are within a few miles of each other. **The Australian (www. australianheritagehotel.com)**, one of the oldest pubs in the country, has rein- vented itself as a contemporary boutique hotel in the heart of a historic and tourist area. The Rocks is the site of the first European settlement in the country and where the first fleet pitched their tents in 1788.

Despite its federation-style architecture, The Australian has something very English about it, with chintzy décor, antique furniture and decanters of port and sherry in the living room. But if you go down to the bar and ask if there are any German beers, you will be met with a firm: 'We only have Australian beers here' and offered a menu of pizza with emu, crocodile or kangaroo. Across the street are 'housing commission', or council, terraced flats, and within spitting distance is the great arc of the Sydney Harbour Bridge. Every night of the week, the pavement outside is filled with drinkers and diners and the hotel is booked out years ahead for the ringside seats the private roof terrace gives to guests for the annual show of the New Year's Eve fireworks.

The Observatory just up the road couldn't be more different. This is an Orient Express hotel and decidedly traditional, offering afternoon tea with either a specially made brew or with champagne. The stars of the southern constella- tion are embedded in the ceiling above the pool in the renowned spa which offers a free 30-minute session in the flotation tank for all international guests as a treatment for jetlag. Around the corner, the award-winning **Four Seasons** hotel definitely has the best view in town, with suites giving near 180 degree views of the best part of the harbour.

When the **InterContinental** hotel in central Sydney started broadcasting the Today breakfast television programme from its rooftop, the channel needn't

Just west of the Central Business District, **Darling Harbour** forms the re- vamped waterside area in the centre of the city. Once a decidedly down-at-heel neighbourhood, it now features major hotel chains and popular restaurants, as well as chic apartment residences. This part of town continues to be improved, with **Cockle Bay**'s restaurants and bars a recent and welcome addition. **Glebe** and **Balmain** are further west again; these are old working-class docking areas, which today are home to the most left-wing residents in Sydney. Both of these neighbourhoods are famous for their weekend markets, independent cinemas and alternative lifestyles.

Newtown is close by, more rugged than the middle-class areas of Glebe and Balmain, and with a lively nightlife. Neighbouring **Redfern** is something of an Aboriginal community, which still suffers from being characterised as rough. Even further west is **Homebush Bay**, the site of the 2000 Olympics, and **Parramatta**, which is probably best described as Sydney's very own Essex, complete with girls wearing white and too-high stilettos. As has been said have worried that they would alienate those in Melbourne. The response has been phenomenal, and the hotel receives so many requests to use it as a location shoot that it is forced to turn many of them down. Those responsible insist the move does not represent a conflict of interests, maintaining that the set-up all works very well and even the businessmen breakfasting on the stunning terrace at 6am love all the attention.

The **W** hotel in Woolloomooloo is a completely different story. Just a few years ago the government wanted to pull down the historic wharf where ships first called in way back in 1912. It was from here in the heart of the city that the building blocks of a nation were created and where the 'Wharfies' who loaded and unloaded cargoes suffered horrendous working conditions. This was the embarkation and arrival point for Australian troops in the Boer War and First and Second World Wars – many of whom never returned. It was also where, during the 1950s and '60s, new arrivals stepped ashore after their mammoth three-month journey by ship from Europe.

A A$350-dollar restoration means that Woolloomooloo can once again take its place in the contemporary make-up of the city. A strip of chic restaurants make up a kind of millionaires' row of eating establishments. Chic apartments owned by the likes of Russell Crowe and Nicole Kidman, a luxury marina and views of the central harbour make this one of the most desirable addresses in the land. When the **W** hotel opened here it was the first outside of North America, and many Sydneysiders assumed the 'W' stood for Wooloomooloo, but since then, another 'W', complete with state of the art spa has opened in Seoul, Korea (*see* **First Steps**, 'Seoul for the Soul', p.91). Bang in the middle of the Sydney hotel is the Water Bar, a slick, chic watering cathedral (rather than hole), which has been named one of the best bars in the world. And next door is the Spa Chakra, which is generally agreed to be Australia's best.

countless times before, Sydney is multicultural and home to over 200 nationalities. Despite the strong Asian influence, **Chinatown** can disappoint, appearing on a scale much smaller than London's.

The **North Shore** across the harbour bridge can seem bland to some, in the same way as, in New York, Manhattan-dwellers turn their noses up at the 'bridge and tunnel' crowd who live mostly in Brooklyn. There are million-dollar residences lining the shore here, with spectacular views of the bridge and city across the water. But it is not solely a residential area; more and more businesses are locating here, so that executives for the Disney Corporation are happy to live in Darling Harbour near the city centre and make the civilised commute to the north shore by boat.

Despite Sydney's sprawl, it is remarkably easy to get around, whether by bus, boat or train. The city's hubs are Circular Quay and Central Station, from where most transport radiates. The best way is to travel is by boat; commuters lucky enough to be able to take the ferry to work do, while tourists make the most of

The Sydney–Hobart Yacht Race

The annual race, which begins in Sydney Harbour on December 26th, attracts participants from around the world. They take on the challenge of sailing some of the most treacherous waters in the world, which claimed the lives of six sailors in a horrific storm in 1998 and resulted in only 44 of the 115 boats finishing the course. The handicap race began in 1945 and runs along a 630-nautical-mile route from the eastern coast of New South Wales and then Victoria before crossing the Bass Strait. From here it traces the east coast of Tasmania south to Tasman Island, across Storm Bay to Hobart. The vessels that took part in the inaugural race made up a tiny fleet of nine wooden yachts with cotton sails and galvanised wire rigging. The boats today are formidable state-of-the-art ocean racers. The race in 2004 was the 60th to take place.

As many as 400,000 eager spectators gather around and in the harbour to view the start of the race. Every kind of vessel from small fishing boat to sleek cruise ship can be seen on the waters. Key vantage points on land include Taronga Zoo, Middle Head in Mosman and North Head in Manly. On the south shore, Neilsen Park and South Head are good viewing spots.

harbour cruises. Choose from jetcats, water taxis, Italian speedboats and obscenely large yachts. Christmas office parties are frequently held afloat, and on celebratory occasions such as Australia Day and New Year's Day the harbour fills with small and large craft packed with people enjoying the water and the view.

Property prices in Sydney are almost as much of an obsession as they are in the UK, and there is certainly enough property gossip about celebrities in the city – whether the stories are true is another matter. At the end of 2004, Heath Ledger, who was in town filming *Candy*, supposedly 'snapped up' a A$4.5 million glass-fronted house with five bedrooms at Bronte, the small pretty beach right next door to Bondi. Native Cate Blanchett apparently toyed with the idea of Tamarama, an eastern 'suburb' by the beach, but plumped instead for a six-bedroom pile in Hunters Hill for a little over A$10 million. Nicole Kidman and Tom Cruise still have both their names on a luxury apartment in Woollomooloo, sparking rumours that there may be a reconciliation. At the time of writing, Kidman was said to be decorating her Darling Point home while looking at buying another in the eastern suburbs for close to A$15 million. No doubt property gossip will continue to make headline news.

The symbols of the city are the Opera House and the Sydney Harbour Bridge, known affectionately as the Coathanger. Before that, it was called the 'iron lung' because of the amount of work it created when it was constructed at the height of the 1930s depression. When built it was the largest single-span bridge in the world and it is still integral to Sydney's psyche as well as continuing to act as the important link between the city and the North Shore. The Opera House was an ambitious project, and the biggest at the time to make use of computer technology. Spiralling costs and internal politics made the scheme something of a soap opera and ended in the designer resigning in 1966. When the building was finally opened by the Queen in 1972 it had cost over A$1 million, 15 times the original budget.

The Hunter Valley

Although this wine region produces only around two per cent of the country's wines, it is one of the country's oldest wine-producing regions, established over 150 years ago. Some of the 80 wineries are owned by big names, such as Hardy's and Lindeman's, that are familiar all over the world. Others are small concerns, which may offer a small output but often have a large range. Just a couple of hours' drive north from Sydney, the Hunter Valley is now also an important area for tourism as well as offering a nearby retreat for Sydneysiders.

The Brokenback Range has a smoky blue hue forming a dramatic backdrop to the vineyards. The area begins officially in **Cessnock**, a large lively town where the surrounding area is important for coal mining. Other significant communities in the valley include **Wollombi**, a small rural settlement surrounded by woods and hills, and **Pokolbin**, which boasts a number of hotels and restaurants. **Branxton** and **Greta** are known for their markets and festivals, while **Kurri Kurri** is famous for its heritage country pubs. **Denman** and the two historic towns of **Singleton** and **Muswellbrook** are all bases for exploring the region, and **Scone** is a centre for breeding thoroughbred horses in the Upper Hunter. As well as the obvious wine-tasting opportunities, activities such as ballooning, parachuting and sky-diving are popular.

When the vineyards were formed in the 19th century, the coastal areas around Sydney were too wet, while the soil of the Hunter was rich and fertile. However, the valley by no means offers ideal conditions – it has large areas of unsuitable soil and unpredictable weather. The first vineyards were established northeast of where they are now found. **Riverina** produces more wine than the Hunter Valley, but the latter offers those of better quality – most importantly Semillon. Tourism began here in the 1960s, and the industry now brings in more dollars than the wine does.

The Premier State

The rest of New South Wales is known as the Premier State, and not without reason. The state was Australia's first colony, but is today one of the most desirable places to live in the country. It boasts not only spectacular beaches, but the country's highest mountain (which is sometimes snow-covered), tropical banana plantations and remote outback country. The powerful Murray River rushes through the southern part of this region, spawning wool, exotic fruit and enormous vegetables, and silver, lead and zinc are all mined here.

Three of the world's heritage sites are here – the **Central Eastern rainforests**, **Willandra National Park** and **Lord Howard Island**. The Hunter Valley, just a couple of hour's drive from Sydney, is a world-class wine region (*see* p.39).

The **Blue Mountains** are so called because of the colour of the haze given off by the swaths of the eucalyptus trees here. The mountains are not especially high at just 3,000 feet, but offer a cool retreat from the Sydney city heat. In 1813, three explorers stumbled across this grazing region, forging the way for a railway constructed in 1868. As early as 1900, destinations such as **Katoomba**, **Mount Victoria** and **Wentworth Falls** became desirable locations to the well heeled, with these Victorian resorts offering a temporary sanctuary to those not wealthy enough to buy a weekend retreat. Antique shops and quaint cafés dot this region, which also has mountain walks and tourist attractions such as a scenic railway into a plunging gorge.

The **Pacific Highway** leads north, but despite its name it does not hug the coast. The main area of appeal here is the **Hawkesbury River** with the Riverboat Postman at **Brooklyn**. Those wanting to get away from the hustle of Sydney, including the retired, gravitate here or to **Gosford** further north with its fine beaches. Further north again is **Newcastle**, a major mining city and not without its similarities to its English namesake. Off the coast are the tiny islands of **Lord Howe** and **Norfolk**.

Along this part of the coast, which rapidly becomes very tropical, are remnant areas of rainforest. Here, the laid-back hangout of **Byron Bay** began in the 1960s as an alternative community and, while it still has that atmosphere, is now where the rich and famous – including 'Croc Dundee' himself, movie star Paul Hogan – have million-dollar homes. Byron is a popular surfing and tourist hang-out which in January becomes very crowded; other tourist spots nearby include Tweed Heads on the border with Queensland. **Tamworth** in the hills is Australia's answer to Nashville. Back in the 1970s a local farmer organised a country and western music festival, which now attracts close to 50,000 people every January, bringing in thousands of dollars to the local community.

South, a string of quaint beachside towns stretches all the way down the coast to Victoria. Inland, **Broken Hill** lays claim to being a traditional mining town of the highest order. Despite its hardcore history, created when it was found to be full of silver, zinc and lead, it is today something of an arts colony as well as the centre for the Flying Doctor Service, which provides medical care for remote communities in the vast outback. Here the now derelict Pub Silverton lays claim to being the most filmed pub in Australia. It is nothing special, but, because it looks like it is in the middle of nowhere yet is close to facilities, it was a location scout's dream and formed the basis of around 150 film and television locations, including *A Town like Alice*, *Mad Max II* and countless beer adverts.

Victoria

In a sad echo of how Manhattan was bought from the Native American Indians for a handful of beads, Melbourne was purchased from some Aborigines for little more than the same. Victoria grew out of the wealth of the 1850s gold rush and the state still has a faintly genteel air, due to its history of farming and old money earned during this time. Despite the fact that this wealth often funded ornate European architecture, there is a lot of industry in Australia's tiniest state and until just a few years ago it was the epicentre for Australian business, which has now been replaced by Sydney.

The border with Victoria's neighbouring state of New South Wales is formed by the **Murray River**, the waterway that waters the lush vineyards, farmland and orchards of the garden state which produce wheat, wool and cheese. Locals are proud of saying that, unlike other states, everywhere in Victoria is reachable within a day's drive. The **Great Ocean Road**, built to commemorate soldiers in the First World War, winds east of the state capital, forming one of the most scenic drives in the world.

Melbourne

Melbourne is Australia's second-largest city, and the capital of Victoria. The settlement named after England's then Prime Minister, Lord Melbourne, is Sydney's quieter, more cultured younger sibling and is regularly named as one of the world's most liveable cities. Devotees wouldn't live anywhere else and its combination of cooler climate and cultural mix is of real appeal. Other pluses are the historic electric trams, including the free Circle line, and its European cafés and restaurants. Detractors point to the cool, even crazy weather, where there really are often several seasons in one day. One Melbourne resident burst into tears on arriving in England because it felt so much like home, and when actress Ava Gardner was in Melbourne to shoot a film about the end of the world, she was quoted as saying she was already there. Sydneysiders joke, 'What's the best thing to come out of Melbourne?' Answer: ' The Hume Highway' (the road that connects the two cities). People from Melbourne make the same joke.

Many of the country's establishments are in the city, and its local élite and private schools have produced more lawyers, stockbrokers and prime ministers than anywhere else in the country. Melbourne prides itself on being refined because of its wide streets, numerous parks and attractive architecture. In 1895 Mark Twain pronounced:

It is a stately city architecturally as well as in magnitude. It has an elaborate system of cable-car service; it has museums, and colleges, and schools, and public gardens, and electricity, and gas, and libraries, and theatres, and mining centres and wool centres, and centres of the arts and sciences, and boards of trade, and ships, and railroads, and a harbour, and social clubs, and journalist clubs and racing clubs, and a squatter club sumptuously housed and appointed, and as many churches and banks as can make a living. In a word, it is equipped with everything that goes to make the modern great city.

Unlike Sydney, Melbourne was built on a grid system. The River Yarra separates the city socially, with house prices on the southeast side more expensive, and those to the north more industrial. Melbourne has very distinct enclaves and is decidedly multicultural. It famously has the biggest Greek population outside Athens, as well as a significant number of Lebanese and Italians. **Brunswick Street**, with its restaurants and small shops, is very charming and distinctly bohemian, while **Lygon Street** is the city's Little Italy, and V**ictoria Street** is packed with Vietnamese eateries. **Crown Casino** is a more recent feature, built at the cost of over A$1.5 billion. It is a big, brash entertainment complex with the country's largest casino, as well as a hotel, restaurants and designer shops, and pylons that spectacularly belch out fire every hour on the riverfront. In **Acland Street** is a Jewish community with cafés and cakes that would rival Vienna. **St Kilda** is an attractive if faded beach resort, with a lively esplanade and traditional funfair of Luna Park.

The city is very much defined by it sporting history. Although Australian Football League (AFL) has taken football into the field of national sports, the game is still rooted in Melbourne, where it was invented in 1858. The game is played between March and September on Fridays, Saturdays and Sundays at the Melbourne Cricket Ground (MCG) and the Telstra Dome, with the Grand Final as the climax, and there are nine important Aussie Rule football clubs here.

Melbourne is the only city in the world to declare a public holiday in tribute to a horse race and is where the Melbourne Cup has been held on the first Tuesday of November since 1861. Even though workers in other cities should be at their desks, few are glued to them on this day, when almost everyone makes a bet (around A$100 million in total) on one of the horses running at the two-mile Flemington Racecourse. The Spring Racing Carnival starting at the beginning of October launches 50 days of racing, with major country cups held throughout the region, including the Melbourne Cup. Melbourne Cup Week is a huge social event along the lines of Ascot, which is characterised by everything from the glamour of 'Ladies' Day' to Stakes Day, which is popular with families.

A couple of hours drive away is **Phillip Island** – famous for its Penguin Parade, where hundreds of tiny penguins waddle up the beach at dusk – and the historic gold-mining city of Ballarat. Melbourne is the starting point for one of the country's – if not the world's, – most spectacular road trips. The **Great**

Ocean Road stretches for more than 60 miles east of the city along the southern coast, where the eroded rock towers, the 'Twelve Apostles', make an extraordinary sight. Inland is the high ground, home to the title character in Banjo Patterson's 1890 poem 'The Man from Snowy River'.

Mornington Peninsula is a holiday area just a couple of hours south of Melbourne. The skinny peninsula here is dotted with bay and ocean beaches, where beach huts or 'boxes' can go for several hundred thousand dollars. **Sorrento** and **Portsea** are two of the most popular – and therefore most expensive – settlements.

To the north is the **Yarra Valley**, a wine region where Moët and Chandon has just established itself. The **Dandenong Ranges** have mountains which are as blue as Sydney's, due to the eucalyptus trees, and which offer a cool retreat from the city, with rainforest walks, a steam train and exotic birds.

Australian Capital Territory

Plenty of jokes have been made about the Australian Capital Territory, or ACT. It took seven years to create the capital here, along with two royal commissions and various parliamentary debates. In some ways, the decision was a conciliatory one, as Canberra was diplomatically placed halfway between the two powerful cities of Sydney and Melbourne. This fact, along with the argument that it was perfectly placed on the confluence of the Murray and Darling Rivers, made it a natural capital. Today, some still like to say that Canberra won for being equally inconvenient to both the country's major cities.

Canberra

The city is surrounded by beautiful mountains and the state is made up almost entirely of bushland. Although the seat of government was transferred here as long ago as 1927, the city's growth was decidedly slow. Walter Burley Griffin was the city's original architect, whose vision of an artificial lake as the focus for the city was eventually realised in 1963 with the damning of the Mononglo River.

Over 300,000 people live here today, although the fabricated city is not without its detractors. Canberra is widely slammed for being bland, like other man-made cities that act solely as centre of government, such as Brasilia in Brazil and America's Washington DC. With his legendary tact, Prince Philip pronounced it a city without a soul, while it might be more diplomatic to say that the city has no real centre and it is certainly not a tourist destination. Amusingly, the Aboriginal place name of Canberra was chosen only after it was realised that the word meant 'woman's breasts'.

South Australia

The state stretched between Western Australia and Victoria is the nation's breadbasket and known for three things – wine, the Flinders Ranges and the Adelaide Festival. The country's driest state is strangely civilised, its capital is distinctly sedate and the whole of Southern Australia's inhabitants seem to be in love with it. This is the country's third largest state – the size of France, Spain and Portugal combined – and its extreme physical environments produce opals in Coober Pedy, coal fields in Leigh Creek, uranium, copper and gold in Roxby Downs and gas in Moomba. It is also a centre for car manufacturing.

Adelaide

The capital, Adelaide, was founded by English engineer Colonel William Light, in 1836. He was suffering from tuberculosis, which meant he had just two months to complete his task. His original design is still apparent today; from the air it looks like a misshapen figure of eight, cut through by the Torrens River.

The city has Victorian houses, a Mediterranean climate and the Murray River, with its birds and steam boats. It's a stately place known for its conservatism, parks and churches, and is an ideal base for exploring Australia's illustrious wine region, the **Barossa Valley**, less than an hour's drive from the city. Big labels like Penfold, Seppelts and Wolf Blass are here, but take time to sniff out the many smaller but no less outstanding vineyards. Other than its wine, the greatest of South Australia's attractions is **Kangaroo Island**. This is a great place to see native animals. In just one day you can spot wallabies, kangaroos, koalas, kookaburras, echidnas and penguins, as well as sea lions on the beach.

Built on a grid system and flanked by hills on its western side, the city is conservative yet lively. Mark Twain fell in love with it, pronouncing, 'If the rest of Australia or any small part were half so beautiful, it was a fortunate country.' Adelaide has more restaurants per head of population than any other major Australian city, numerous pubs in the city centre and what is said to be the largest fresh produce market in the Southern Hemisphere.

Modern buildings and 19th-century architecture stand side by side. This distinctly cosmopolitan city is home to 1.2 million people, and hosts cultural events from the Festival of Arts to the Fringe Festival, as well as sporting events such as the Test Cricket and the Classic Car Rally. The Festival of the Arts takes place over a fortnight in the first quarter of every even-numbered year, bringing together some of the best visual, written and performance arts in the world. The most expensive houses are north of the river and were originally reserved for the British upper classes. This area is home to the Adelaide Oval.

South of the river is the grid of the business district, encircled by parks separating the centre from the rest of the city.

Coober Pedy

Just a few hours north is another world. Coober Pedy is a strange subterranean town where rich opal-mining attracts hopefuls – some would say no-hopers – from all over the country. Temperatures of 49°C (120°F) or more mean living underground is the only way to survive, and it's not just homes that are built beneath the surface, but hotels, shops and churches too. The town is largely featureless desert, with no trees and abandoned mines, giving it the appearance of a war zone. One of these homes was used in *Mad Max III*. Victor Harbour, Goolwa and Port Harbour are popular beach towns 60 miles or so south of Adelaide where the city's inhabitants gravitate at weekends, all of which are generally cooler than the state capital.

The Barossa Valley

The Barossa Valley is both a favourite holiday destination and an important wine region, which is responsible for more than half of the country's wines. It has an appealing Mediterranean climate, scenic countryside and pretty villages. Cellars open their doors for tastings and hotels and resorts dotted throughout the region cater to the many visitors who come to taste the world-class wine. Around 30 wineries in just a 12-mile by 6-mile area can be visited by private vehicle, on group tours, or even by bicycle.

In the 1830s, German Lutheran farmers were the first to settle here. They planted grape vines and established the industry that exists today, but also enriched the area with their own culture, traditional restaurants, churches and houses. On the eastern side of the valley, the Murray River is one of the largest river systems in the world. In 1887 the area was irrigated, resulting in a lush land with a variety of fruit of wine as well as wildlife and watersports.

Further Afield

Murray River is nearly 1,200 miles long with lovely scenery. William Randell was something of a visionary in that he was the first to put an admittedly ramshackle steam boat on the water here in 1853, with the aim of transporting flour to the Victorian gold fields, and only 20 or so years later there were a couple of hundred of these kinds of vessels on the river. Today it is a peaceful spot, and the boats offer river cruises to tourists, and houseboats for rent.

The **Flinders Ranges** are a mountain range that begins at the north of Adelaide and reaches far into the outback. Dating back one billion years, they

The Ghan Railway: A Living Legend

This train, which runs through the heart of a continent, forms one of the great railway journeys of the world. When the first carriages steamed into Alice Springs from Adelaide on 6 August 1929, the idea was that the route would run all the way to Darwin. It took more than 70 years to turn that dream into a reality, but in February 2004 the route was made twice as long. The new extended train is made up of two locomotives with 43 carriages that weigh over 2,000 tonnes. Those 330 passengers lucky enough to get to ride on the new train – tickets sell out months in advance – are given good food and comfortable berths.

The new railway, which opened up the heart of the country to commerce and tourism, played an important part in Australia's history, but was not without its mishaps. It had to cross through one of the most unforgiving environments in the world, where frequent flooding meant the train could be delayed for up to several months. The train travelled at such a slow pace that most people could walk faster and it is said the driver sometimes had to shoot wild animals to feed the hungry passengers. Once in the 1970s it did not appear in Alice Springs for three long months, forcing supplies of milk to be flown in every day. In 1980 a new line was built, which followed a less hazardous route, with bridges crossing the troublesome rivers. A local businessman bought the old railway, which he cut up and polished and sold as souvenirs; in 1988 a museum was opened at the Macdonnell Siding.

Before the railway was built, all goods had to arrive by camel trains that were driven by Afghan tribesmen who were skilled at driving these tough 'ships of the desert'. They drove hundreds of miles in the searing heat and had to deal with blinding dust and incessant flies. This is how the railway got its name. These beasts of burden brought in everything from pianos and cars to long-awaited letters and cosmetics. The Afghans arrived in Australia without any women and often ended up marrying with the Aboriginal population. When the railway was completed, the cameleers were forced out of work and had to let their camels loose into the outback. Descendants of these early Afghan drivers still live in Alice Springs and the local cemetery holds a number of their ancestors.

are rich in geological interest as well as attracting artists, poets and writers throughout the seasons, especially when the after spring rains bring multi-coloured wildflowers. **Wilpena Pound** is an unusual 30-mile square basin encircled by high cliffs which is home to a rich collection of wildlife.

Whyalla is South Australia's second city, situated near the head of the **Spencer Gulf**. Although it has a distinctly rural setting, the city boasts the full range of services, as well as an airport, marina and maritime museum. There is a strong sporting and outdoor culture here, including activities such as camping, surfing and bushwalking.

Western Australia

This enormous state spans over one million square miles and occupies around a third of Australia. It is practically another country, with distinct regions, each with their own climatic zones. When it is warm and dry in the north, it is cool and wet in the south. Many Australians tend to go a bit misty-eyed when talking about Perth and 'WA', although few have ever been. This is the most remote of all the states – even more so than the Northern Territory – and distance and high air fares work against it, which is unfortunate, as it is one of Australia's most wild and beautiful regions. Flanked mostly by desert to the east, to the west the state is fringed by white sandy beaches and nearly 8,000 miles of the most pristine coastline in the country.

Although the French beat the English to Western Australia in 1779, they did not actually claim it, so that when the British got here nearly 50 years later they were able to form a colony. At first, no one wanted to live here because of the mosquitoes and mud swamps, so convicts had to be brought in. Gold rushes in the 1880s and 1890s laid the foundations for its future and brought an influx of people, increasing the population by a mammoth 700 per cent. Few of the Victorian buildings that sprung up during this time still remain, and the city is largely characterised by modern skyscrapers.

Perth

Around 80 per cent of the state's population of 1.7 million are settled in the state capital of Perth, with the remaining few concentrated around its coast. The city is green with parks and gardens, and has a thriving yachting community and diving just 10 miles off its coast. The southwest has lush towering forests and spectacular surfing beaches. East of Perth are gold fields and the mining town of **Kalgoorlie**. East again is the **Nullarbor Plain**, which extends all the way to the border with South Australia. The north is un-mistakably wild and peppered with isolated communities and the pearling port of **Broome**.

Since the first Dutch navigators set eyes on Western Australia's shores in the 17th century, more than 700 vessels have come to grief on the rocky coast. Nowadays these waters are better known as the arena for world-famous yacht races, such as the Whitbread Round-the-World Race and the America's Cup, and some of the best game fishing in the country. The North West Cape's seas are full of whales in season (March to June), which you can swim alongside, and are also home to one of the country's best-kept secrets, a second barrier reef called **Ningaloo Marine Park**. The reef runs for 160 miles, where there is snorkelling with manta rays. **Shark Bay** is a World Heritage Site nearly 500 miles north of Perth, famous not for its sharks but for its dolphins, which come so close to the shore that children can paddle in the shallow waters as the animals swim.

Perth is the most isolated city in the world and physically closer to Singapore than it is to Sydney. The nearest city is Adelaide, 1,500 miles away. Rich in gold, silver, diamonds and pearls, Perth became a base for mining and oil companies and a brash city to rival Dallas, complete with corruption scandals, until it all came crashing down in the 1980s. Some say that Perth still has the largest number of millionaires in the country, who rub shoulders with around 80,000 students at the various colleges and five universities. The city not only has a warm, sunny climate but the highest number of average daily sunshine hours of any in Australia. The metropolitan area of Perth has miles upon miles of coastline, with some of Australia's best beaches, popular for water sports.

Fremantle

Fremantle is Western Australia's principal port, just 12 miles west of Perth's central business district (CBD). Ideally located at the mouth of the Swan River on the shores of the Indian Ocean, Fremantle is a thriving tourist centre and attracts hundreds of visitors each week. Charles O'Conner is the man responsible for putting Fremantle on the map. After Captain Fremantle sailed in here in 1829, nothing much happened until O'Conner, an engineer, constructed a harbour out of the unforgiving rock, which allowed bigger ships to call in, making it a centre for the dockyards. Today, the population of 250,000 gravitate towards upmarket South Terrace with its strip of historic architecture and colourful markets.

Further Afield

In the southwest 'hook' of the continent lies the **Margaret River** wine region with wild forests, thundering surf, dramatic cliffs and rich bird life. Only 30 years ago this was simply a farming region, before it was discovered by surfers, bohemians and wine buffs; today it is where the people of Perth love to come for their weekends and holidays. Dolphins flock to **Bunbury** and the tourists follow them. Inland, the state is mostly wheat fields and desert, but approaching 380 miles from Perth is the gold-mining town of Kalgoorlie, with the world's largest open-cast gold mine and fine old pubs lining the wide streets.

The Kimberley has such a tiny population and is so remote that few people ever visit it. Less than 25,000 people live in this part of the country permanently, even though it forms an area as large as California. Most residents are here for a year or two to work in the local mines, and this is real frontier country, with harsh mountains and extreme weather. There are only three towns in this part of the state – Broome, Derby and Kununurru – and the main road was only paved in the 1980s. On the eastern edge, close to Kununurra, is a million-acre cattle station, **El Questro**, where you can camp in tents or stay in an upmarket resort. There are also the ancient **Geikie and Windjana gorges**, pearl farms with the world's best South Sea pearls.

Broome is in the remote northeast corner of the state and its 20-mile long Cable beach is one of the most gorgeous in the world. The beach takes its name from the first overseas cable that was laid here in 1889 to link the country with London. When pearl shell was discovered here in the 1880s it created a community that was named after the then governor. It took less than 30 years for it to become the pearl capital of the world, pulling in more than 80 per cent of the world shell found on the planet, which was used mostly for buttons. It was a real melting pot, with Chinese, Arabs, Malaysians and Japanese all congregating here to work on the hundreds of pearling boats. But it was a dangerous job and the industry had died out by the 1930s.

Thankfully, Broome was saved from the attentions of English property tycoon Sir Alistair McAlpine, who fell for the town and decided in his wisdom to build the flash Cable Beach Club. A combination of a slump in the economy and McAlpine's chickens coming home to roost meant that he didn't get to transform the community further. The original Chinatown still remains, although of course it is small by global standards. Camel rides and spectacular sunsets are a real draw here.

Inland from Perth, **Kalgoorlie** is unmistakably an outback town as well as an important stop on the Indian-Pacific train ride. In 1893 Paddy Hannan, an Irish man, miraculously stumbled across gold nuggets under a tree here, prompting the last of Australia's last gold rushes. Just a few years later, the town boasted a population of around 6,000. Revenue created here helped to fund a 350-mile pipeline to bring in clear water to this desert region, and by 1903 there were 30,000 inhabitants, which is the number of people living here today.

Queensland

This is the holiday state, Australia's Cornwall, although of course with a better climate. The best beaches in the country are here, along with tropical islands, stunning mountains and the mini Miami of the Gold Coast. Tropical heat and humidity can make the pace of life positively Caribbean. There are also pockets of brash high rises and slick developments in the state that is four times the size of California yet with a population of just over three million.

The state's background is not at all glamorous, beginning as so many do with the brutal treatment of convicts. However, as early as the 1840s 'free settlers' came here in their thousands, attracted not only by the obvious natural resources in the sea, but by the opportunity to grab land on a huge scale. By 1859, Queensland had become a state in its own right, breaking away from New South Wales, and to the surprise of everyone it became relatively wealthy from sheep, gold and sugar. However, in the eyes of many, the state remained a cultural backwater, with a poor reputation for its treatment of Aborgines. One man who did not help Queensland's image was Sir Johannes Bjelke-Peterson, who managed to keep it in some kind of time warp right up until 1987, when he was voted out of power.

The biggest draw for visitors to Queensland is the **Great Barrier Reef**, teeming with colourful coral and exotic creatures. The reef runs for 1,250 miles along the coast, as far south as Bundaberg, 238 miles north of Brisbane. There are also many white-sand beaches, the best of which are on the Gold Coast in the state's south, and on the Sunshine Coast, a two-hour drive north of Brisbane; there are others in Cairns and Port Douglas. However, deadly box jellyfish, or 'stingers', halt swimming at beaches in the northern third of the country in the months between October to May.

Brisbane

Brisbane, or 'Brissie', is the third largest city in the country with around 1.5 million inhabitants living in the arm of the Brisbane River. Moreton Bay, where the city was founded, is 20 miles from the city. This is where many of the country's worst convicts were brought in 1824 and kept in such appalling conditions that a large number of them died. A terrible fire in 1864 practically destroyed the whole city; the most attractive buildings date from the 1880s.

Further Afield

The Gold Coast became a holiday destination way back in 1884 when city coaches began operating from Brisbane three times a week. This 25-mile strip of unrelenting development runs from Coolangatta on the New South Wales border up to Surfer's Paradise. Over-zealous development resulted in a thick wall of brutal skyscrapers, which cast giant afternoon shadows over the beach. Apart from the 300,000 or so people who live near the beach, there are numerous holiday apartments and hotels here and the area is a popular tourist destination both for visitors from abroad and for native Australians. Many people have made millions from soaring property prices in this area in recent years.

The Gold Coast is not the place to come if you are searching for either peace or civilisation: theme parks, brash nightlife and louder-than-loud attractions are the main feature of this region. However, it is a different world inland, with farming country, historic **Warwick** city, national parks, scenic waterfalls and attractive mountain areas. The **Glasshouse Mountains** 60 miles north of Brisbane are volcanic and dramatic; the **Blackall Range** are sedate pockets reminiscent of 19th-century England, and the 17-mile stretch from **Maleny** to **Mapleton** is dotted with waterfalls and rain forests.

The **Sunshine Coast** is a dense string of holiday resorts north of Brisbane, reaching all the way from the Glasshouse Mountains to Rainbow Beach. This stretch tends to attract families and retirees who are attracted to the quiet life. **Noosa** is a popular and wealthy tourist spot that combines Noosaville, Noosa Heads and other communities. Noosa Heads is the undeniably classy spot on the whole coast, sandwiched between two national parks. Surfers have gravitated towards its shores since the 1960s. No buildings are allowed to be constructed higher than the trees here, saving the area from the overdevelopment of some of the other parts of the coast. Rockhampton is a commercial centre that is big on beef. This is a modern, hot city of over 65,000 people.

Townsville is the country's largest tropical city, and is industrial rather than attractive. The city was founded in 1863 by two men who built a wharf and a cattleman plant here. It came into its own during the Second World War when it acted as an important base for American and Australian forces. Dominated by the 1,000ft high Castle Rock, it is the jumping-off point for popular **Magnetic Island**.

Cairns is a huge national and international tourist destination and a Mecca for the Great Barrier Reef, mainly because it offers rainforest to the west and world-class diving in its waters to the east. It has come a long way since its origins as a base for small-time fishermen in the 1860s. Gold and tin finds in the nearby Atherton Tablelands soon changed its fortune and in 1924 a railway was built to connect it with Brisbane. As recently as the 1980s, Cairns found its feet as a tourist destination, in some ways sadly consuming the original settlement.

One of the most appealing of Queensland's destinations is the aquatic playground made up of the 74 **Whitsunday Islands** in the Great Barrier Reef Marine Park. These mostly uninhabited islands are a paradise for kayaking, snorkelling, diving, fishing, bird-watching and bareboat sailing. Another big attraction is the lush 110-million-year-old **Daintree rainforest**, just north of Port Douglas.

Like many settlements in the area, **Port Douglas**, 50 miles north of Cairns, was built on the Gold Rush in the late 19th century. Situated between the rainforest and the coral sea, as recently as the 1980s it was a sleepy fishing village. The five-star resorts, golf courses and upmarket marinas haven't blighted its appeal and it has welcomed the likes of holidaying Bill Clinton. In fact, wander along the wonderful Four Mile Beach here and you might just bump into Jerry Seinfeld or Sean Penn.

Northern Territory

This is the land known affectionately as the 'Never Never', which has an almost mythical status within the country. Many Australians regard NT as the real Australia, even though few of them have ever been there. The northern 'Top End' is soaked by monsoon rains, which water the lush land of Kakadu National Park, while the south is the 'Red Centre' and home to the magical **Uluru (Ayers Rock)**. The Northern Territory is six times the size of Great Britain, even though it has one of the lowest populations of any state in the world at a little over 200,000. Darwin and Alice Springs are the two main centres – the rest of the territory's inhabitants live in out-of-the-way cattle stations, Aboriginal missions or mining communities.

Near the tropical city of Darwin, the territory's capital is **Kakadu National Park**, where you can cruise past crocodiles on inland billabongs (ponds), bird-watch and visit ancient Aboriginal rock-art sites. Closer to Darwin is **Litchfield National Park**, where you can take a dip in fern-fringed swimming holes surrounded by red cliffs – hill scenes straight from Eden. You can cruise the waterways of Katherine Gorge, a few hours' drive south of Darwin, or explore them by canoe. Near **Katherine** you can canoe along rarely explored, crocodile-infested inland rivers and learn to make your own didgeridoo (a large wooden, traditional Aboriginal musical instrument).

Darwin

The state capital of Darwin began life as Palmerston before being renamed Darwin after the naturalist who came into the bay here in 1839 and rather hopefully believed it would rival the now sophisticated city of Singapore. Despite earlier settlement, Darwin was not fully established until the gold rush of the 1880s. The Second World War changed the face of the city once again when it became a major base for Allied forces and major highways and airstrips were constructed.

Darwin is relatively close to Asia, giving it a mix of nationalities, and still attracts those drawn to its frontier feel, with many of its workers on short-term contracts and enjoying a hard-drinking lifestyle. Nearly a quarter of the population here is Aboriginal – the highest percentage anywhere in the country. Almost half of the land is given over to the original inhabitants and permission is required to visit it. There are only two seasons here in the tropical north – wet and dry. During the wet season, in summer time, the heat, high humidity and rains make life difficult. In the dry period (April to September), the heat and drought can be equally difficult to bear.

If you expect Darwin to be a remote backwater, you are in for a surprise. It is a city of 80,000, with a thriving business district and a distinctly modern feel.

This is partly due to Cyclone Tracy, which practically destroyed the city on Christmas day in 1974, so that it had to be rebuilt almost from scratch. Its more sophisticated neighbourhoods are indistinguishable from the most desirable parts of Melbourne or Sydney. That said, the old timber houses with wrap-around balconies are rarely seen, having been replaced by sturdier versions in brick. Darwin has good beaches and boating in the harbour.

Tasmania

The very last stop before Antarctica is the island state of Tasmania, 200 miles or so off the southeast coast. Wet and green, with lakes and forests, 'Tassie' is something of a mini New Zealand. This heart-shaped state is around the same size as Scotland and can be crossed by car in just a couple of hours. Like England's northern neighbour, it has trout-filled lakes, mountains and green forests. It also has an altogether more relaxed way of life than the rest of the country from which it is separated by the stormy waters of the Bass Straights. This stretch of sea is crossed by a regular overnight ferry service from Melbourne, but the Roaring Forties is an area of particularly strong winds from the west, forming some of the roughest waters in the world, so if you don't have sea legs, think twice before making the journey.

Although the Dutch explored Tasmania in the mid-17th century, they largely ignored it, and it wasn't until 1803 that the British set up a penal colony here with some of the harshest prisons in the country. Convicts stopped being sent here in 1852, but the island's violent history continued, with the Aborigines suffering probably more here than anywhere else in Australia. During the first years of the 19th century, these new arrivals fought with the 5,000 natives, whose ancestors had been living here for more than 10,000 years, since they had walked across the Bass Straight during the last Ice Age .

The first settlers simply decided to kill them all, which they largely succeeded in doing. They poisoned the men, took the children into slavery and raped and killed the women. Finally, in a particularly hideous chapter of the island's history, a 'Black Line' was formed, in 1830, in which 2,000 civilians marched shoulder to shoulder for nearly a month, shooting Aborigines on sight. Only 150 survived and they were effectively imprisoned on Flinders Island. Forced to become Christians, most of them died of either grief or disease.

A third of the state's population lives in the capital of **Hobart**. The country's second oldest city has a tight grid of streets with pastel-painted timber houses and sandstone warehouses on the waterfront, which have been transformed into galleries shops and restaurants. The historic Georgian houses and twisting alleyways of Battery Point are protected by the National Trust.

Mount Wellington, 1,220m (4,000ft), sometimes gets snow, and has been climbed by many, including Darwin and George Bass, who gave his name to the perilous straits. Anthony Trollope, the outspoken novelist, was unimpressed, declaring it to be 'just enough of a mountain to give excitement to ladies and gentlemen in middle life'. The east side of Tasmania seems particularly English, with its cream teas, shops selling antiques and names like **Brighton** and **Somerset**. **Huonville Valley** at the heart of the island is an area of apples and pines, the pine trees here produced timber known as 'green gold' because of its great value.

Port Arthur, 70 miles southwest of Hobart, can seem like a different country. Mark Twain described it as a 'bringing together of heaven and hell' because this peaceful and pretty landscape was the birthplace of so much brutality in the prison camps. This is where the most violent criminals from Sydney were sent and a kind of Alcatraz was set up, so that if the dogs and guards didn't get would-be escapees, the sharks and the waves of the water would. Then, in 1852, the idea of sensory deprivation arrived from England. In a kind of early version of Guantanamo Bay, prisoners wearing hoods and chains were isolated for 23 hours a day and not allowed to speak. Most of them went insane. The solution was to set up a lunatic asylum, which is now a popular tourist site visited by 200,000 people each year. They take boat trips to the **Island of the Dead**, the final resting place for nearly 2,000 convicts.

Australia Today

Images of Australians as crocodile-wrestling Paul Hogan types who live in a country removed from the rest of the world, where the men are men and the culture is nil, are all but a distant memory. When the tsunami struck at the end of 2004, Australia pledged more money than any other country. Australia today is a vibrant, contemporary country, with world-class artists, a thriving film industry and a confident identity. The 1988 bicentennial of British settlement indicated a new-found confidence, while the referendum on republicanism in 1999 and the Olympic Games in 2000 heralded a more contemporary, outward focus for Australia.

While closely allying itself with Asia, the country's problems, such as the crisis in the wool industry and the plight of its indigenous people, are purely its own. When author Donald Horne coined the phrase 'the lucky country' in his book of the same name, published in 1964, it was generally realised that he was being ironic. It was only in the years that followed the release of the book that the phrase was sabotaged by politicians, the media and the general public. Horne was referring to the country's cultural cringe, its foreign policy and the White Australia Policy. He says that he was in fact talking about a 'not too clever country'. In his book, Horne wanted to explore such issues as the lack of innovation in manufacturing and enterprise generally. The title came from his idea that while other countries had to work to be industrialised, Australia was lucky enough to be formed as a nation when it could simply reel in the technological, economic and social innovations from the rest of the world. While these other countries were clever, Australia was just lucky.

Politics and the Monarchy

The Political System

The political system in Australia is made up of a bicameral federal parliament, which includes an Upper House of 76 senators and a Lower House with 150 members. The government is formed in the Lower House, and the leader of the majority party in the House of Representatives is the prime minister. The members of the **Lower House** are elected from single-member constituencies, known as 'electorates' or 'seats'. This is organised in relation to population, so that the more populous the state, the more members it will have. In the **Upper House**, representation is made up of 12 senators from each state and two senators from each mainland territory, regardless of population. **Elections** for both houses take place every three years and are for six-year terms using proportional representation and the single transferable vote.

There are three inter-connected arms of government:

- **Legislature**: the commonwealth parliament; responsible for all laws and the legal framework of the other two arms.
- **Executive**: the prime minister, the cabinet ministers, ministers and their departments; administers laws.
- **Judiciary**: the High Court of Australia and subsidiary federal courts; hears cases using both statute law and the common law.

States and Territories

Each of the individual states in Australia is led by a premier who has won a majority (or working minority) in the Lower House. Their sovereignty and juris-diction is ruled by the constitution and cannot be affected by the Commonwealth, unless a referendum is called. In addition to the states, there are also three self-governing territories: the Australian Capital Territory, the Northern Territory and Norfolk Island.

Political Parties

Confusingly, the **Liberal Party** in Australia is centre right. Representing business and middle-class voters, it is most closely allied to the Conservative Party in England. The **National Party** or 'Nationals' is another party of the right, whose supporters are in the main those with rural interests (they used to be known as the Country Party). The **Australian Labor Party (ALP)** (*see* box, p.58) is comparable to the UK Labour Party, with members from the working and middle classes. The differences between Liberal and Labor voters have, as in the UK, become increasingly blurred in recent years.

Smaller parties include the **Australian Democrats,** whose supporters are mostly middle-class centrists; the **Australian Greens**, a radical environmentalist party; **One Nation**, a populist anti-immigration party (formed in the late 1990s and now almost nonexistent); and the **Family First Party**, a party appealing to conservative Christians. Although these smaller parties have only ever won a handful of seats, together with the independents they hold the balance of

50 Years of Politics
1949 Robert Menzies becomes prime minister. The Liberals (Australia's Conservatives) remain in power for 23 years.
1972 The Labor Party, led by Gough Whitlam, is elected.
1975 Liberals, led by Malcolm Frazer, regains power.
1983 Labor elected with Bob Hawke as leader.
1991 Paul Keating takes over from Hawke until 1996.
1996 The Liberal-National Party coalition comes to power led by John Howard.
2004 John Howard wins a fourth term.

The Australian Labor Party

Gough Whitlam was the charismatic character the Labor Party needed to bring them to office, which finally happened in 1972. This heralded a time of important change: conscription was abolished, Australia pulled out of Vietnam and the welfare system was overhauled. Although Labor with Whitlam won again in 1974, a sudden world recession and a series of scandals brought pressure on Whitlam to resign, prompting a constitutional crisis that resulted dramatically in his 'dismissal' by the governor-general, who represented the Queen. Malcolm Fraser, leader of the Liberal-National Party opposition took over. Labor came back in 1983 with the election of Bob Hawke, an ex-union leader. Even at this stage, Labor had become more conservative. Labor continued in power, with Paul Keating becoming prime minister in the early 1990s. Medicare (national healthcare), was introduced only at this late stage.

The Labor Party in Australia is the oldest in the country, with a history that precedes Federation. That said, before the 1980s, the party had very little success electorally. Just as in England, the party was formed to represent the rights of workers, and, while it is still affiliated with the trade unions, it has moved away from its roots over the years. In 1921, socialism was formally embraced by the party, which declares itself to be committed to 'the democratic socialisation of industry, production, distribution and exchange' and to 'eliminate exploitation and other anti-social features in those fields'. However, Labor's chief aim is to civilise capitalism, not to replace it, and the party's members include a significant number of liberals, social democrats and nationalists who would not align themselves to socialism.

Instead, two main threads of ideology run through the Labor Party's history. There is the centre-left element of social liberalism, which seeks a positive equality that is expressed by politicians such as Hawke and Keating as the idea of social justice. Then there is Laborism – a centre-right concept that can be defined as a commitment to protect those in the working classes who are in need, and to endeavour to provide them with full employment for a fair wage with decent working conditions. Later, a third strand of thought came to light, when in the 1980s and 1990s the governments of Hawke and Keating took on board market conditions, which was criticised by some as a move to the right. The criticism levelled at UK prime minister Tony Blair – that he compromised his ideology to get into power – has also been thrown at Hawke and Keating.

power in the senate. Further, as disillusionment with the major parties increases, these minorities enjoy greater appeal. For example, those frustrated with internal wrangling within the Australian Democrats have been drawn towards to the Greens.

Although voting is compulsory, there is a tendency for Australians to dismiss politicians as 'bastards who are all the same'. You will be able to vote only if you are a citizen; not even immigrants with 'resident' status have this right.

The Monarchy

Australia is a federation that was formed in 1901, and has a constitutional monarchy. Its written constitution defines the relationship between the Commonwealth (or national government) and the various states. It is an independent nation within the Commonwealth of Nations, and Queen Elizabeth II is the official sovereign. She is represented in Australia as a whole by a governor-general and by a governor in each state. Australia is now completely independent from the UK, a process which took place over a period of years. In 1999 there was a long-awaited referendum on the proposal to make Australia a republic, which would have meant that the Queen would be replaced by a president. Although it was widely expected that the Australian people would vote in favour of the proposal, it was defeated owing to its flawed wording.

Recent History

In 1996 the Liberal Party-National Party coalition came to power and John Howard became prime minister, ending 13 years of ALP government. Howard was elected again in 1998, 2001 and 2004. His government has attempted to bring down the current deficit and to speed up the privatisation process, but perhaps its most controversial move has been to bring in a goods and services tax along the lines of British VAT. In the future, he is expected to strengthen relations with the USA, Britain and his closer neighbours, China and Japan.

Howard's election win in 2001 was something of a surprise, which some say was due to his harsh line on illegal immigrants and asylum-seekers. At this time, Australia's relations with its neighbours in Asia were somewhat strained. Anxieties about world terrorism were brought to a head in October 2002 with the Bali bombing and only increased with the bombing of the Australian embassy in Jakarta in September 2004. The campaign for the 2004 election was fought on fierce support for the Iraq war and consistently successful economic performance. In December 2004 John Howard became the second-longest serving prime minister in Australia, just overtaking Bob Hawke.

Internal Issues

Australian politics is largely ignored from the European corner of the world, but two of its prime ministers did make world news and have been immortalised for bizarre acts. In 1954, Bob Hawke made the *Guinness Book of Records* for sculling 2.5 pints of beer in 11 seconds. Then, in 1967, Prime Minister Harold Holt went for a swim off a beach in Victoria and was never seen again. Conspiracy theories abounded, including one that he had been captured by a Chinese submarine, although it seems likely he was just taken by the strong current. In typically irreverent Australian style, locals remember him by naming a swimming pool after him and now refer to 'doing a Harold Holt' – a bolt.

The Environment

Australia's environmental record is – perhaps surprisingly for a country that is so proud of its natural beauty – very poor. It has persistently refused to ratify the

World Heritage Sites

At the time of writing (2005), Australia has 16 Australian sites on the World Heritage List. These sites have been so designated because of their importance to all the peoples of the world. Australia has national legislation in place to protect World Heritage values through a strict environmental assessment process and strives for community and Indigenous involvement in management.

The **Great Barrier Reef** was one of Australia's first World Heritage Areas and is the world's largest World Heritage Area. It is thought to contain more than 1,500 species of fish and over 300 species of hard, reef-building corals. In addition, more than 400 species of sponges have been identified on the Reef.

Kakadu National Park was inscribed on the World Heritage List in three stages. It is one of the few sites that is listed for both outstanding cultural and natural universal values. This park forms a breathtaking natural environment and contains internationally important wetlands.

The **Willandra Lakes Region** in the Murray Basin area in southwestern New South Wales is a large area of arid land that features dried salt lakes, saltbush, sand dunes and woodlands.

The **Tasmanian Wilderness** is another site listed for its outstanding natural and cultural universal values. It forms one of the largest conservation reserves in Australia and covers around 20 per cent of the land area of the island of Tasmania. It is important as one of only three temperate wilderness areas in the Southern Hemisphere.

The **Lord Howe Island Group** lies 700km northeast of Sydney. The Lord Howe Island Group is made up of Lord Howe Island, Admiralty Islands, Mutton Bird Islands, Ball's Pyramid and associated coral reefs and marine environments.

Uluru-Kata Tjuta National Park was inscribed on the World Heritage List in two stages, first for its outstanding universal natural values and then for its outstanding universal cultural values. The park includes arid ecosystems and the national icon of Uluru (Ayers Rock). It is close to the centre of Australia in the traditional lands of Pitjantjatjara and Yankunytjatjara Aboriginal people.

Central Eastern Rainforest Reserves. In 1986, a number of rainforest reserves on the Great Escarpment of eastern New South Wales were inscribed on the World Heritage List for their outstanding natural universal values. Large extensions, including reserves in southeast Queensland, were listed in 1994.

Kyoto pact on global warming, despite pressure from the 15 countries of the European Union who have already signed the protocol. Signed in Japan in 1997, the pact decrees that signatory nations reduce greenhouse gas emissions by 8 per cent of their 1990 levels between 2008 and 2012. For it to take effect, the nations that account for 55 per cent of global greenhouse emissions must ratify it, but to date it is supported by countries responsible for only 36 per cent of such gases. Howard refuses to budge, declaring with disarming honesty that

The **Wet Tropics of Queensland** are between Townsville and Cooktown on the northeast coast of Queensland. This is a very beautiful area with fast-flowing rivers, deep gorges and spectacular waterfalls. There are high mountains and large areas of undisturbed rainforest.

Shark Bay on the most western point of the coast of Australia is one of the few properties inscribed on the World Heritage List for all four outstanding natural universal values. The Shark Bay region is where three major climatic regions collide, forming a special environment for botanical specimens.

Fraser Island, on the southern coast of Queensland, is the largest sand island in the world. This unusual and very beautiful environment includes pristine white beaches and stunning lakes, and teems with plant and wildlife.

There are two **Australian Fossil Mammal Sites**: on the Gregory River in Riversleigh in northwestern Queensland, and in Naracoorte, South Australia, on flat ground near the coast with a series of stranded coastal dunes.

The **Heard and McDonald Islands** lie in a remote place off the Australian mainland and were not discovered until the 19th century. They are near the meeting-point of Antarctic and temperate ocean waters.

Macquarie Island became a World Heritage Site in 1997. The island is about 1,500km southeast of Tasmania, about halfway between Tasmania and Antarctica. It is important internationally as it is the only island in the world made entirely of oceanic crust and rocks from deep below the earth's surface.

The Greater Blue Mountains Area was added to the World Heritage List in December 2000. This area of scenic mountainous landscape and eucalypt forests lies just west of Sydney. These forests are one of the reason it is important; along with its exceptional biodiversity, including ancient species.

Purnululu National Park in the East Kimberley Region is where Australia's tropical and arid zones meet, and is famous for its Bungle Bungle beehive formations. It was inscribed as a World Heritage Site only in 2003, when it was recognised for its geology. Purnululu also has had a rich Aboriginal cultural heritage over 20,000 years.

The **Royal Exhibition Building** and its surrounding **Carlton Gardens** in Melbourne are the latest to achieve World Heritage listing, for their cultural value, in 2004. The building is Australia's first to attain a World Heritage listing and is important because it represents the global influence of the international exhibition movement of the 19th and early 20th centuries.

such a move would cost Australia jobs and affect its national industries. By staying out, the USA and Australia will be unable to benefit from the valuable economic resources created under the protocol.

Australia created the second national park in the world in 1879 when it designated an area in the south of Sydney a Royal National Park. However, until remarkably recently, national industries were able to do pretty much whatever they liked to the environment. Oil-drilling threatened the Great Barrier Reef, and logging and sandmining nearly destroyed the pristine nature of Fraser Island, both of which are protected as World Heritage Sites. The Green Movement really began in Australia in 1972 in Tasmania when the United Tasmania Group was formed. Its aim was to stop the damming of Lake Pedder and, although it lost that battle, it is still the country's most formidable green army. Its successes include the protection of the Frankin River, which resulted in the declaration of the Southwest Tasmania World Heritage Area.

The exotic wildlife and flora of Australia are among the many attractions of the country, which has over a million different species of plants and animals, many of them unique to this part of the world. For example, some 80 per cent of native mammals live only in Australia. Earlier generations of Australians might have been impressed, but their actions had a devastating effect on their environment. Over the past 200 years, Australia has lost 75 per cent of its rainforests and has the world's worst record of mammal extinctions.

Nowadays Australians are increasingly concerned to preserve their environment. They express this by giving a high priority to national parks and reserves, by educating people about the impact of humans and imported animals on the native habitat, and through conservation efforts in the community. There can often be controversy when conservation and economic interests clash. An example occurred in the 2004 parliamentary election, when the extent to which logging should be permitted in the native forests of Tasmania became a major point of debate. There are wildlife protection societies in all the states, which have active branches at local level. For these groups, practical conservation and campaigning go hand in hand. They work on projects like tree-planting, restoring wildlife habitats and protecting rainforest remnants, and advise on helping wildlife in the suburbs. They also campaign for threatened wildlife areas and promote the importance of national and marine parks.

Native species are not only threatened by humans, they also suffer from the impact of European animals in the wild. Some of these, like red foxes and rabbits, were wild animals originally imported for sport. But pigs and goats imported as domestic animals have also gone feral in large numbers. And that cuddly domestic pet, the cat, has become lethal both as a widespread feral animal and as a marauder from suburban homes. The now wild rabbits, pigs and goats compete for food with native animals and can destroy native flora. The foxes and cats actively hunt and kill birds and mammals, not always consuming their prey. State governments have taken a number of measures, including culling, to reduce the effects on native wildlife. One controversial measure tried in parts of Victoria is a 'cat curfew' to reduce the night-time attacks on the threatened population of lyrebirds.

Even when native species adapt to an increasingly urban environment, they are in danger of being seen as pests when they co-exist with humans in suburban areas. Bandicoots cause problems by eating lots of grubs and garden pests and sometimes leaving snout-shaped marks on your lawn. You can encourage them into other sections of the garden, or build bandicoot-proof fencing. Possums are common visitors to backyards, and sometimes get into roof cavities. You can get advice on how to remove them safely and build a special possum box. There are plenty of snakes in Australia, but they are not naturally aggressive, and will attack humans only if hurt or provoked. If you find one in the backyard, you can call your local council office to arrange for it to be removed.

Asylum-seekers

Perhaps even more controversial than Australia's environmental policy is John Howard's tough stance against asylum-seekers. He has commanded the Australian navy to intercept ships carrying asylum seekers and re-direct them towards Papua New Guinea and other locations in the Pacific. His argument is that he is protecting the integrity of Australia's borders and is doing it in a humane and compassionate way. This treatment of asylum seekers has appalled some international observers. In 2004, Amnesty International declared that the Australian government's ongoing and indefinite detention of asylum-seekers is an abuse of human rights and breaches its international obligations. Amnesty went on to condemn the ongoing detention of children and of 100 Iranian detainees who had been held in Australia for more than three years. A series of hunger strikes and acts of self-harm carried out by this group have caused concern for their mental health.

The Wool Industry

The country has long been said to have ridden to economic wealth 'on the sheep's back', and even today the wool industry is worth A$3 billion. Extraordinarily, animal rights activists have turned this situation on its head. Just a few years ago, wool was a major export for Australia, bigger even than beef, of which it is the world's largest exporter. In just a couple of hundred years, the country has built up a flock of around 150 million sheep, which supply 70 per cent of the wool used by the world's clothing industry. Some fleeces produced in Tasmania are 'golden fleeces', in that they are literally worth more than their weight in gold.

But in 2004, the American animal rights organisation 'People for the Ethical Treatment of Animals (PETA) began an international campaign for a boycott of Australian wool. The group takes issue with the practice of 'mulesing', in which sheep are strapped to metal bars and skin is cut away with wool so that blowflies are unable to lay their eggs. The farmers argue that it is a necessary procedure and without it three million sheep would be at risk, but the wool industry says the practice will be phased out completely by 2010. At the time of writing, the major American clothing retailers Abercrombie and Fitch had introduced a boycott and others were threatening to join.

American Influence

In many ways Australia has more in common with America than with England. America's influence is of course felt the world over through its films, music and media, but perhaps nowhere else has its language infiltrated deep into the culture as in Australia, where you are, for example, much more likely to hear 'awesome' than the English 'brilliant' and where friends are 'dudes' and girls are 'babes'. American television is much more pervasive here, although English programmes are also popular.

Australian life has in recent years absorbed some American influences to an extent that is not noticeable in the UK. Go to a yoga class in this increasingly litigious country and you will be asked to sign a mitigation form in case of injury. According to recent news reports, some people who have been fed a constant diet of American crime programmes have dialled 911, the US emergency number, instead of the Australian version, 000.

William Howitt predicted:

It will take a century to work this miscellaneous gathering of rude people out of the scum. As they get money, they will, however, as in America, in time give their children some education; but out of them will grow, as is plain to see, a go-ahead, self-confident sort of people – Yankee sort of people.'

The 'have a go' attitude so integral to the Australian psyche has much in common with those acting out the American dream. The two countries share a history in which poor immigrant workers worked every hour of the day to make something of themselves and their new life. As a young country, Australia has always had its own version of the 'American Dream', but the country is now adopting more of its values of raw ambition and materialism. Not so long ago, someone down on their luck would be called a 'battler' by the non-judgemental Aussies, now they would more likely be labelled a 'loser'.

D.H. Lawrence declared after his visit:

This is the most democratic place I have ever been in. And the more I see of democracy the more I dislike it. It just brings everything down to the mere vulgar level of wages and prices, electric lights and water closets, and nothing else.

Mateship

Australians have a tendency to call everyone – men, women and children – 'mate' and it is deeply entrenched in the nation's psyche. 'Thank you' as a phrase is hardly complete without a 'mate' at the end, while 'maaate' can be used to emphasise any point. Members of parliament say it to their constituents, the prime minister uses it in public speeches and it was even proposed that 'mateship' should be written into the constitution, with John Howard declaring, in a speech delivered at Australia House in London on 10 November 2003:

It is one word in all of this which is so unarguably, distinctively and dramatically and proudly Australian... I want us always to be seen as Australians, not as Americans or as Europeans or as Englishmen or as Asians. As distinctive Australians having those great qualities of classlessness and mateship and fairness which have been the hallmark of Australians through all experiences and all generations. The two World Wars exacted a terrible price from us – the full magnitude of that lost potential, of those unlived lives can never be measured. And yet, some of the most admirable aspects of Australia's national character were, if not conceived, then more fully ingrained within us by the searing experiences of those conflicts. None more so than the concept of mateship – regarded as a particularly Australian virtue – a concept that encompasses unconditional acceptance, mutual and self-respect, sharing whatever is available no matter how meagre, a concept based on trust and selflessness and absolute interdependence. In combat, men did live and die by its creed. 'Sticking by your mates' was sometimes the only reason for continuing on when all seemed hopeless. I was moved by an account written by Hugh Clarke, who, like thousands of other Australian and British servicemen, endured years of senseless cruelty as a prisoner of the Japanese after the fall of Singapore. He couldn't recall a single Australian dying alone without someone being there to look after him in some way. That's mateship.

Aboriginal People and Racism

The 1996 election saw a hideous element of Australia's psyche rearing its ugly head, when One Nation Party Pauline Hanson was elected to parliament with a stark policy which came down to anti-immigration, anti-Aboriginal aid and anti-globalisation. Hanson declared herself representative of the white community and not the Aboriginal and Torres Strait Islanders. Although Hanson's maiden speech was openly racist, Howard refused to condemn her, and chose instead to criticise political correctness. Howard also resisted pressure for him to apologise to Aboriginal people for the generation of Aboriginal children taken from their parents.

Sadly, Australia has a history of racism that dates back to the time when the first Europeans settled in the country. *See* pp.4–11 for the historical context.

Relationship with Europe and the EU

Despite the American influence, Australia's relationship with Europe runs deep. Way back in the 17th century, explorers from Spain, Portugal, France, Holland and England reached these shores and from the end of the 18th century a constant flow of Europeans settled in Australia; this turned into something of a flood after the Second World War. When England joined the then European Community, Australia's economic relationship with the country changed, but today the European Union is its more important economic partner. They share similar democratic systems and participate in the United Nations and the World Trade Organisation. Committed talks began in 1976 and covered issues such as trade, aid programmes, education and environment, and within the next decade these had become formal annual meetings. An EU–Australia Joint Declaration adopted in June 1997 has strengthened this relationship, even though Australia refused to sign a human-rights clause desired by the EU. Issues in the Asia Pacific region, such as stability in Indonesia, bringing peace to East Timor, dialogue with China and boosting the Southeast Asian economies, are regularly discussed in formal dialogues each month. One sticking point is Australia's view that the EU should accept Myanmar (Burma)'s membership of ASEAN without democracy being re-established.

Education and Childcare

Education and childcare were key issues in the 2004 election. John Howard has kept his promise of providing millions of dollars of additional funds to improve facilities in schools and he also vowed to create technical schools as an alternative to university. However, his commitment to providing parents with a 30 per cent rebate on child care has already been compromised with the introduction of a ceiling amount, which rules out a significant number of families.

Healthcare

Health is another major issue. Howard's government has embarked on a multi-billion-dollar scheme to bolster the publicly funded health system and to introduce strategies to combat specific diseases. Sadly, political parties across the board fail to address the pressing issue of the indigenous people. Aboriginal people have such a poor standard of health that the United Nations has declared it worse than what prevails in many developing countries. Aborigines are quite poorly represented in the political system, with just one indigenous Australian senator; the one body dedicated to campaigning for their rights – the Aboriginal and Torres Strait Islander Commission (ATSIC) – was abolished by John Howard last year.

The Economy

When it was first settled, Australia struggled to establish its economy, but eventually wool became its mainstay. The situation was transformed when gold was struck in 1851, and during the next hundred years a broad-based economic sector emerged. Impressively for a country so young, by the end of the 20th century Australia had a per capita GDP equal to that of the four major western economies. Today, despite a recession in the early 1990s and an economic downturn in the last few years, the country's economy is thriving, domestic output has increased, inflation is low and unemployment is 5.2 per cent – the lowest level since the late 1970s.

This is partly due to the sweeping reforms introduced first by Bob Hawke in the 1980s and continued by John Howard from 1996. While some have praised the deregulation of the labour market, which created important flexibility in the work force, detractors point to the negative effect on workers' rights and wages. During this time, union powers have been restricted and a number of industries deregulated. What is without doubt is that a transformation has taken place and what was once an inward-looking country is now one that holds its own in the world of international exports.

Australia's services sector accounts for as much as 65 per cent of its GDP, but its agricultural and mining products account for the majority of its exports. Sometimes called the 'world's farm', the country has a vast untapped source of natural resources, but the government has chosen to develop its tourism and technology markets. It is also looking to increase the amount of manufactured goods that are exported within a tough international market.

Religion

Around 70 per cent of Australian people consider themselves to be Christian, of which a third are Catholic. Because of the diversity of nationalities now living in Australia, Buddhist, Jewish and Muslim communities are increasingly common. Australia has one of the lowest church attendance records in the world. Although three-quarters of Australians believe in God, on a Sunday morning only around 20 per cent of them will be found in church.

The Family and Role of Women

Few people are aware that Australia was the first country in the world (in 1902) to secure the right for women to vote as well as the right for them to stand for election to parliament. However, the next hurdle proved much more difficult to surmount and it wasn't until nearly 30 years later that the first woman was elected to state parliament, and it took over 40 years for a woman to enter federal parliament – ironically, the longest time lag in any western country. Today, there are 59 women in parliament, but that represents only one-quarter of the total seats.

In 1903, Vida Goldstein became the first woman in the British Empire to stand for election to a national parliament. Although she did not win the seat, Goldstein continued to have an important role in the women's suffrage movement in Australia, as well as campaigning for women's rights and social justice. She was a powerful speaker and campaigner and during the war formed the Women's Peace Army. At one point she was gaoled for her political activities. When Adela Pankhurst arrived from England, Goldstein quickly recruited her to her cause. After the war, Goldstein began to extend her concerns to the global arena, pushing for improved living conditions and disarmament internationally.

The Australian A$5 note features a picture of Caroline Chisholm, who arrived in Australia in 1838 and was the first person to put together a cookery book for Australian women, *The Bush Cookbook*. She tried to help young girls arriving in New South Wales and became known as the 'emigrant's friend'.

Despite the contribution of Australian women to the war effort, it had little effect on the attitude towards women, and in the 1950s Australian men were possibly the most macho anywhere on the planet. The 'ocker' still exists – a vest-wearing, beer-drinking man who thinks a lot of himself and very little of women – but Australia's treatment of women in the 21st century is on a par with any other westernised country.

Just as in many developed countries in the world, women in Australia are marrying and giving birth later than in the past. Today, the average age for a woman to give birth is 30, and by 2010 some 60 per cent of newborns will have a mother aged over 30, compared with 25 per cent in 1975. It is predicted by the same experts that if current trends continue, then 25 per cent of women in Australia will be childless.

Major Media

Media in Australia are generally well advanced, although privately owned television and radio lay claim to the highest viewing and listening figures. In print and broadcast media, ownership is confined largely to four main groups who own around 80 per cent of newspaper titles in Australia.

Freedom and regulation of the press is limited when compared with other developed countries. In 2004 Australia was ranked 41st in terms of press freedom, compared with the UK (28) and New Zealand (9). This rating was partly a reflection of prime minister John Howard's condemnation of reporters who brought up the question of whether Australia should have taken part in the invasion of Iraq. The Australian Broadcasting Authority (ABA) regulates radio and television as well as online content, while the Australian Press Council monitors print media and deals with public complaints.

Newspapers

The main national or state dailies are:

- the *Sydney Morning Herald* – daily
- the *Herald Sun* – Melbourne-based daily
- the *Australian* – national daily
- the *Daily Telegraph* – Sydney-based daily
- the *Courier-Mail* – Brisbane-based daily
- the *West Australian* – Perth-based daily
- *The Age* – Melbourne-based daily
- the *Advertiser* – Adelaide-based daily
- the *Australian Financial Review* – business daily

There are also 35 regional dailies and nearly 500 other regional newspapers. Australia has one of the highest magazine readerships in the world: out of 1,500 magazines, 30 have circulations of over 80,000.

Australia's media ownership is very highly concentrated, with newspapers dominated by just two companies: the News Corporation and John Fairfax Holdings. The News Corporation publishes the *Australian*, the country's only daily national newspaper, as well as a daily newspaper in every capital city except Perth. It also owns the *Courier-Mail* (Brisbane), the *Daily Telegraph* (Sydney), the *Herald Sun* (Melbourne) and the *Advertiser* (Adelaide). John Fairfax Holdings owns the *Sydney Morning Herald*, the *Age* (Melbourne) and the *Australian Financial Review*. Rural and regional media is dominated by Rural Press Ltd, which owns titles such as the *Canberra Times*, *Queensland Country*, *Life*, *Stock and Land* in Victoria and *Farm Weekly* in Western Australia.

Television

There are three major commercial television networks: Seven, Nine and Ten. In addition, there are two public broadcasters: Australian Broadcasting Corporation (ABC) and Special Broadcasting Service (SBS), which are publicly funded. Most residents in the country have access to all these stations, although in some rural areas reception is restricted. At the beginning of 2001, digital free-to-air broadcasts began and it is thought that by the end of the decade all analogue broadcasts will have been phased out. Currently, nearly 25 per cent of households have Pay TV.

The **ABC** functions very much like the BBC in Britain as a public service broadcaster with debates raging about whether its role should continue. Detractors argue that American shows have just as much validity as and are much more popular than home-grown programming. Yet Australian TV programmes have had huge international success over the years, for example *Skippy* in the late 1960s, *Prisoner: Cell Block H* (just *Prisoner* in Australia) and *Neighbours* in the 1980s and *Home and Away* in the 1990s.

SBS broadcasts a variety of high-quality programmes and documentaries and is the only channel that reports from around the world, including all-important football games. Other channels tend to be dominated by reality TV shows, re-runs and American sitcoms. All commercial broadcasters in Australia are required by law to transmit a certain percentage of Australian-made programmes. **Pay-TV** is a significant sector, although it is not as strong as it once was, partly due to the growth of digital television.

UKTV is Australia's only television channel dedicated to bringing audiences the 'Best of British' television. Available in Australia through subscription TV carriers, it was launched in August 1996 and is a joint venture between BBC Worldwide, one of the BBC's commercial subsidiaries, FOXTEL and Fremantle Media. Programmes includes *EastEnders*, *Coronation Street*, *Family Affairs*, *The Bill*, *Casualty*, *Holby City*, *Mersey Beat*, *Top of the Pops*, *Only Fools and Horses*, *Red Dwarf* and *Yes, Minister*.

The main Australian TV channels are:

- **ABC: national public network**
- **SBS TV: national multicultural public broadcaster; programmes in English and 60 other languages**
- **Seven Network: national commercial**
- **Nine Network: national commercial**
- **Ten Network: national commercial**
- **Australian Broadcasting Authority (ABA): licenses and regulates TV stations; station lists available**
- **Foxtel: pay-TV operator, owned by Rupert Murdoch's News Corporation, the Packer group and telecommunications**

Radio

On top of 264 commercial radio stations, there are over 300 community stations. The BBC World Service broadcasts on different short-wave frequencies throughout the day. Between 5am and 10.30am GMT it can be found on 15360kHz; between 10pm and midnight GMT it can be found on 11955kHz; and between 11am and 4pm GMT it can be found on 9740kHz. The main news and talk radio station in Australia is Radio National on 576 AM.

The main Australian radio channels are:

- **ABC: public radio, operates speech-cultural network Radio National, rolling news station ABC NewsRadio, youth-orientated Triple J, classical and contemporary music network ABC Classic FM and local-regional services**

- **Radio Australia: ABC's external service, targeted at Asia-Pacific region via shortwave and Internet**

- **SBS Radio: national multicultural, multilingual public network, broadcasts in 68 languages**

- **Australian Broadcasting Authority (ABA): licenses and regulates radio stations; station lists available**

Media Moguls

Kerry Packer is regularly ranked one of the world's richest men. The Packer family is the dynasty of the Australian media, with Kerry's son Jamie officially at the helm, although it is widely believed Kerry Packer has by no means relinquished control. In 1987 he famously sold Channel Nine for nearly £500 million, only to buy it back just three years later for a bargain £100 million.

Today the Packer empire also includes 25 per cent of Foxtel, as well as owning significant publishing (60 per cent of all magazines sold in Australia) and gambling interests.

Melbourne-born **Rupert Murdoch** is one of the most powerful figures in the media today. He built the 'News Corporation' from a low-key Australian newspaper into a global force, which includes television, publishing, magazines and newspapers around the world. His sharp business sense and refusal to compromise has made him few friends, particularly within the unions, and he is regularly accused of dumbing down. However, it is difficult to overestimate the effect Murdoch has had on the global media. Having in many ways conquered Australia, the UK and the US, he has for some years now been setting his sights on China.

Alan Bond was somewhat less successful. A ruthless business man, he gained support from the government in Western Australia and various bankers. His group once owned the Nine Network, a series of newspapers and had vast property investments. Although a great showman, he made some rash decisions, which brought about his downfall, and he spent a stint in prison. His corporation went into receivership with the biggest debt ever in Australian history, and much of its business was folded.

Culture and Art

You never knew anything so nothing, nichts, nullus, niente, as the life here...
I feel as though if I lived in Australia for ever I should never open my mouth
to say one word that meant anything.

D.H. Lawrence

The old joke that Australia doesn't have any culture cannot legitimately be made today. Long gone are the days when its residents suffered from 'cultural cringe' and felt inferior to other countries, and to Britain in particular. At one time it seemed that anyone with artistic talent packed their bags and went off to London, complaining about the unsophisticated audiences in their home country. Times have changed and the government has introduced arts subsidies. The years following the 1970s were a period of great successes in the arts. Although the country is bombarded by secondhand imports from America and Europe, it successfully holds its own in the fields of cinema, music, television and the arts. Its contemporary arts scene reflects both the diverse population of the country and its ancient landscape.

Australian Film-making in the 20th Century

In 1933, **Errol Flynn**, the wild boy from Tasmania, starred in his first feature film, *In the Wake of the Bounty*. It was directed by **Charles Chauvel**, who was a major figure in Australian film-making right up until the late 1950s. At this time the rest of the world saw Australia as little more than an out-of-the-way location for 'kangaroo westerns'. In 1959, **Stanley Kramer** directed Ava Gardner, Gregory Peck and Fred Astaire in the post-Holocaust drama, *On the Beach*. The classic portrayal of outback itinerant labour, *The Sundowners*, with Deborah Kerr and Robert Mitchum, came out just a year later.

Government funding in the 1960s and 1970s brought a healthy burst of creative activity. **Peter Weir** was a major player in Australia cinema, first with the still powerful *Picnic at Hanging Rock* in 1975, and then with his much praised *Gallipoli*. In 1978, **Gillian Armstrong**'s *My Brilliant Career* propelled her and actors **Sam Neill** and **Mel Gibson** into the global spotlight, and shortly afterwards the *Mad Max* trilogy made a massive mark on the hard-to-penetrate US market.

In many ways the 1980s is seen as a golden age of Australian cinema. The international box office success of *Crocodile Dundee* in 1985 had almost as much of an impact on tourism to Australia as *The Lord of the Rings* has had on visitor numbers to New Zealand. Australia, momentarily at least, became a popular destination and Kakadu National Park was catapulted to worldwide fame. *A Cry in the Dark*, with Meryl Streep playing the woman who claimed 'a dingo ate my baby', had the same effect on Uluru (Ayers Rock). Rupert Murdoch took over 20th Century Fox in 1985 before he began bolstering the Australian

Australia's Big Things

Australia's 'Big Things' are a bizarre collection of giant structures specific to one area. They have become something of a cult phenomenon and the ABC even produced a documentary about them. The very first Big Thing was the Big Banana which 'appeared' in 1964 in Coffs Harbour, New South Wales. Today there are more than 50 of the things. There is the Big Crocodile in Western Australia, the Big Lobster in South Australia, Victoria's Giant Ned Kelly, Tasmania's Big Penguin and Queensland's Big Barramundi.

film industry in the late 1990s. When he set up Sydney's Fox studios, it hit the headlines almost immediately for hosting first the production of the Star Wars films, and then *Mission: Impossible 2*. But it was *Moulin Rouge* that really put the facility on the world cinematic map. This time it was not just the production that was Australian – so was the director, **Baz Luhrmann**, and Hollywood star **Nicole Kidman**. A whole new breed of Australian A-list actors, including luminaries such as **Cate Blanchett** and **Russell Crowe**, has replaced Mel Gibson, who was anyway born in America.

Cinemas in Australia are usually in huge shopping centres nowadays, part of entertainment complexes with smaller screens so that several films can be shown at the same time.

Music

Many of us will have a tendency to think 'rock' when Australian music is mentioned, partly because of the phenomenal international success of heavy rock band **AC/DC**, as well as the thriving contemporary Australian rock music scene. But there is a wide variety of music that has come from this part of the world, from the folk group **The Seekers** in the 1960s, followed by pop band **INXS**, to disco diva **Kylie Minogue**. The garage rock band Jet and artists such as **Ben Lee** and **Kasey Chambers** are popular, and **Triple J** takes a key role in supporting new talent.

Live music is big in Australia, both in cities and smaller communities, but particularly in Melbourne. Some say the **Australian Chamber Orchestra** is the best of its kind in the world and there are excellent symphony orchestras in the capital cities.

Opera

Opera became important in Australia during the 19th century and by the 1850s large opera houses had been built, allowing important productions to be staged. **William Lyster**'s opera company, established in 1861, was the country's first real Australian opera; it was incredibly successful, putting on the country's first full-scale productions of European opera.

Sydney Opera House

Although it has been open only since 1973, iconic Sydney Opera House has come to symbolise Australia as much as the Eiffel Tower represents Paris. Located on Bennelong Point at a strategic point of Sydney harbour, the sculptural building appropriately enough evokes a ship at full sail.

In the late 1950s the Government of New South Wales set up a competition for the design of the building, which was won by renowned Danish architect, Jorn Utzon. Some say his design was too ambitious for its time; for whatever reason, Utzon had to spend a few years reworking his original design. As a result, the project went way over budget, with problems reaching a head in 1966 when the Government stopped payments and Utzon resigned. In the end the building was completed in 1973, but more than 30 years later the Sydney Opera House is to have its reception hall designed by Utzon – the first time he will be responsible for its interior.

The Sydney Opera House is the busiest performing arts centre in the world and its performances are not confined to opera. The building is in fact a complex of theatres and concert halls, hosting theatre, musicals, contemporary dance, ballet and all kinds of concerts from classical to rock, as well as exhibitions and film showings. There are around 3,000 events every year and some 200,000 people take a guided tour of the building annually.

One of the early shining stars of Australian opera was **Dame Nellie Melba**. Born Helen Porter Mitchell in 1861 in Melbourne, Victoria, she changed her name to Melba in honour of the city of her birth. Five years after she began studying singing seriously, she made her operatic debut in Brussels in 1887. She went on to win wide acclaim at London's Royal Opera House, at the Met in New York and at many other opera houses around the world. After playing extensively in Europe and around the world, Melba last performed in Australia in 1928 and died in 1931. The Australian **Joan Sutherland** is one of the world's greatest operatic sopranos living today. She was born in Sydney in 1926, and performed in Australia extensively before launching herself on the international opera stage with the 1959 production of *Lucia di Lammermoor*. Her last performance was in Sydney in 1990.

When the **Sydney Opera House** (*see* box) opened in 1973 it became the permanent home of the Australian opera and did much to boost the international profile of the art. And, as a way of bringing what is sometimes criticised as an élitist art to remote parts of Australia, a team called **OzOpera** was established in 1997 and tours around the whole country.

Opera has evolved dramatically in Australia in the last 20 years or so and a strong contemporary operatic scene has developed. For example, **Trepang** ('Moon Spirit Feasting') draws on on the traditions of Chinese street opera, using puppetry and karaoke. In 1996 the Australian Opera and the Victoria State Opera merged to form **Opera Australia**, now resident in Sydney Opera House.

Thus Australia has made its mark on the international opera scene. Big names like Dame Joan Sutherland and Nellie Melba have been replaced more recently by younger, female rivals Deborah Riedel, Lisa Gasteen and Yvonne Kenny. Today Opera Australia is the third most important opera company in the world.

Art

Although Australia has had a significant school of painting since the early days of European settlement, the visual arts have really taken off in the last 30 years and helped to portray an image of the country as a whole. A key part of this has been the development and recognition of Aboriginal and Torres Strait Islander artists. Of course this art form goes back to the time of indigenous settlement in Australia, but the relatively recent use of canvases as opposed to sand paintings made it much more accessible. There are also artists such as Emily Kngwarreye and Kitty Kantilla who have successfully created modern interpretations of their Aboriginal traditions. Important non-indigenous artists include Arthur Boyd, Sidney Nolan and Russell Drysdale.

Indigenous art in Australia is the oldest continuous art tradition in the world. The very first forms of this kind of expression date back over 30,000 years, taking the form of rock carvings, body painting and drawings in the earth. For Aborigines, art is not about just presenting a body of work but is crucial from a spiritual point of view as a way of connecting their past and present life, as well as expressing their relationship with the landscape and the supernatural.

Aboriginal art today is an important part of the country's identity, and is now recognised by Australians and the international community, demonstrated by

The Angry Penguins

In Adelaide in the 1940s a group of four angry young poets got together to form 'The Angry Penguins', a literary movement that aimed to challenge the artistic élite. Its ringleader was Max Harris, who published a magazine of the same name. In his words, the penguins sought 'a noisy and aggressive revolutionary modernism' and wanted to express themselves in a language that spoke more directly to their readers.

There was even a Penguin painting group made up of Arthur Boyd, Albert Tucker and Sidney Nolan. Looking to surrealism and other movements taking hold in Europe, the movement's members expressed a frustration at Australia's cultural isolation. As a result they were condemned for their 'Europeanism' and obscurity, but few deny they played an essential role in the development of modernism in art and literature in Australia.

The Archibald Prize

Where else in the world could an art prize get top billing on the front page of a major daily newspaper? The Archibald Prize for portraiture gets that sort of coverage each year in the *Sydney Morning Herald*, and is Australia's oldest and best-known visual arts award. The winning artist gets prize money of A$35,000, but it is the publicity and recognition the award generates that is the real prize. As part of the selection process, entries are exhibited in the Art Gallery of New South Wales in Sydney, and the winner is then selected by the gallery's trustees.

The annual Archibald Prize competition and its winning entries generate great public interest within Australia. It is important because it stimulates discussion about painting and portraiture, as well as larger questions about art. Criteria for entry include that any artists submitting works must know the subject of the portrait and, in turn, the subject of the portrait must be aware of the artist's intention. There also has to be at least one sitting by the subject for the portrait.

One quirky aspect of the Archibald competition is the Packing Room Prize, awarded by the workers behind the scenes who receive, unpack and hang all the entries. First awarded in 1991, the Packing Room Prize is adjudicated by the Gallery's Storeman, Steve Peters – who continues to claim his right to 51 per cent of the votes. This prize is traditionally awarded a couple of days before the Archibald, after the hanging of the finalists.

In 2004 there were 732 entries from around Australia for the Archibald Prize, with 40 of these shortlisted. The winner of the 2004 prize was Craig Ruddy who won with his portrait *David Gulpilil, Two Worlds*. Gulpilil is one of Australia's best known Aboriginal actors. Craig Ruddy said of the subject of his portrait:

David is a man who crosses the lines that still divide two contrasting worlds... One is an infinite world of spiritual connection with the land and universe as a whole, and the other a materialistic conformation of western civilisation. Simplicities and complexities infiltrate both worlds and David seems to strike a balance.

the opening ceremony of the 2000 Olympic games, which included an Aboriginal event. However, this situation has taken many years to come about, and has been achieved through the considerable combined effort of Aboriginal and Torres Strait Islander artists. Australian indigenous art now uses modern technology and new media. Indigenous Art Online (**www.fineartforum.org/Gallery/cybertribe**) and Maningrida art and culture (**www.maningrida.com**) are two good resources.

Literature

The Aboriginal people were the first storytellers in the country by several thousand years – an oral tradition that was first recorded in 1929 in *Native Legends*, a book by Aboriginal author **David Unaipon**. Contemporary authors who have achieved international fame include **Nevil Shute**, **Thomas Keneally**, **Les Murray** and **Colleen McCullough**. Australia's two most famous literary exports are **Patrick White**, who won the Nobel Prize for Literature in 1974, and **Peter Carey**, who was awarded the Booker Prize for *Oscar and Lucinda* in 1988.

Dance

Like all arts forms in Australia, there is a strong indigenous dance tradition. From the 1960s, Aboriginal dance, which was once performed only in cere-monies, began to be expressed outside of the communities and brought to a wider audience.

There are strong European influences too in the form of ballet, theatre and pantomime. In the years of the Australian gold rushes, where money was plen-tiful, romantic ballet in particular became very popular, and in the 1920s and 1930s visiting Russian ballets were fashionable. By the middle of the 20th century, Australia had begun to form its own ballet companies and in the years that followed a number of contemporary dance companies were founded. Important contemporary dancers include **Sir Robert Helpmann**, **Kathleen Gorham**, **Martin Rubinstein** and **Edna Busse**. **Bangarra Dance Theatre** is a successful indigenous company, while **Legs on the Wall** is a radical physical theatre organisation.

Spectator Sports

For participatory sports, *see* **Living in Australia**, pp.177–82.

Australians love their sport – an obsession that can begin in the playground and continue all the way to the retirement home. As a country that is often on the sidelines in the global political arena, it makes itself heard worldwide through its sporting achievements. Australia has had resounding successes in sports and is one of the keenest sporting nations. Australians' love of supporting the underdog is often shown in their decision of which team to support – given the choice, most would pick the team most likely to lose – partly because they love nothing better than to win against all odds.

The Melbourne Cup

It's a day when the nation stops whatever it's doing to listen to the race call, or watch the race on TV, and even those who don't usually bet try their luck. At

3.10pm AEST, on the first Tuesday in November, Australians everywhere stop for one of the world's most famous horse races – the Melbourne Cup.

Since 1861, when the Melbourne Cup first took place at Flemington race course, it has been held every year, come war or depression. American writer Mark Twain said when he visited the country, 'Nowhere in the world have I encountered a festival of people that has such a magnificent appeal to the whole nation. The Cup astonishes me.' On Melbourne Cup Day – always a Tuesday – showy hats and cold champagne are brought out and an ostentatious display is made that rivals Ascot.

It is one of the most difficult horse races in the world and offers a staggering A$4.6 million in prize money. Because it is run over 3,200 metres and is a handicapped race, punters have a good chance of picking a winner and it can seem that almost every adult in Australia has a try. Although everyone in Melbourne is given a day off on Cup day, even in Sydney few are glued to their desks and manage to join in the spirit of the peak of the Spring Racing Carnival where champagne and extravagant hats are the order of the day.

Phar Lap is a legendary figure and still carries an incredible resonance considering he is a dead horse. He ran his last Melbourne Cup in 1931 with a 10-stone handicap and lost to a horse called White Nose. During his life he won more than £65,000 in prize money and in his final two years was favourite in all of his races except one. When he died, conspiracy theories abounded and many believed he was poisoned. In a rather bizarre division of body parts, his bones were given to a Museum in New Zealand, his hide was displayed at the Museum of Victoria, and his heart was put on show at the National Museum of Australia.

Melbourne, the Sporting Capital

Following the resounding success of the Olympic Games in Sydney in 2000, the Commonwealth Games are due be held in Melbourne in March 2006, with 72 countries and 4,500 athletes taking part. Melbourne is the fourth city in Australia to host the Commonwealth Games, after Sydney in 1938, Perth in 1962 and Brisbane in 1982. Melbourne has a tradition of hosting major sporting events and the games will open at the Melbourne Cricket Ground (MCG). Way back in 1956 it welcomed the Olympic Games, and every year Grand Slam tennis and Formula One are held every year.

In fact, Melbourne is undoubtedly the country's sporting capital. The Australian Open Tennis is held at Melbourne Park every January, and the Australian Formula One Grand Prix at Albert Park in March. Most of the Aussie Rules teams play from spring through to the Grand Final at the Melbourne Cricket Ground in September or October, and the traditional cricket Boxing Day Test Match rounds up the sporting calendar.

Sydney has its sporting arenas too, including the state-of-the-art Stadium Australia,s constructed for the Olympic Games.

Football

Football is a winter sport, played from March to September, and can be rugby league, rugby union, soccer or Aussie Rules. As is the case so often in this country, there are huge differences between the states, so that Victoria, South and Western Australia favour Aussie Rules, while NSW and Queensland go for rugby league. Australians probably love their football as much as your average English person and the support of their team is a serious business. There are four major football codes, each with a professional league:

- **Australian Football League (AFL)**
- **Australian Rugby Union (ARU)**
- **National Rugby League (NRL)**
- **National Soccer League (NSL)**

Usually known as Aussie Rules, AFL is far and away Australia's favourite sport. It originated in Melbourne as a means of keeping cricketers fit out of season, and is now taught in establishments across the country. The first game was played in 1866 and until 1987 there were only 12 clubs involved. Today there are 16, including two from South Australia and Western Australia, and one from New South Wales and Queensland, with additional teams from Melbourne, Victoria.

Rugby was first played in Australia in the 1820s, but rugby union can be traced back to England in the 1880s. Australia's international team is the Wallabies, who won two World Cup titles in the 1990s. Despite the worldwide reputation of the Wallabies, rugby union is much less popular than rugby league, but since they defeated France to win the World Cup in 1999, union has grown in popularity. Matches such as the Super 12 tournament and Tri-nation series, which Australia, South Africa and New Zealand participate in, often pack stadiums and pubs.

In 2003, the first Rugby World Cup final, the biggest sporting event after the Olympics and the Soccer World Cup, was played in Australia. The rules of rugby league differ from rugby union and there are only 13 players per side rather than 15. It has been played in Australia since 1907 and is now one the country's best-loved sports. The national league competition ends with the National Rugby League (NRL) final in September. The only match that approaches the popularity of the NRL final is the State of Origin series in June, when the states of Queensland and New South Wales compete with each other.

Cricket

Cricket is the summer sport, played from November to March. In 1877, Australia's cricket team visited England for its first international test against the mother country, and were victorious. It was an historic event for the Aussies

Australian of the Year

Each year on 26 January, Australia Day, the prime minister of Australia announces who is the Australian of the Year, and also presents the Young Australian of the Year, Senior Australian of the Year, and the Local Heroes awards. The Australian of the Year is one of the country's most prestigious accolades and open to all Australians regardless of age. It pays tribute to outstanding achievement, and an individual's role in inspiring fellow Australians and contributing to the nation.

In 2004 Australian of the Year was cricketer Steve Waugh, AO, who believes that being Australian is about 'looking after your mates, taking care of your family and being able to have a laugh at yourself'. In previous years Australians of the Year have included Australia's first Aboriginal senator, Neville Bonnor, AO (1979); the adventurer Dick Smith (1986); eye surgeon Fred Hollows, AC (1990); artist Arthur Boyd, AC, OBE (1995); Army Chief Lieutenant-General Peter Cosgrove, AC, MC (2001) and Professor Fiona Stanley, AC (2003).

The first Young Australian of the Year Award, recognising the achievements of young people aged 16 to 24, was announced in 1979. In 2004 it was given to Hugh Evans, founder of the Oak Tree Foundation, Australia's first entirely youth-run aid and development agency. Past winners include conductor Simone Young (1986); Olympic champions Cathy Freeman (1990) and Kieren Perkins, OAM (1992); and medical student James Fitzpatrick (2001). The Senior Australian of the Year Award began in 1999 as a way of honouring Australians aged 60 years and over who make a significant contribution to the nation.

to take off with the ashes of English cricket, and ever since then the two countries have been in fierce competition to win the small, symbolic urn – the trophy that is presented to the winners.

Other former British colonial countries including South Africa, India and Pakistan also take part. In the months of December and January, teams arrive for a tour of five test matches, which take place in Melbourne, Sydney, Perth, Adelaide and Brisbane, as well as smaller one-day matches.

Australia has more than 200 major cricket grounds, which is a ratio of one per 100,000 citizens. Most of these are located in the major cities. Brisbane Cricket Ground, or the Gabba as it is better known, has a seating capacity of 36,000. The Adelaide Oval is around the same size. The MCG, or the Melbourne Cricket Ground, is the largest cricket ground in the world. It staged both the first Test Match in March 1887 and the first One Day International Match in January 1971. Its seating capacity has recently been increased from 70,000 to over 100,000. The Sydney Cricket Association Ground (SCG) has a seating capacity of 45,000. The Western Australian Cricket Association Ground in Perth holds a maximum of 26,000 spectators.

From humble beginnings in the late 1970s, indoor cricket has grown into a major sport in its own right. In Perth, Western Australia, where the game originated, the 1996 Sports Census showed indoor cricket to be the fifth most popular of all sports.

Tennis

The first recorded tennis tournament played in Australia was held in 1880 and the country's first national tennis body, The Australasian Lawn Tennis Association (ALTA), was formed in September 1904. The prestigious Davis Cup competition began in 1907; since then the country's players have won 28 Davis Cup titles, most recently defeating Spain in the 2003 final in Melbourne. The women's equivalent of the Davis Cup is called the Federation Cup, which Australia has won seven times. Australia's tennis champions are household names and their progress is eagerly watched by the nation. In 2003 Lleyton Hewitt, then the number one player in the world, was named the Young Australian of the Year; Pat Rafter and Evonne Goolagong have also won the award in the past.

Australian men and women tennis players have risen to the pinnacle of their sport. Australian professionals have consistently stood out at the four Grand Slam tennis events held each year (the Australian Open, the Roland-Garros, the US Open and Wimbledon). It is the ultimate in the career of a tennis professional to 'win the Grand Slam' – all four Grand Slam events in a year. Australia's Rod Laver is the only professional to have achieved a Grand Slam twice, in 1962 and 1969. Margaret Smith Court won a singles Grand Slam in 1970 and also achieved a mixed doubles Grand Slam in 1963. Predictably, of all the Grand Slam events, Australians have been most successful in the tournament played on their home ground – the Australian Open. It began as the Australasian Open in 1905, became the Australian Championships in 1927 and the Australian Open in 1969. To date, Australian men have won 51 singles titles and Australian women 43 of the women's titles.

Australians have claimed victory on several occasions at the French Open, since Ken Rosewall first won way back in 1953, then again in 1968. Norman Brookes was the first Australian to win the men's singles at Wimbledon in 1907 – making him the first male outside Britain to win the Championships and the first of 12 Australian men to take the title.

Lleyton Hewitt's victory in 2002 made him the most recent Australian Wimbledon champion. Other great Australian Wimbledon champions include Rod Laver (1961, 1962, 1968, 1969), John Newcombe (1967, 1970, 1971) and Pat Cash (1987).

The first Australian woman to win Wimbledon was Margaret Smith Court, who won the first of her three titles in 1963. Evonne Goolagong Cawley is the only other Australian female to have won the title – in 1971 and 1980. Australian players who have excelled on the hard court at the US Open have included Ken Rosewall (1956), Margaret Smith Court (1962, 1969, 1970, 1973), John Newcombe (1967) , Pat Rafter (1997, 1998) and Lleyton Hewitt (2001).

First Steps

04

This chapter gives you a taste of what it might be like to live in Australia and tells you the best way to get there. The section 'Why Live and Work in Australia?' discusses the pros and cons of living and working in Australia, and includes two case studies. The 'Getting to Australia' section gives advice on how to choose flights, and lists the telephone numbers and websites for all the major airlines servicing Australia. It gives other practical details, information about jetlag and some tips on how to make that long flight as painless as possible.

Why Live and Work in Australia?

Australia's appeal is obvious. It boasts a superb climate, a relaxed way of life and gorgeous white beaches. The country has an enormous coastline, an unbelievable expanse of outback, ancient green mountains and great stretches of national park land. It is a vast country, whose name is synonymous with the great outdoors and where even city living can mean having a jungle in your back garden.

As a result of the size of the country and its very low population, houses and accompanying land tend to be larger than is common in other Western countries. Apart from laying claim to some of the world's most beautiful scenery, Australia can also boast one of the most pristine environments anywhere on the planet.

Australia is one of the few countries in the world in which an English person feels familiar, yet at the same time it can seem exotic, with tropical beaches and almost year-round sunshine. The language is English (with a few variations) and, aside from all those jokes about whingeing Poms, the Brits have an almost sibling-like relationship with the Aussies.

The country consistently enjoys high popularity ratings when it comes to polls. The Economist Intelligence Unit in London recently evaluated 130 cities around the world in terms of their 'liveability' and no fewer than five of Australia's state capitals appeared in their top 10, with Melbourne as number one. In 1995, the World Bank declared Australia the richest country in the world, based not on economic factors like GDP, but on standard of living and the well-being of its population. In 2004 readers of luxury travel publication *Condé Nast Traveller* magazine, voted Australia their favourite holiday destination because of its climate and landscape, and they declared Sydney their second favourite city in the world.

Australia has a stable government and a well-established democratic system. Partly as a result of its being 'on the other side of the world', it has generally escaped political violence and, despite the Bali bombings, it has in the main been mercifully removed from the acts of international terrorism that have

Case Study: A Country for Children

When Sarah Purnell and her husband, Neil, decided to live in Australia, their first priority was whether the move would be the right one for their two children, Molly, 5, and Daniel, 3. Sarah says, 'Of course we knew that they would have much more of an outdoor lifestyle, but what surprised us was the level of cultural activity open to them. Where we live, in Melbourne, there are so many events, concerts and exhibitions for the children to go to and for very little cost. It just doesn't compare to where we used to live outside Bristol. My sister is still there with her three kids and I am well aware that they only have a fraction of the opportunities that my children have.

'It's a very child-friendly country in general, for several reasons. Australians, like Americans, are big on convenience. For example, from our house in England it was nearly an hour's drive to the nearest shopping centre, but where we live in Melbourne, there are four, each just 10 minutes away. There are other things, too, which just make life with children so much easier here. Australians are very relaxed so they are not likely to get uptight about children in the way some British people do. It may also be due to the American influence again, as Americans are incredibly good at dealing with children socially. The outdoor life is another factor. Families are not hidden away indoors, but take their kids to the beach and to cafés and restaurants. Also, because so many people living in Australia emigrated here from other countries, many don't have extended families or the support network in the home, so are much more likely to live a life outside the home.

dogged other countries in recent years. As a young country, Australia still has something of a pioneering spirit and seems to have avoided the political and religious intolerances of some countries in Europe. However, the attitude towards indigenous Aboriginal people and even to some other ethnic minorities is still largely racist.

One of Australia's appeals is the laidback attitude of its people, who are known for their 'she'll be right' attitude. Most Australians live near the beach, and city workers can be seen jumping out of their suits and into their surfing gear in the early afternoon. Class differences are less pronounced than in the UK and the country can claim true ethnic diversity, with nearly one quarter of the population having been born outside of Australia. Perhaps because it is a young country, there is a feeling of optimism, opportunity and freedom.

The country's economy is healthy, with a per capita GDP to match the most economically powerful countries in Western Europe. The Australian dollar has been weak against the pound for several years and at the time of writing is still relatively low, making investment, retirement and relocation prospects very attractive for English expatriates.

Case Study: 'No Worries'

When Rebecca and Robert Sabelinski flew down to Australia with their working holiday visas they had no idea what to expect, but they seemed to land on their feet. Robert was a promoter in London and soon found a job running big entertainment venues – work that it would have been very difficult for him to find at home. Rebecca was looking for a job as a journalist: 'I remember having an interview at a big news agency in the city and kind of panicking. I had been travelling around Australia for three months and the red dust of the desert was barely off my shoes. This agency was very corporate and seemed a bit too grown-up for me and I was worried about working in an office every day as I was used to being freelance. But the money was good – unbelievably good – and the job was just what I was looking for.

'Straight after the interview I was told I had the job, but there was a hitch. They didn't have room in the office for me. Would I mind taking a laptop away and working from home? I nearly leapt up out of chair, and practically skipped all the way home with my computer under my arm. I always put in the hours and got the job done, but my optimum writing time was in the evening. So I would get up late, work on the sunny terrace, meet Robert for lunch, carry on working until around 10pm and, because Robert was promoting clubs, I would go out with him at night. Then, one morning at around 9am I got a call from my boss. I was basically still asleep when I was talking to him and was convinced I was in trouble, but the next time I saw him all he said was. "You're not a morning person, are you?" and that was it.

'I think that would be unlikely to happen in England. And although of course not everyone will be lucky enough to get a boss like mine, Australians generally do have a much more relaxed attitude to work than we do. In fact, they have a much more relaxed attitude to everything. We had a great year, living in the equivalent of Soho, going to bars and clubs on our doorstep, and I don't think we cooked once because eating out was so cheap.'

Opportunities

Australia has a long tradition of welcoming, even courting, settlers from overseas, and many of them from the UK and Europe. The first wave came with the convicts – English prisoners effectively banished to this land on the other side of the world – and their legacy lives on in the language, food and culture. In the 1960s huge numbers of Europeans came over by ship, often with no more than their passage paid for and the promise of a better life. The skills shortage has largely been satisfied, but there are still many opportunities not available to those in the UK.

The country pursues an official policy of multiculturalism, which encourages educated, highly trained professionals from around the globe to work and live in Australia. In 2003, nearly 10,000 Britons were granted permanent residence in Australia. Although the wages for senior positions does not match those for professionals in the UK, the pay-off is the lower cost of living and a less stressful environment, both in and out of the workplace.

The working holiday visa programme means thousands of British residents aged under 30 have spent a year in Australia. In 2003, nearly 40,000 British citizens under the age of 30 headed down under as part of the 12-month working holiday visa scheme.

Leisure

Leisure time in Australia is, where possible, spent outdoors. During evenings, weekends and holidays, the makings of a barbie or a picnic are thrown into the back of a car for a few hours at the beach or a national park, with maybe a bit of fishing or walking thrown in. It is not only the sunshine and the outdoor life that encourage a healthy lifestyle. Just about everywhere you go on the coast you will find fresh juice bars, shops selling organic fruit and vegetables, and health food outlets.

And of course this is wine country too. Australian producers have an impressive reputation on the international market and their wines here are a real bargain for someone coming from England. Add to that the fact that many restaurants allow you to bring your own (BYO) alcohol, so there is little mark-up on the cost of having a good wine with your dinner, and you really are on to a good thing.

One Drawback

Of course, the main drawback to emigrating to Australia is the distance. It is literally on the other side of the world, 10,000 miles away and 24 hours by plane. Being so far away from friends, family and the country you grew up in can feel isolating, even frightening. And the logistics and expense of a 24-hour flight mean that for most people a visit from loved ones is going to be every couple of years at most.

Preparing the Way

Moving house, even if it is only down the road, can be a stressful experience; if you are moving to the other side of the world, the practicalities are much more complex and the emotional effects can be more intense. You are not just vacating a building, you are leaving your country, your family and your friends. No doubt you will have spent a lot of time considering the implications of what you are doing before you finally pack your bags, but it is easy to brush aside the psychological implications of such a move when in the throws of dealing with its physical aspects.

One of the most significant ways to avoid the move being stressful is to allow as much time as possible. Feeling rushed only adds to the pressure and the sense of being out of control. Don't underestimate how long it will take to get everything arranged, practically and emotionally. Visa applications can be drawn out, but also have a time limit, so timing is crucial (*see* **Red Tape**, 'The Basics', pp.99–110). Discuss the move with family and friends as far ahead as possible to give them time to get used to the idea. Your move may be harder for the people who are left behind to adjust to than it is for you. They do not have the excitement of the prospect of a new life in a new country and could feel abandoned.

There are lots of ways to be in communication with family and friends: calls between Australia and the UK need not be expensive – phone cards offer rates of around £3 an hour, which you could buy as gifts before you leave; e-mail is a great, cheap way to stay in touch and is not affected by the time difference between Australia and the UK; if you have children you might think of buying webcams so you can see each other as you talk. (For more practical information *see* **Living in Australia**, pp.122–30.)

Getting to Australia

Getting there takes a long time and is expensive. The long flight is a horror for many, and a minimum fare of £500 means that for most people it's not a trip to be undertaken lightly. If you are a family of four that is £2,000 at least just to get out there, never mind the cost of going back home for visits. If you have young children or pets (*see* **Living in Australia**, 'Taking Your Pet', pp.175–7), or are elderly, there are even more factors to consider.

It is worth doing some research to find the airline to suit you; if you have any special needs – either because of a fear of flying or an illness – let the airline know as far in advance as possible. Airlines are usually very sympathetic and will do all they can to accommodate you. Let them know of special requests before the flight so they can make things as comfortable as possible for you, rather than leaving them to find out during the flight when a problem has occurred.

Consider, too, how to get to the place you decide to live. If you are going to live in a city you won't be too far from an airport, but plenty of Australia is remote and it can take days to reach the nearest terminal.

By Air

Melbourne, Sydney and Brisbane are the main centres for flights into Australia, and the three most popular destinations for immigrants. They are followed by Perth, Adelaide, Hobart, Darwin and Cairns.

Flight Times to Australian Cities
These are approximate flying times only, depending on the airline.
From London:

- Adelaide: 24hrs 30mins
- Brisbane: 23hrs 25 mins
- Cairns: 25hrs 45 mins
- Darwin: 21hrs 25 mins
- Melbourne: 23hrs
- Perth: 21hrs 50 mins
- Sydney: 23hrs 30 mins

Around 30 international airlines fly into Australia from the UK. Although the vast majority depart from London Heathrow, some also fly from London Gatwick, Manchester and even Birmingham. When choosing an airline, most people will consider cost, convenience (in terms of flight times and connections), in-flight service and seat pitch – the distance between your seat and the one in front. You might want to consider flying with a particular airline that offers reduced rates of internal travel.

A huge range of flying and ticket options is available. Around-the-world tickets to Australia are often a great deal as they offer airline flexibility and a number of stops. You can fly direct or stop over in Thailand or Singapore, break your journey in the States or island-hop across the Pacific.

When to Go?

Ticket prices range dramatically according to the time of year. Predictably, you will pay a huge premium for travelling during holiday periods. Australia's seasons are the opposite of the UK's. Winter is between June and August and summer from December through to February. Just like most places in the world, it is more expensive to travel in the middle of summer. The fact that this is also Christmas time in Australia means that flight prices can go through the roof and availability can be scarce.

Transport from Airports

- Sydney Airport (Kingsford Smith) is just 5 miles (about half an hour) south of the city. Be prepared for long queues at customs if arriving in the morning; because no flights are permitted between 11pm and 5am, there are lots of landings at this time. The airport has good public transport connections. Airport Express is a bus service that runs into Kings Cross and the city. Airport Link connects the airport with central train stations. There are also coaches, courtesy shuttle buses and of course taxis.

- Adelaide Airport is 4 miles (20mins) west of the city. Transport connections include coaches, buses and taxis.
- Brisbane Airport is 8 miles (35mins) northeast of the city. Coaches link the airport with the city, major hotels, the Gold Coast and the Sunshine Coast.
- Darwin Airport is 8 miles (20mins) northeast of the city and has coaches and taxis.
- Melbourne Airport is 14 miles (30mins) northwest of the city. There is a 24-hour Skybus Coach as well as taxis and regional buses.
- Perth Airport is 7 miles (25mins) northeast of the city, with airport buses and taxis.

The Boomerang Pass

Air Pacific, Air Vanuatu, Australian Airlines, Polynesian Airlines and Qantas offer the Boomerang Pass for international travellers. It allows travel within Australia and to selected airports in Fiji, New Caledonia, New Zealand, Samoa, Solomon Islands, Tonga and Vanuatu. You must purchase the passes (a minimum of two per person) before arriving in Australia.

See **Living in Australia**, pp.151–3, for information about internal air travel.

The Main Airlines

- **Qantas, t** 0870 850 9850, **www.qantas.com.au**. The national airline, which operates in partnership with British Airways. It has an excellent safety record and flies to all the major cities, with up to six daily departures from the UK.
- **British Airway, t** 0870 850 9850, **www.britishairways.com**. Flies to Perth, Sydney and Melbourne from London.
- **Singapore Airlines, t** 0870 608 8886, **www.singaporeair.com**. Operates to the five major gateways in Australia – Adelaide, Brisbane, Melbourne, Perth and Sydney – with departures from London and Manchester. It has a high reputation for passenger service and now boasts a new personalised in-flight entertainment system in every seat, which offers more than 30 video and audio channels.
- **Malaysia Airlines, t** 0870 607 9090, **www.malaysiaairlines.com**. Has departures from Heathrow and Manchester to Adelaide, Brisbane, Melbourne, Perth and Sydney, with stopovers in Kuala Lumpur.
- **Cathay Pacific, t** 0845 408 5988, **www.cathaypacific.com**. Has up to 18 departures a week from Heathrow and Gatwick to Adelaide, Brisbane, Cairns, Melbourne, Perth and Sydney, and three daily flights to Sydney. Stopovers in Hong Kong, as well as other Asian destinations, are available.

Seoul for the Soul

The modern mega-capital of Korea is a less obvious stopover than Bangkok or Hong Kong, but it could be just what you need to soothe your soul halfway through your long flight. Book yourself into a luxury hotel and indulge yourself for 24 hours with the money you have saved by buying a flight on this route. Enter the world of the Korean bathhouse where scented pools of green tea detoxify, warm ginseng baths energise and aromatherapy Jacuzzis relax. There are gem-walled saunas, invigorating body scrubs, edible face masks and wonderful, pummelling massages.

Retail therapy in the Insadong district comes in the form of glorious antique shops and exquisite art galleries. For more local colour, there's traditional Namdaemun Market, which sells just about everything – including kitchen sinks – at bargain prices. Food for the soul comes in the form of 'kimch'l' – grated vegetables mixed with chilli, garlic and ginger, and *pulgogi*, or 'fire beef' – strips of beef marinated in soy sauce, sesame oil and chilli. Outer districts are pockets of the 'land of the morning calm' – the Korea that was once just gardens, palaces, tea-houses and temples.

Korea Air and Asiana Airlines both fly to Sydney from London via Seoul. Even if you decide not to make the stopover, with several hours in Seoul while the plane refuels, you can still snatch a taste of Korea at the airport. There's free Internet access for transit passengers, a television lounge and a playroom. For real relaxation, head to the massage and shower room or maybe even the hotel, where six hours' sleep can be had for about £40.

- **Emirates, t** 0870 243 2222, **www.emirates.com**. One of the fastest-growing airlines. It flies to Brisbane, Melbourne, Perth and Sydney from London's Heathrow and Gatwick airports, as well as from Manchester and Birmingham, offering stopovers in Dubai on return UK flights. It has daily flights to Sydney, Melbourne, Perth and Brisbane.

- **Korean Air, t** 0800 0656 2001, **www.koreanair.com**. Flies from London Heathrow to Sydney and Brisbane via Seoul, Korea. Flights are highly competitive, although most involve a several hour wait in transit in Seoul (*see* box, above). The airport here is state of the art, with free Internet access, massage services and a hotel that charges only around £40 for six hours.

- **Air New Zealand, t** 0800 028 4149; **www.airnz.com**. Flies to Brisbane, Cairns, Melbourne and Sydney via Los Angeles.

- **Thai Airways, t** 020 7491 7953; **www.thaiair.com**. Flies to Australia several times a week from London Heathrow. Service is of a very high standard and Thailand is an attractive stopover destination.

Stopovers

You might think that it is a waste of time making a stopover and that you would rather get to your destination as quickly as possible. Bear in mind, though, that stopping halfway for a night, a day or even a day or two gives your body time to adjust to the changing time zones, which could save you being knocked out for several days when you arrive at your destination. It is also a great way to see a part of the world – usually either the States or Asia – for little extra cost, as most airlines don't charge for stopovers.

If you decide to travel straight through, take note that all flights to Australia will stop to refuel, which usually involves a wait of around 90mins in transit (and you won't be allowed to leave the airport).

Jetlag

Owing to the distance involved, the worst jetlag you are ever likely to encounter is on a flight between the UK and Australia. Because our bodies are synchronised to day and night through brain chemicals, especially melatonin, those bodily functions that are linked to this 24-hour cycle – for example, digestion, temperature, hormones and heart rate – can be particularly affected by jetlag. Flying east usually results in much more severe symptoms because travelling eastwards takes the body in the opposite direction from its body clock, while going west simply extends the usual day-to-night cycle. If you suffer from severe jetlag, it might be worth considering a westward route to Australia.

Symptoms of jetlag include fatigue, general malaise and insomnia. Many existing conditions are made worse by flying, because it affects the immune system and hydration levels. If you tend to suffer from constipation, it will probably be exacerbated by flying, but it can be prevented by drinking lots of water and eating foods that are easily digested – fruit and vegetables, rather than protein and carbohydrates. Other symptoms that may occur are anxiety, diarrhoea, headache, nausea, sweating and even confusion.

There are some things you can do to minimise the effects of flying. Don't think you can catch up with sleep on the plane. Flying below par is a recipe for disaster. Get as much fluid intake (still water) as you can both before you leave and while on the flight, and try not to drink dehydrating beverages, such as alcohol, tea, coffee and carbonated drinks. Bring at least two large bottles of water with you, as the small glasses you will be served in flight will not be enough. Try to drink at least one glass of water for every hour you are flying. The air inside a plane is drier than the Sahara.

When air crew fly for pleasure, they make a point of wearing comfortable, loose-fitting clothes during the flight and changing into something smarter before arrival. Walk up and down the aisles as much as possible to increase your circulation and even make small movements in your seat. Travel accessories can work wonders. An eye mask and earplugs can be great aids for sleep and all

Jetlag? What's That?

As a travel writer, I am well used to long flights, thinking nothing of jumping on a plane to India or Brazil, and have never had any problem with jetlag. Then, as author of this book, I got on a plane to Australia, which instead of the 10-hour or so flights I was used to, meant 24 hours in the air. I was fine for the first day or so, which is apparently common. Then I began feeling nauseous, my lower back ached and when I wasn't feverish and sweating I was shivering and vomiting violently.

Looking up all my symptoms on the Internet, it looked like a classic case of jetlag. I took to my bed for two days, unable to eat and surviving on painkillers. In the end I went to a doctor who told me I had a severe kidney infection and that I was on the point of being hospitalised. Although what I had wasn't jetlag as such, there is no doubt that the long flight brought on the symptoms by affecting my immune system and causing dehydration.

airlines on long-haul flights provide pillows and light blankets. Some people swear by melatonin as an antidote to jetlag. It is available without prescription in the States as well as on the internet.

Try to get as much natural light as possible, as this will help your body adapt to the new time zone. On arrival, immediately change your watch to local time and eat at local meal times. If you arrive in the daytime, try to stay up until the evening, so that your body will adjust more quickly to the local time zone. If you have flown east, energy levels will be higher in the evening, while those travelling west will find themselves more lively in the mornings.

How to Avoid Long Haul Becoming a Long Haul

It's always a good idea to travel midweek when flights tend to be less full. Check in early if possible so you can have your choice of seat and if the flight isn't full ask if you could have extra seats reserved next to you.

Seat Pitch

On long flights the distance between a seat and the one in front is crucial. This is known as the seat pitch, and is not the same as leg room. With highly publicised cases of deep-vein thrombosis, customers have become more aware of the issue of adequate seating room and the great variations between airlines. As a result, airlines have been put under pressure to provide for passengers.

The UK travel company Bridge the World, which specialises in long-haul travel, broke new ground when it informed its sales staff to give clients information about seat pitch provided by the various airlines. It soon became clear that customers were basing their choice of airline on the seat pitch provided and rejecting traditionally popular airlines such as British Airways, Qantas and

Online Agents

- www.bargainholidays.com
- www.bridgetheworld.co.uk
- www.cheapflights.com
- www.deckchair.com
- www.ebookers.com
- www.expedia.co.uk
- www.flynow.com
- www.lastminute.com
- www.majortravel.co.uk
- www.opodo.co.uk
- www.statravel.co.uk
- www.teletextholidays.co.uk
- www.thefirstresort.com
- www.thomascook.co.uk
- www.trailfinders.co.uk
- www.travelocity.co.uk

Cathay Pacific, which have ungenerous seat pitches, in favour of airlines such as Malaysia, Thai and Air New Zealand. Of course, if you travel business or first class (or in the case of British Airways, World Traveller Plus), the seat pitch will be significantly bigger.

There are various websites (for instance **www.uk-air.net** and **www.seat guru.com**) that give up-to-date information about seat pitch on the main airlines; these sites also have seating plans, so you can ask for a seat with a non-restricted recline, or one that is in a quiet area. The list below shows the seat pitch provided by the major airlines operating to Australia:

- Air New Zealand: 34ins
- British Airways: 31ins
- Cathay Pacific: 32ins
- Emirates: 32ins
- Malaysia Airlines: 34ins
- Qantas Australia: 31ins
- Singapore Airlines: 32ins
- Thai Airways: 33ins
- British Airways World Traveller Plus: 38ins

Air Miles and Loyalty Schemes

Air miles gained on flights between the UK and Australia soon add up and if you are going to be making several journeys it is well worth looking into the points offered by the various airlines. Also, many airlines have alliance schemes, so that if you fly with any of a group of companies you accrue points that can be used interchangeably. Generally, it is worth registering for any loyalty schemes or air mile programmes; bear in mind that you must usually do this before you embark on your journey.

By Sea

Obviously, travelling to Australia by boat is not the cheapest or quickest way to go, but for those who can't or don't want to fly, it's a real lifesaver. Doing one leg, such as London to Singapore, by plane and the Singapore to Australia segment by cruise ship is also a good option. Cruise ships have moved on leaps and bounds in the last few years, so put aside those images of elderly passengers shuffling around the captain's table. State-of-the-art vessels with spas, theatres and sushi bars are now becoming the norm. November 2004 saw the maiden cruise of Sydney's largest liner, the Titanic-sized *Pacific Sun*, as well as P&O Cruises' boutique Australian liner, *Pacific Princess*. The 2,700-passenger *Sapphire Princess* was the largest liner ever to sail to Australia in December 2004, and Cunard's famous *QEII* arrived in February 2005.

Cruise liners call in at the ports of Adelaide, Brisbane, Hobart, Melbourne, Perth and Sydney. Major international lines include Cunard, Norwegian Cruise Lines, Orient Lines, P&O and Princess Lines. For information on all the major cruise lines, check **www.cruisedirect.co.uk**.

AMIS pvs proprietary Limited
Level 9, 56 Berry Street North Sydney NSW 2060
Australia

Phone +61 2 9959 5944 Fax +61 2 9954 0490 .www.amis.com.au

Migration agent of AMIS pvs
Wayne Parcell PSM,
Solicitor (9790656); Karen
Mathie JP (0209525); Hadi Assanteh JP (0320689);
Anita Skipps JP (0321906);
Joanne Miller, Solicitor (0425707); Komathy
Rajaratnam, Solicitor (0429276).

Red Tape

Gone are the days when it was relatively easy to get into Australia. The country has set increasingly higher standards in its immigration rules. There are all sorts of hurdles to get over and the process can take years. On top of that, the regulations are complicated and constantly changing, making it almost impossible to outline the visa system accurately. For example, there are more than 10 different permanent visas, each with a different set of requirements, and for the skilled permanent visa alone, the Australian government publishes a 76-page instruction booklet to accompany the relevant forms.

There are a few general rules though. First, the immigration department wants young people and is unlikely other than in exceptional circumstances to consider for skilled migration applicants over the age of 45. Secondly, Australia is mostly interested in attracting migrants with post-secondary educational attainments and a high level of recognised skills. Most of the permanent visas granted are skilled visas, which involve an independent skills assessment by a prescribed assessing authority. This takes different forms, depending on your occupation.

Unless you are applying for a straightforward electronic travel authority (ETA) or a working holiday visa, you will probably want to put your application into the hands of a skilled immigration lawyer. Just make sure they are registered and belong to the Migration Institute of Australia (MIA). There are plenty of horror stories of inefficient professionals happily taking their fees while misadvising their clients.

A Little Bit of History

The 'White Australia' policy is the term used to describe Australia's approach to immigration from federation until the end of the 20th century, which favoured applicants from certain countries. It was also formed according to religious criteria, in that, for example, Lebanese people who were Christian were considered white, and therefore eligible for migration, while Muslim Lebanese were deemed black, and therefore rejected.

The abolition of this policy took place over a period of 25 years. After the election of a coalition of the Liberal and Country parties in 1949, the immigration minister Harold Holt permitted 800 non-European refugees to stay in Australia and a number of Japanese war brides to enter the country. Over the following years, Australian governments gradually dismantled the policy, but there is still some evidence that Australia's immigration policy is not entirely just to all ethnic groups.

After the Second World War an official migration programme began. From October 1945 to June 2000, over 6 million people (a little more than 3 million males, and just short of 3 million females) have settled in Australia, and about one million people have left the country permanently. Economic and humanitarian events around the world have influenced the number and the source countries of people arriving in Australia. At various times the Netherlands, Germany, Italy, Greece, Turkey and Yugoslavia have been important migrant source countries. Since planned migration started after the war, almost 600,000 people have arrived under humanitarian programmes, as displaced persons or refugees, and Australia's total population has risen from 7 million to nearly 20 million.

Today, almost a quarter of Australia's 20 million people were born abroad. From 2001 to 2002, the number of immigrants reached nearly 100,000. Arriving from over 150 countries, 17.6 per cent came from New Zealand, 9.8 per cent from the United Kingdom, 7.5 per cent from China, 6.4 per cent from South Africa, 5.7 per cent from India and 4.7 per cent from Indonesia.

The Basics

The Australian migration programme has three major 'streams' – Skill, Family and Humanitarian. For the first, migrants must score a certain number of 'points', work in a specific occupation, be sponsored by an employer, or have successful business acumen or significant capital. For 'Family', a relative – for example, a spouse, fiancé, child or parent – must sponsor the applicant. The last category is for persons determined to be refugees under the United Nations Convention or to be of a limited class of people who have experienced certain human rights violations.

The immigration authority is keen to exclude people with serious health problems or serious criminal convictions. The joke goes that it used to be a requirement that you had a criminal record to enter Australia, and now it's the opposite.

ETAs

Anyone arriving in Australia who is not an Australian citizen must have a valid visa. Electronic Travel Authorities (ETA) are 'paperless' visas available only to certain passport holders, including UK passport holders, and can be applied for online; they are usually issued immediately. As they are electronic, ETAs do not appear as labels in your passport. Available for both tourism and short-stay business purposes, tourist ETAs and short-validity, single-entry business ETAs are free of any Australian government charge, but there is a charge for long-validity, multiple-entry business ETAs.

For more information, or to apply, visit **www.immi.gov.au**. Participating travel agencies and airlines can issue ETAs, usually for a small administration fee. If you are not a citizen of a country eligible for an ETA application, or if you want to stay in Australia longer than 3 months, you need to apply for a non-ETA 'label' visa. Tourist visas usually allow a stay of up to 3 months on each visit, although in special circumstances it may be possible to obtain a tourist visa for a stay of more than 3 months.

Working Holiday Visas

If you are aged between 18 and 30 at the date of application and are a citizen of the UK (or Canada, the Netherlands, Japan, Republic of Ireland, Republic of Korea, Malta, Germany, Denmark, Sweden, Norway, the Hong Kong Special Administrative Region of the People's Republic of China, Finland, the Republic of Cyprus, France, Italy, Belgium, Estonia or Taiwan) you can apply for a working holiday visa, which allows you to undertake incidental work in Australia for up to 12 months while on holiday. Working holidaymakers are permitted to do any kind of work of a temporary or casual nature. As the main purpose of the visit is for holiday and travel, work for longer than 3 months with any one employer is not allowed.

There are other criteria. You must:

- **hold an eligible passport and have no dependent children.**
- **not intend to study in Australia – except for courses or training that last a maximum of three months.**
- **be able to prove you have enough money for your return air fare.**
- **be able to prove you have sufficient funds to support yourself during the time you are away.**

Student Visas

Student visas are available for those of primary school age up to adults who are studying on courses full time run by a registered educational provider (**www.studyinaustralia.gov.au**). Depending on the type of student visa applied for, applicants must have – and must be able to prove they have – access to enough money to support themselves and their family for the entire time they are studying. There are quite complicated formulas used to determine how much these funds should be and how they should be evidenced. In some cases, funds for the support of family will be required to be demonstrated even where the student will be in Australia alone.

While studying, students may be able to work for up to 20 hours a week, or full time during holidays. Students can apply for a visa with the right to work only after arriving in Australia, and, once the student has begun studying, there is also an application charge. Student visas are necessary only for students studying in Australia for over three months; if studying for less than three months, a short-stay visa may be sufficient.

Normally, students are given a multiple-entry visa, which means they are allowed to travel into and out of Australia. Members of immediate family (spouse and unmarried dependent children under 18 years of age) are allowed to accompany students to Australia and are granted visas in the same visa subclass. The guardian visa allows a parent or other close family member to accompany a student or students while they undertake their Australian education.

Business Visas

Business long-stay visas are for those who are sponsored by an Australian or foreign company; a business must first apply to be approved as a business sponsor, and that approval can be granted to genuine businesses intending to directly employ the nominee with economic benefit to Australia. The sponsor undertakes to meet specified obligations to the Australian government and meet training undertakings to Australian employees. Next, the position to be

Skilled Occupations

The two most popular categories of skilled migrant are the independent skilled and skilled Australian sponsored (SAS) programmes. Applicants for skilled visas must score a certain number of points before their application is considered for visa grant. Those who score less than the required amount may be held for future processing if the pass mark changes. For independent skilled migrants, points are earned in areas such as work experience, formal qualifications, age and English language competency. For SAS applicants, the same criteria apply, but in addition family relationships and the status of sponsors is also taken into account.

At the time of writing, the South Australian government is recruiting policemen but nationally, doctors, accountants and hairdressers are all in demand. The 'Migration Occupations in Demand List (MODL) has details of the occupations for which demand is high and which therefore attract preference in migration applications. This list changes frequently. It's the same in England. There are times when nurses are in demand and the British government advertises overseas. Another year it may be accountants. It's important to keep your eyes open to see what professional skills are in short supply during that year.

People who have 'skilled occupations' that are needed are permitted to make an application for migration under the skills programme, which can be found on the 'Skilled Occupations List' (SOL) on the Department of Immigration website (*see* 'Useful Addresses', p.110). If an occupation is not on this list then, regardless of the academic level attained in acquiring the skill, a successful points-tested skilled migration application is unlikely through this channel.

occupied by an applicant must be nominated and approved; even after a prospective employer is approved as a business sponsor, only certain occupations can be nominated for these long-stay business visas. Finally, applicants must be approved to fill the approved position nomination. Business long-stay visas are granted to enable applicants to work temporarily, for a periods of validity of up to 4 years at a time.

Short-stay business visas allow holders to stay in Australia only for up to three months for business purposes.

Partner Migration

To apply to live in Australia with your partner, whether a married or a de facto spouse (a de facto relationship is where two people live as if married without having gone through a religious or civil ceremony), you must have lived with your Australian partner for at least a year. You must prove this by demonstrating your joint financial commitments, household bills and showing the social aspects of the relationship in the form of declarations from friends and family, joint travel and so on. If you are in a same-sex relationship, or in a relationship that is domestic but not intimate, then you need an **Interdependent Partner Migration Visa**.

The Regional Sponsored Migration Scheme

Because of the concentration of the workforce in the major urban centres, the Australian government is desperately trying to encourage people to live in rural and low-population-growth areas, and preference for visa applications is given to them. The **Regional Sponsored Migration Scheme (RSMS)** visa was introduced on 1 July 2004 to encourage immigration to the regional areas of Australia (determined by postcode), away from the more densely populated urban areas.

Applicants must apply for a position that is of a skilled nature and they are required to meet certain skill, age and language requirements. The process involves regional bodies declaring genuine skilled vacancies for positions that will be available for at least two years.

Resident Return Visas

Only Australian citizens have the right to enter Australia without a visa. Permanent residents who are not citizens must have a valid **Resident Return Visa (RRV)** if they wish to enter Australia and retain their permanent resident status. Valid for between three months and five years, depending on your circumstances, an RRV allows Australian permanent residents to travel to Australia as often as they wish within the validity of the visa, permitting them to remain indefinitely in Australia on each entry. Renewal of an RRV is not -

Case Study: Four Weddings and a Funeral

It took Elizabeth de Angelis three long years to get her residency through her de facto relationship. During that time she could have been made to leave the country at any point and she was unable to make work or college commitments. The strain that it put on her relationship was significant. Fifteen years later, the stress was not over. 'I had my heart set on getting married in England, in a church in rural Norfolk which had particular significance for my family, and for six months we made the necessary arrangements. Then, just three months before the wedding, I was told that although I was still a British citizen I was not legally allowed to get married at the church unless I had been resident in the parish for 15 nights prior to the wedding.

'It just wasn't practical. As it was we were taking five weeks off work for the wedding and the honeymoon. After a lot of tears, we married in Scotland, which has no such quirk in the law, and had a blessing in the style of a traditional wedding in the church. Sadly my great aunt, who had been married in the same church around 70 years previously, died months before the blessing. My in-laws live in Melbourne, a several-hour plane ride from where we are in Sydney, so we had a celebration for them and my husband John's family, which my father attended from England. Finally, we had a big cocktail party for all our friends in Sydney.

'It was a lot of work, but they were all wonderful celebrations. The whole thing highlighted for me how important England is for me. As much as I love Australia and living here, my roots will always be there.'

automatic, and extended absences from Australia, without maintaining suitable ties or involving activities in Australia's interests, can make renewal of the RRV less than straightforward.

The Visa Scheme

Anybody who is not a citizen of Australia must have a visa to enter or remain in Australia. Furthermore, anyone from any country can apply to migrate, regardless of their ethnic origin, their gender, colour or religion. If a person satisfies Australia's selection criteria, he or she stands an equal chance of being selected.

Importantly, under Australian law a person can be granted a visa only if he or she meet all the legal requirements. If all legal requirements for a visa are met, then the visa must be granted. If all requirements for a visa are not met, then the visa will not, except in very limited circumstances, be granted.

The Australian Migration Scheme is highly prescriptive and complex, with visa classes and visa subclasses. A class of visa is a group of similar subclasses of visa. When you are applying for a visa, you are applying to be granted a visa of a particular subclass.

Visa classes are complicated and can best be understood by reference to the **Migration Regulations Schedule 1**, which details what you need to do to make an application for all visas. Schedule 1 of the Migration Regulations gives details such as:

- **Where a visa application must be made.**
- **On what form or forms it must be made.**
- **The fee that must be paid at the time of lodging the application.**
- **In some cases, where the applicant must be at the time of lodging the visa application.**

It is crucial that all requirements of Schedule 1 are complied with, as failure to do so will result in an invalid visa application and it will not be considered.

A **visa subclass** details the eligibility criteria for a visa application, but eligibility is not the same as validity. The structure of a visa subclass is best explained by referring to the **Migration Regulations Schedule 2**. Consideration of an application for a visa of a particular subclass is broken down into two stages:

- **Criteria to be satisfied at the time of application.**
- **Criteria to be satisfied at the time of decision.**

Additionally, there are primary criteria (which apply to the main applicant) and secondary criteria (which apply to any spouse or dependent child) to be satisfied at each stage.

For some visa subclasses, every person who applies for the visa is a **primary applicant**. A good example of this is the subclass visitor visa. Every applicant for this visa applies in their own right and must independently satisfy all the legal requirements, regardless of whether or not they are travelling at the same time as another family member. Other visa subclasses require that only the primary applicant satisfy the important (primary) eligibility criteria. A good example of this is the skilled independent subclass 136 visa (a permanent visa) for which it is necessary that only the primary applicant meets the age, skill, education and work-experience requirements, and his or her eligible dependents need satisfy only the secondary criteria, such as the health and character requirements.

If all eligibility criteria are met at the time of application and at the time of the decision by each of the primary and secondary applicants, then the standard structure of the Schedule 2 visa subclass information further prescribes how and when the visa should be granted and evidenced, and details any conditions which will or may be imposed on the visa to be granted.

It is important to select the right subclass of visa, as different rights and obligations attach to permanent and temporary visas, and even between different subclasses of temporary visa. **Permanent visas**, once granted, usually have no conditions on them that restrict either the holder's activities in Australia or the time he or she can spend in Australia. Permanent visa-holders enjoy many rights that temporary visa-holders do not, including:

- Rights to access 'free' public schooling for children.
- Universal 'free' healthcare.
- Unrestricted property ownership.
- Rights to employment.
- After a qualifying period, the right to apply for Australian citizenship (and an Australian passport if citizenship is granted).

Temporary visas are usually issued with one or more visa conditions. These conditions are endorsed on the visa so that the holder can engage only in activities consistent with the purpose for which the visa subclass was created and granted. An example is the **visitor visa**, which is quite simple to apply for and obtain – in many cases online and in minutes for a small fee. However, the visitor visa prevents the holder from working in Australia. Other conditions can also be applied to visitor visas, including a condition that the holder of the visa may not – after entry to Australia – apply for another visa while they remain in Australia.

Breaching a visa condition can have serious implications for visa-holders. A person who applies, for example, for a visitor visa, but whose intention is to work in the hopes of securing more permanent residence once in Australia, might find that the perceived shortcut provided by the visitor visa did not assist them to achieve the long-term goal they were hoping for because the conditions imposed on the visitor visa, or non-compliance with the conditions, prevents them from applying successfully for a further visa inside Australia.

There are in total more than 100 different permanent and temporary subclasses of visa that one can use to secure entry to or residence in Australia. The name given to each of the visa subclasses is supposed to be descriptive of the type of person that the visa is intended to attract and be granted to. Schedule 2 of the Migration Regulations includes a comprehensive list of visa subclasses and their eligibility criteria.

The temporary or permanent nature of the visa is determined with reference to the policy objectives for creating the visa subclass, and heavily affects the level of effort required to apply for, process and be granted a visa. As a general guide, the longer the visa validity and the more favourable and permanent the rights associated with a visa, the more cost and effort you will need to put into the application.

Usually, if you apply for the wrong type of visa (a visa for which you do not meet the criteria), apply at the wrong time or in the wrong place, or submit an application for a visa without, for example, the prescribed forms, supporting documentation or correct fees, it is likely that it will be invalid or refused. This will happen even if you could have applied successfully in a different manner, at a different time or place, or for a visa of a different subclass.

Health and Character

For all visas, applicants need to be of good health (not including minor ailments) and good character.

The details into which the **Australian Department of Immigration and Multicultural and Indigenous Affairs'** website (**DIMIA; www.immi.gov.au**) will first enquire about, and then check into, about a person's health or character are:

- **the likely risk of harm to Australian citizens or permanent residents.**

- **the cost to the Australian community of any adverse health or character condition affecting an applicant if they were granted a visa and permitted to enter Australia.**

As a general rule, the shorter the intended stay in Australia, the less intrusive the examination of a visa applicant's health or character. Tourists intending no more than a simple three-week vacation are not normally required to undergo a health examination before a visa is granted to them, although the law does not exclude this possibility, and applicants from some countries where there is a high known incidence of serious contagious disease may be asked to undergo a radiological or physical examination. An application for a permanent visa, or a temporary visa that is likely to place the applicant in close contact with work colleagues or fellow students, for example, will be required to complete health examination procedures.

Applicants with less than perfect health or past misconduct should not necessarily be discouraged from applying for a visa. Some health conditions are transitory or respond to appropriate treatment even if contagious and may therefore be unlikely to be a long-term cost or threat to the Australian community. If an applicant has been or is being treated for a medical condition, it is important in making a visa application that they honestly declare the matter and document the nature of that condition and its treatment and medical management.

Anyone with past misconduct that fails to meet society's expectations might seek to include evidence of the offence for which they were charged, or of which they were guilty, and include current statements and evidence showing that such behaviour is not habitual. Past misconduct need not be a permanent bar to the granting of an Australian visa, but you should consider seeking professional advice in connection with any visa application.

Failure to disclose health and character issues in any visa application is a serious matter and can count against a visa applicant. Should DIMIA call for medical examinations or police records checks before making a decision about a visa application and subsequently discover that answers given on any visa application form or an incoming passenger card were at that time incorrect, they might consider future visa applications from that applicant in a less than favourable light. All visa applicants have a duty of continuous and candid disclosure of all matters relevant to their visa application, and failure to meet this requirement might adversely impact DIMIA's views of the *bona fides* of an applicant and can lead to the refusal of visa applications.

Visa Selection

It is important, in approaching the visa selection and application process, to determine first your objectives for entry to and residence in Australia. If you are is interested in spending only a year working, holidaying and living in Australia, there would seem little advantage in applying for a permanent visa. Permanent visas involve time, effort and cost to conclude successfully. Conversely, a person who is planning a major family resettlement in Australia, involving, for example, the sale of assets, resignation from employment or sale of business, and withdrawal of children from school, might consider the cost, effort and time involved in making a permanent visa application worthwhile, given that without a permanent visa their rights in Australia are likely to be restricted in some way if they hold only a temporary visa.

After determining one's objective(s) for entry to and residence in Australia, the next step is to select the subset of visa subclasses that will permit, either alone or in combination, that objective to be achieved. It may well be that one's ultimate objective cannot immediately be achieved by an application for a single visa subclass. There are people who wish to settle permanently in Australia but because their present circumstances do not enable them to meet the criteria for any of the available permanent visa subclasses, they need to apply for a temporary or conditional permanent visa subclass that can lead to eligibility for permanent residence in the future.

One example is a young person whose post-secondary academic and employment achievements in their home country are not of the standard prescribed for immediate approval under Australia's skilled permanent migration stream. This person may decide that they will enrol in an Australian university to complete an Australian qualification as a student visa holder (a temporary visa), and, following successful completion of the course in Australia, apply for permanent residence under a special visa class designed specifically to reward foreign students who have completed the required level of tertiary study in Australia.

Another example is a skilled professional or specialist who wishes to relocate to Australia reasonably quickly and experience working life before committing to the permanent residence process. Such a person, who secures an offer of employment in Australia from an Australian employer, may be able to enter quickly using a temporary business visa. This person may be sponsored by the Australian employer for a temporary visa for employment purposes and thereafter, if mutually agreed and the criteria are able to be met, the Australian employer may decide to nominate the sponsored employee for a permanent business visa in Australia.

Business owners who fail to meet the rather complex processes and requirements for a permanent visa subclass under the business skills programme in the first instance may decide to accept the risk associated with a conditional business skills visa. This would enable them to be granted a visa that works somewhat like a temporary visa in the initial stages, but can lead to a permanent visa should certain business outcomes be achieved by any business that they establish in Australia.

Summary

The Australian migration scheme is composed of many different visa subclasses, all designed to be granted with a certain type of person in mind. There are visas for the partners, parents and children of Australian permanent residents or Australian citizens. There are visas for students, professionals, tradespersons and specialists to live and work temporarily in Australia. There are visas for business owners and investors. There are visas for refugees and humanitarian applicants. There are visas for people with an Australian sponsor and those who do not have any Australian party to support their visa application. There are even visas for traditional fishermen, spies and witnesses in judicial proceedings!

It cannot be stressed too greatly that the Australian migration system is highly regulated and can be complex. Where the stakes are not high, say in the case of applying for a visitor visa for a short holiday in Australia, a person should be able in most cases to apply for a visa without professional assistance. Where the reasons for a visa application to Australia involve important family, professional, educational or business objectives, there seems little merit in approaching the process in a manner less seriously than any other matter involving such a complex area of law, which means enlisting professional help.

Australia has instituted a system of universal registration of all Australia migration advisors. The system requires that persons giving paid immigration advice and assistance be registered with the **Migration Agents Registration Authority (www.mara.com.au)**. Lawyers and non-lawyers alike must be registered and registration is renewed annually on completion of prescribed continuing professional development and adherence to the Migration Agents Code of Conduct.

Professional migration agents and lawyers tend to specialise. Some focus on the needs of corporate clients and their expatriate employees. Others deal in court matters and appeals. Some specialise in the business skills programme for entrepreneurs, business owners or investors. Refugee and humanitarian applications deserve their own particular brand of advocacy and not every migration professional is equipped to provide the level of expertise required.

Good agents will always refer you to a colleague better placed to assist you, rather than take on work for which they are ill-equipped, and they will usually indicate on their website the client type in which they specialise.

As in any profession, there are good agents and not so good agents. Choosing the right migration professional need not be impossibly difficult but certainly is key to ensuring your risks are properly managed and your objectives are achievable. Some of the qualities that you can expect of a competent migration advisor include:

- **size and capabilities suitable to your needs.**
- **experience.**
- **clearly defined and written agreements addressing service level and fee scale.**

There are a reasonable number of enthusiastic amateurs in the migration profession in Australia and, although you might form a useful relationship with such a person or their firm, you could just as likely find that they are not there for you throughout the entire immigration lifecycle. The average life of an Australian migration agent is about three years – that is, once registered, the majority of migration agents last only about three years in the profession before they move on elsewhere.

Finally, whatever your needs, it is worth remembering that Australian migration law is a complex area of law that changes with unnerving regularity. The legislative scheme enables the Australian government to amend its policies and the system quickly, and in many cases without advance notice to parliament and applicants. The current Australian government has made it abundantly clear that it will exclusively determine who will be permitted to enter and remain in Australia, and it fine-tunes the system as and when it sees fit, using simple and very quick devices such as regulations and gazette notices.

Citizenship

Immigrants and refugees are eligible to apply for Australian citizenship only after becoming permanent residents, and thereafter meeting the residential requirements. Generally, people are eligible for Australian citizenship when they have been present in Australia as a permanent resident for a cumulative total of two years in the previous five years, including 12 months in the two years immediately before they apply.

Applicants generally must be present in Australia when they apply and must also intend to live there permanently or to maintain a close and continuing association with Australia. They must also be of good character, be able to speak and understand basic English, and have an adequate knowledge of the responsibilities and privileges of Australian citizenship. See **www.citizenship.gov.au** for more information.

Useful Addresses

The website of the Australian **Department of Immigration and Multicultural and Indigenous Affairs'** (**DIMIA; www.immi.gov.au**) is not as user-friendly as it could be, but is comprehensive and has lists of answers to frequently asked questions in each section. Applications can be made online for some new and replacement visas, from ETAs right through to citizenship, and there is a range of booklets to assist potential visitors.

The **Australian High Commission** (Strand, London WC2B 4LA), does not provide a direct telephone enquiry service. For all public information, visitors are directed to the website or the 24-hour recorded information service on **t** 09065 508 900 (£1 per minute, accessible in the UK only). Client counter hours are Mon–Fri 9–11am, for general information and forms only. No visa applications can be lodged over the counter; these must be posted to the above address with a self-addressed special-delivery envelope.

The main high commissions and consulate generals are:

- **British High Commission in Australia, www.uk.emb.gov.au.**
- **British Consulate**, Level 22, Grenfell Centre, 25 Grenfell Street, Adelaide 5000, **t** 00 61 08 8212 7280.
- **British Consulate-General**, Level 26, Waterfront Place, 1 Eagle Street, Brisbane 4000, **t** 00 61 07 3223 3200.
- **British High Commission**, Commonwealth Avenue, Yarrlumla, Canberra, ACT 2606, **t** 00 61 02 6270 6666.
- **Honorary Consul**, 1A Brisbane Street, Hobart, Tasmania 7000, **t** 00 61 03 6230 3400.
- **British Consulate-General**, 17th Floor, 90 Collins Street, Melbourne 3000, **t** 00 61 03 9650 3699.
- **British Consulate-General**, Level 26, Allendale Square, 77 St George's Terrace, Perth 6000, **t** 00 61 08 9221 5400.
- **British Consulate-General**, The Gateway, Level UK (16), 1 Macquarie Place, Sydney, NSW 2000, **t** 00 61 02 9247 7521.

The legislation relating to immigration and visas, including the Migration Act and Regulations, can be consulted online from the **Attorney General's Department (http://scaleplus.law.gov.au)** and the **Australian Legal Information Institute (www.austlii.edu.au)**.

Living in Australia

06

The majority (90 per cent) of Australians live in towns or cities on the coast and most are within 30 minutes of a beach. Australia is one of the most urbanised countries on earth. The Aussie dream is to own a home in a good area, with a quarter acre of land, complete with a 'barbie' and the classic Australian circular clothes line, the Hills Hoist. Housing tends to be low-rise, so that cities are spread outwards rather than upwards. There are some key differences between European and Australian house styles. While larger communities and cities have a wide range of housing available, including a large amount of European and American styles, there are plenty of examples of uniquely Australian buildings. High-rise residential areas are rare in Australia, although inner-city living has become increasingly popular. The vast majority of houses have three bedrooms; around 15 per cent have four bedrooms and just 5 per cent have five bedrooms. A 'backyard', or garden, is standard.

Finding a Home

Some new arrivals will be lucky enough to have friends or relatives to stay with to kick start their move to Australia. For most, though, it will be necessary to find somewhere to rent and then perhaps a home to buy. Renting or buying can be done either privately or through an estate agent. The criteria for how to make your choice will be pretty much the same as at home, although you may find you need to do more preliminary research into locations. Factors to consider include proximity to facilities, transport, your place of work and the beach. If you have children, the location and quality of nearby schools is important. Don't rely on other people's information, especially if those people are estate agents, and don't make assumptions. One nurse from the north of England accepted a job and housing in Sydney's district of Liverpool and looked forward to lunchtimes at the beach until on arrival she found she was an hour and half from the coast.

Renting a House or Flat

Even if you know that you want to buy a flat (known in Australia as a 'unit') or house, the chances are you will need to rent somewhere first. The rental situation is not unlike that in the UK. Most estate agents (known as real estate agents in Australia) have lists of properties to let as well as to buy. If you want to do it privately, look through the 'to let' section of local newspapers or search on the Internet.

Contracts are usually for a minimum of 6 months, which should be enough time to establish which area you want to live in long term. Again, as in the UK, tenancy agreements ask for a month's rent in advance and a refundable deposit (known as a '**bond**') of a month's rent. The **Residential Tenancies Authority (RTA)** outlines the terms for renting, which are designed to protect both parties. It is standard procedure to make sure the bond is lodged at the Department of Fair Trading in case there is any dispute when you move out.

The bond can be withheld if any damage is done by you to the property or its contents. When leaving the property, make sure that everything is clean and all rubbish removed; you do not want any reason for the landlord to withhold the bond. Obviously, any repairs necessary due to standard use are the responsibility of the landlord, such as malfunctions with the boiler or the toilet, for example. It is not a bad idea to write down any problems – such as marks on the walls or ill-fitting doors – and get the landlord to sign as confirmation. Keep this and the rental contract safe.

Looking for somewhere to rent can be a demoralising experience. The procedure can take a long time, especially if you don't have all the necessary paperwork to hand. A good tip is to get your tax file number (TFN) from the Tax Department and a bank account as soon as you can. Two references are usually required and will normally be followed up. If you are not working, proof of funds may be required. English references may not be accepted in Australia and some landlords won't accept tenants without employment.

The initial start-up costs involved in renting can make a significant drain on resources, so make sure to budget properly. Before embarking on your search, find out the average rental values of the areas you are looking at. Before committing yourself to a property, consider hidden costs and also whether other charges can be met. Telephone companies in particular may ask for connection or advance payments. Don't forget to include removal costs.

Narrow down your search by deciding on one or two suburbs where you would be happy to live. Finding a location to suit your lifestyle is crucial. Do your research: find out about local transport, facilities, schools, shops, and so on. The following checklist may help you in your search:

- **public transport**
- **proximity to workplace**
- **services and shops**
- **schools**
- **park**
- **beach**
- **parking**
- **recreational facilities**

With regard to the property itself, some people find it helpful to draw up a list of 'musts', such as a garden or the number of bedrooms you want.

Arranging an inspection is an important step and is best done as soon as possible to ensure the best chance of beating off any competition. Check for

The Cost of Living

Obviously, a key question when considering a move to Australia is: what is the cost of living compared to England? Many potential migrants have the idea that living in Australia is much cheaper than at home. While this is generally true, when you take into account lower incomes and higher taxes in Australia, you may very well be worse, not better, off. Of course, just as an individual's earning capacity varies enormously, so does their ability to spend it, so it is difficult to define cost of living. Just as in the UK, apart from housing, the cost of living does not differ that much between different parts of the country.

obvious problems, such as rising damp or leaks, and make sure that appliances, such as oven and boiler, are in working order. You are within your rights to ask for any problems to be fixed before agreeing to move in, although a landlord may decide it is easier to go with a less demanding tenant.

When you have decided on a property, you will probably be asked to complete an application form, which will include details of your employer and income. In addition, it may ask for details of your personal finances, such as loans and savings, although in some states this is illegal – regional tenants' advice services can advise. Questions about your marital status, race, religion and sex are illegal nationwide and you are not obliged to answer them. The application may very well take several weeks, during which time it is wise to keep in regular contact with your landlord. Some states charge an application deposit. If this is the case get a receipt for this and find out if the fee is refundable once the decision has been made.

Most people rent privately, taking a lease on housing that is owned by businesses or individuals. Short-term rentals are usually for one- or two-bedroom furnished flats, which will normally have everything from a television to a washing machine. You will pay a premium for renting somewhere short-term, and in holiday periods prices may rise again. Co-tenancy involves two or more people sharing the accommodation, with each signing the tenancy agreement and each having equal responsibility for rent. For those looking to share a property, **www.flatmates.com.au** may be able to help. In general, accommodation is much more modern and of a much higher standard than at home.

Unlike in the UK, most accommodation is let unfurnished, so you will need to buy furniture and white goods, bring your own over from home, or rent them from a local company. Sub-letting means that one person with their name on the lease holds all responsibility. Boarding is when just a room is rented, such as in a private house with a family, and involves standard tenancy laws.

Student Accommodation

Those coming to Australia to study may be eligible for student accommodation, either on or off campus. There are distinct advantages to living in this environment, which offers convenience, services, a ready-made social life and usually relatively cheap rent. Student housing officers attached to the college or university concerned can supply information and are best contacted as soon as possible in advance as this type of housing is quickly snapped up.

It is quite unlikely that as a new arrival to the country you will be eligible for public or community housing. This is usually offered only to disadvantaged members of the community, such as those on low incomes or those with a disability. As demand for this kind of housing is high, long waiting lists are usually involved.

Buying a House or Flat

Only Australian and New Zealand citizens and people with Australian residency can buy a property in Australia. Others need permission from the **Foreign Investment Review Board (FIRB), www.firb.gov.au**, which also features downloadable guides. Even if you do get permission, you will need to meet a number of conditions. Buying a property is not something to rush into anywhere; make sure you do your homework. It needs to suit you in terms of price, 'suburb' (neighbourhood), proximity to the Central Business District (CBD), size and any specific requirements you might have, such as a 'backyard' (garden).

Prices are significantly lower than in the UK. Sydney has the highest house prices in the country, closely followed by Melbourne and then Brisbane. Properties in Perth, Darwin and Adelaide are around half the price of those in Sydney. In most city suburbs, two-bedroom apartments and houses are available from under £40,000. Sydney property costs at least four times as much, although central one-bed apartments are still available for under £150,000.

An Early Visitor

Way back in 1841, John Hood visited his son in Sydney just after convict transportation had ended. He may have been one of Australia's first tourists, but he certainly wasn't one of the happiest ones. In his memoir, *Australia and the East*, Hood was repulsed by the convicts, drunks and Aborigines he encountered in Sydney. When his son Alexander – who had left for Australia 10 years before – took him out past the Blue Mountains to his settlements, his opinion did not improve. He despaired at the journey, the town of Bathurst and finally his son's sheep farm. He couldn't bear the basic accommodation, flies or remoteness, and was convinced they would be attacked by robbers. Things came to a head at Christmas when Hood wrote, 'The sultry heat is a disagreeable contradiction to all our impressions of that happy season of frosts and snows and fireside comforts.' Although it was with some regret that he would never see his son again and that he had ever sent his son there, he could not leave soon enough, writing, 'For me such a life has not charms to compensate for the disadvantages.'

Three-bedroom suburban bungalows start at £60,000 or so. Terraced homes in Paddington, Sydney, are available for under £300,000. Melbourne is also expensive – Toorak in Melbourne has many properties topping the £1 million mark – but it is still cheaper than London.

With 70 per cent of Australians paying off home mortgages, the country has one of the highest rates of home ownership in the world. Australians are just as property-obsessed as Brits and can often be found glued to home-grown home-improvement programmes such as *Burke's Backyard*, as well as to all the UK versions. For Australians a house is a national symbol of security and it is easier to buy property in Australia than in the UK. You need to be in a job only for six months to be financed for up for 30 years, and the government is currently providing incentives for first-time buyers. The meteoric rise in property prices over the last few years (in 2003 many properties rose by as much as 55 per cent) has only fuelled the national obsession. Dinner-party conversations frequently revolve around investment values and the high level of ownership is one of the reasons why it is relatively easy to rent; many individuals own two or three houses to let out.

Finding a Property

Homes on the market can be found through newspaper advertisements, particularly on Wednesdays and Saturdays under the 'Real Estate' section. If you use an agent, choose one that is a member of the **Real Estate Institute of Australia**. Websites and auctions are other sources; auctions are much more common than in the UK. One major difference is that viewings are usually done over the weekend, with several potential purchasers arriving at the same time.

Financing and Mortgages

Arranging a mortgage can be a complicated business in any country. The administration process can be slow, with unpredictable demands made for specific documents. There are around 40 lenders to choose from, offering a variety of products, some of which are different from those in the UK. In the same way as in the UK, most lenders will want to see that you are creditworthy and are a 'good risk' financially. If you have no 'credit history' in Australia, it is a good idea to bring copies of any mortgage arrangements you had at home.

Home loans can be charged at various rates:

- **Standard variable rate:** changes depending on the market.

- **Discounted variable rate:** rate usually lower than standard variable rate.

- **Honeymoon rate:** reduced rate for the first 6–12 months, often used to attract new customers.

- **Fixed-rate home loan:** set rate of interest for an agreed period, usually 1–5 years, before returning to the standard variable rate.

A 'line of credit' means that the borrower does not have to draw the full amount of the loan, or to make regular repayments, but interest is normally paid monthly. The websites of the four major banks show the current standard variable rates at any time:

- **National Australia Bank, www.national.com.au.**
- **Australia and New Zealand Banking Group, www.anz.com.**
- **Westpac Banking Corporation, www.westpac.com.au.**
- **Commonwealth Bank of Australia, www.commbank.com.au.**

The loan you choose will feature the best interest rate for you, the flexibility you need and a minimum of fees. The length of the loan is normally 30 years. Watch out for fees charged by banks, such as an application fee, a property valuation fee, a loan repayment fee and so on. Credit providers and finance brokers are required by the **Australian Securities and Investments Commission (ASIC), www.asic.gov.au,** to give consumers a comparison rate. This rate is the total cost of credit, taking into account all fixed charges.

You can arrange the loan yourself or use a **broker**. You may think that going to a bank directly will save you paying a broker's fees, but usually brokers get better deals than individuals, so any commission is cancelled out. The advantage of using a broker is that they are well used to dealing with lenders and can find the best deal for you. A word of warning, though: some disreputable brokers may point you towards a product that is in their best interests, not yours. Compared with the UK, the mortgage-broking industry is relatively young in Australia and still largely unregulated. For more advice on how to choose a mortgage broker, look at:

- **Finance Brokers Association of Australia (FBAA), www.fbaa.com.au.**
- **Mortgage Industry Association of Australia (MIAA), www.miaa.com.au.**

How Much Can You Borrow?

When budgeting for a home, take into account the cost of conveyancing, which can be carried out by either a solicitor, licensed conveyancer, or the buyer or vendor. On top of these fees, statutory fees, stamp duties, transfer and registration fees are payable. When added together, such charges can amount to as much as 7 or 8 per cent of the final purchasing price.

How much you are allowed to borrow is decided by a number of factors.

Income Level, Source and Security

These factors are crucial because they indicate your ability to repay the loan. It is very difficult to secure a home loan without a job. Investments, or whether you are about to start a job, may be taken into account, but in this case only a percentage of the value of the property may be loaned because you will be considered high risk. In addition, you may be charged interest at a higher rate and you might be asked to supply additional mortgage insurance.

Even if you are employed, lenders may be resistant if you have been in a job for less than three months, or if you do part-time or contract work. In this case, you might be charged 1 or 2 per cent higher interest rate and be allowed to borrow only 80 per cent of the value of the property. If you are in this position, try to get as much documentation to support your case, such as a letter from your current employer stating the level of security of your job. It may also help if you get a letter from your previous employer to demonstrate that you have been contin-uously employed in the same profession. For those running their own business, lenders will not usually be prepared to help you until you have been operating for two years. They need proof of income in the form of contracts, tax returns and so on, and may then offer a loan for up to 95 per cent of the value of a prop-erty for 1 or 2 per cent higher than the standard variable rate.

Only certain lenders will accept overseas income when considering applica-tions for mortgages. International banks such as **Citibank, www.citibank. com.au**, and **HSBC, www.hsbc.com.au,** tend to have a more flexible approach to foreign earnings. That said, you will still be required to provide full documenta-tion from home, including pay slips, tax returns, bank statements; and your maximum borrowing would be 80 per cent. Try to gather any records and copies of credit history before leaving for Australia.

Financial Commitments and Expenses

Those people with a large number of outgoings will be likely to have their borrowing reduced. Potential lenders will ask for details of any credit card debts, rent, loans and so on. Don't be tempted to be dishonest about your commit-ments. Information you give will be put on file and banks can check most of the information you give them. If you are declined a loan, you may then have prob-lems with another lender, as details are shared.

There are no set ways of calculating living expenses – the only real rule is that the higher they are, the less you can borrow. Lenders will look at household costs and the number of dependants you have. It is clearly advisable to get any application for a loan right first time. Do your research first and choose your lender and mortgage carefully to try and ensure approval. Making a number of applications to different lenders will make them nervous about offering you a loan.

Credit History

If you have just moved to Australia, you will not have a credit history in the country. This information is held on a credit file and every time you make an application for any kind of loan, details of your request will be added, which can be accessed by lenders. If it is clear that an individual has made a number of unsuccessful applications, potential lenders are likely to be cautious and even refuse a loan. An even more serious situation occurs if you are shown to have a default on your credit history, for instance by not paying a bill after a series of demands, or not meeting a commitment with a bank. Even subsequent payment of a bill does not automatically clear your history. To view a copy of your credit file, contact **Baycorp Advantage, www.baycorp.com.au**.

Amount of Deposit You Can Pay

As is the case anywhere in the world, you will be expected to pay something towards the purchase of a property. The money can be a gift, savings or proceeds from another investment, but it must be 'your own', which means that it has been in your possession for at least six months. If your relatives or friends offer to help you financially they need to give written evidence of the deposit. And if they are to act as guarantors, they need to sign a guarantee to the loan, which makes them fully liable for the debt repayment. Before taking on such a responsibility, it is a good idea to seek independent legal advice.

Quality and Condition of Property

Most people will be using the property they are buying as security for a loan. In this case, the lender calculates its worth, based on a number of criteria. If your chosen flat or home is either very small or very large, in a rural or undesirable city area, you may have problems getting a loan.

Australian residents may be eligible for a first home owner's grant of up to A\$7,000, provided by the government, which can be put towards your deposit. This was brought in to offset the impact of the goods and services tax, introduced in 2000. Obviously, conditions apply. More information is available at **www.firsthome.gov.au**.

The Process of Buying a House or Flat

Each state and territory has its own laws and regulations concerning land and property transactions. In the ACT (Canberra), for example, no land is sold freehold; all property is sold on long leases.

The process of buying property is similar to that in the UK. Exchange of contracts is called 'settlement'; when the vendor accepts your offer, a contract is signed stipulating the date of settlement, and in between the offer acceptance date and the settlement date, the legal formalities – searches, conveyancing, survey, financial arrangements – take place. If settlement does not happen on the agreed date, the defaulting party must pay a penalty.

The contract is fairly standard, issued by the Real Estate Institute, and will simply state the sale price and agreed deposit (officially 10% but negotiable), the date of settlement, and which fixtures and fittings are included in the sale. You should check that the property has a current certificate stating that it is free of white ants, a common pest.

You can choose to use either a solicitor or a 'settlement agent' (a conveyancing specialist) to do the conveyancing; the latter will be cheaper, but fees will be in the region of A\$500–1,000. Costs of buying average around 5 per cent of the purchase price and include legal fees, stamp duty, which varies from region to region, and a small land transfer registration fee.

Checklist When Buying a House or Flat

It is worth asking an expert to carry out an inspection, but if you want to make one yourself, or to check that the professional you have employed has done a thorough job, here is a checklist of points to look out for.

- **Title**: make sure that the description in the title accurately matches the property in terms of size, number of rooms and so on.
- **Plot**: the boundaries of the land need to be identified and any disputes with neighbours investigated; pipes, cables and tanks as well as public areas on your land in the form of footpaths should be marked.
- **Outdoor areas**: if there is a swimming pool, check the condition and costs of maintenance.
- **Structure**: check for subsidence and damp, displayed in obvious signs like cracks and discoloured patches. Who has responsibility for shared walls?
- **Roofs**: remember that repairs can be costly; check for external signs of problems, such as missing tiles, and take professional advice if necessary. If buying a flat, you are likely to have joint responsibility.
- **Pipes and guttering**: look out for loose pipes, leaks and repairs.
- Woodwork: look out for rotting door and window frames.
- **Floor**: rotting or in need of repair? What is the condition of the joists?
- **Interior walls**: look out for cracks, damp or sagging.
- **Electrical system**: is it in good working order?
- **Gas system**: is it in good working order?
- **Water**: what system is used?
- **Central heating/air-conditioning**: is it in good working order?
- **Water drainage**: is it running smoothly?
- **Repairs, additions and improvements**: find out what the details are.

Some useful websites:

- **www.buyersolutions.com.au**.
- **www.domain.com.au**.
- **www.property.com.au**.
- **www.propertypursuit.com.au**.
- **www.reia.com.au**.
- **www.wotif.com.au**.
- **www.yellowpages.com.au**

Photo essay
by Jane Egginton

1 Melbourne at night
2 Tropical palm grove, Cairns
3 Whale off Queensland
4 Surfers at sunset, Sunshine Coast, Queensland
5 Islands off the Queensland coast

The Devil's Marbles, Northern Territory

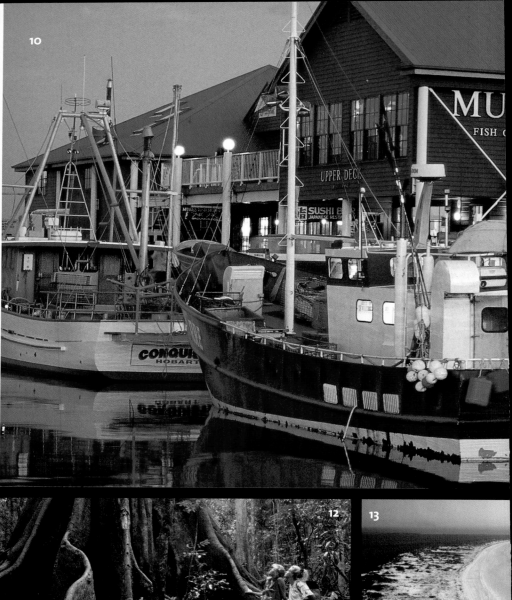

15 Aboriginal rock art
16 The Kimberley, Western Australia

17 Lake Oberon, Tasmania

18 Lawn Hill National Park, Queensland

19 Wildflower

20 Decorated boomerangs

21 Maria Island National Park, Tasman

Home Utilities

Once you have made all the arrangements to either rent or buy your new home, the next step is to arrange connection to all the utilities. While this is by no means as complicated as the first process, it still takes time and effort and may take longer than you expect because some procedures are different from home. Further information for immigrants to Australia about setting up home – in particular in connection with utility bills and costs, electricity and gas supply, water and insurance – is available from the **Department of Immigration and Multicultural and Indigenous Affairs, www.immi.gov.au.**

Council rates are levied to pay for local shared services such as refuse collection; these are paid by property-owners, but not by tenants.

Electricity and Gas

The voltage in Australia is 240–250AC. Electrical plugs generally have three pins but are smaller than British plugs. You will need a 'universal' (not 'continental') adaptor to use electrical equipment from home, which can be found in electrical stores and chemists in Australia, but are best brought from home.

Newer homes tend to have both electricity and natural gas connections. Both are supplied by the local state electricity or gas authority, the contact details of which you can easily find in a local phone directory.

Many houses have some form of air-conditioning, ranging from a simple electric ceiling fan to reverse-cycle a/c. In any case, you will get used to keeping your home cool by keeping windows and blinds firmly closed during the day and open from sunset onwards, to help regulate the indoor temperature.

Water

Water and sewage rates are charged per annum in addition to a metered water usage charge, see **www.overseas-emigration.co.uk/australiaguide/home.php.** Water is supplied to homes by state authorities.

Australia suffers periodically from water shortages. Sydney is not only the biggest but one of the thirstiest cities in Australia, although it receives more rainfall than Melbourne. In 2004 levels at the Warragamba dam, which provides 80 per cent of Sydney's water, reached record lows. The situation rang alarm bells throughout the country as it proved that the country's water crisis had moved from the dry desert of the outback to its coastal suburbs and towns. Just a couple of hours' drive southwest of Sydney, in the suburb of Goulburn, long-term tough water restrictions were imposed. At the time of writing, residents here are allowed to use no more than just 150 litres per day, the equivalent of three five-minute showers. At the time of writing, for example, the following restrictions apply to all Sydney Water customers including residents, businesses and local councils:

- **No hosing of lawns and gardens except handheld hosing before 10am and after 4pm on Wednesday, Fridays and Sundays.**
- **No filling of either new or renovated pools of more than 10,000 litres except with a permit from Sydney Water.**
- **No sprinklers or watering systems at any time.**
- **No hosing of hard surfaces including vehicles at any time.**

Some commentators are saying that these restrictions to domestic use are out of proportion, given that the bulk of water consumption is by industry and that huge amounts of the arid continent's water supply are used to support politically sensitive industries. As one expert put it: 'The Murray River is dying so that Australia can export rice to China.'

Telephones, Internet and Post

Telephones and the Internet

The telecommunications industry was deregulated in 1997 and there is now competition for landline supply. The national government-owned provider, which was called Telecom, is now rebranded as **Telstra**, and its major competitor is **Optus**. Although there is now a wide range of choice, complicated pricing options can make choosing a provider difficult. In Australia a system of 'preselection' exists in which you choose a telephone company for any or all local, national and international calls, and calls to mobiles, although Telstra (like BT in the UK) remains responsible for the maintenance of the line. Contact either provider or one of their many smaller competitors to connect a phone line to your home. Bills are paid quarterly and there will be a connection fee and a deposit required. Local (and usually Internet ISP) calls are a single fixed price, not per minute, and therefore are generally cheaper than in the UK.

Internet Access

Australia is one of the cheapest countries for online access. Check the rates on offer from a number of different companies, bearing in mind the kinds of calls you are likely to make. Some companies offer incredible deals for international calls, which can work out as cheap as a couple of dollars for half an hour to the UK. Unlike in the UK, charges for local calls are usually fixed and irrespective of the length of the call. This can make a huge difference if your Internet service provider (ISP) is local, as you can stay online for several hours for a fixed low cost. This means it is important to make sure that your ISP has a local telephone number for Internet dial-up access.

Many ISPs limit the amount you can spend online or the volume of information you can download, and others discount some of their costs if you take more than one service from them (such as preselection and Internet access). Contact your chosen telecoms company and open an account over the telephone or via the Internet. Setting it up will usually take a couple of weeks.

Because there is such a huge choice, picking an Internet service provider can seem as easy as picking a needle out of a haystack. Which one you choose will largely depend on the level of your Internet use. Before taking an option to pay for access to the Internet, consider the possibility of connecting for free. A number of ISPs offer free access because they are funded by advertising or sponsorship. There are limitations to these kind of providers, though. For example, they may offer a limited range of functions – no POP e-mail or news options – or a restriction on the duration of each online session and a limit on the number of websites you can visit. It can often be difficult to connect to these ISPs, especially at peak times.

You may be given a free starter kit from an ISP when you buy your computer, which usually includes a certain period of free access. Bear in mind the phrase, 'there is no such thing as a free lunch'. The so-called 'free' hours may mean you have to sign up to the service for a fixed amount of time, and the software in the kit may be outdated.

Consider the estate agent's adage: 'location, location, location'. It is important to get an ISP that you can dial into for the cost of a local call. This can be offered because the company has what is known as a point of presence (POP) in your area or simply because dial-up access is offered for the price of a local call. It is relatively easy to find a list of ISPs in your area. Telstra Big Pond provides local call dial-up access numbers throughout Australia.

If you live outside a city, but work within a metropolitan area and want to access the Internet from both locations, you need to look for either an ISP that has a POP in each area or one that offers a local call access number. Some large international ISPs such as **AOL, www.aol.com.au**, and Compuserve, **www.compuserve.com.au**, provide access in several countries. But you don't need such a service to access your e-mail when you are out of Australia.

Finding impartial information – regarding costs and performance – about the several hundred ISPs in the country can be difficult. It is reasonable to assume, however, that the larger the provider the faster the service. Various computer magazines publish reports on ISPs, which can be accessed online. Some examples are **www.netguide.com.au**, **www.apcmag.com** and **www.pcworld.idg.com.au**. Bear in mind, though, that information can date very quickly and there are no standards by which to measure performance. Also, these reports tend to ignore smaller providers.

One of the key things to consider is your price plan. The one you choose will depend on your Internet use. If you are a 'casual user' – you tend to be online for just a few hours a month – you will probably want a basic arrangement in which you are charged a fee for your hourly use. If, however, you use the Internet a lot, a plan in which you are given a block of hours per month for which you pay a set fee might suit you better. If you go over the agreed amount, a charge is then made for each additional hour, or part hour. Unlimited access options are becoming increasingly popular. This means you could, in theory, be online constantly for a set charge. Watch out, however, for companies offering what they say is unlimited access, but is in fact restricted in some way.

If you need help setting up or if something goes wrong, the amount of assistance a help desk can give you is crucial. Sadly, the standards of some ISPs' customer support are appalling, or high charges are made for calls to helplines. The main Internet providers are:

- **AAPT Smartchat Internet, t** 138 888, **t** 1800 688 842, **aaptchat@aapt.com.au, www.smartchat.net.au.**
- **Aardvark Internet, t** (03) 9629 8833, **t** (03) 9629 8233, **info@aardvark.net.au, www.aardvark.net.au.**
- **Access Net Australia, t** (03) 9686 4192, **t** (03) 9686 4189, **info@access.net.au, www.access.net.au.**
- **AOL Australia, t** 1800 265 265, **www.aol.net.au.**
- **AR Internet, t** 1800 000 890, **t** (02) 9809 9199, **info@ar.com.au, www.ar.com.au.**
- **AT&T Global Network, t** 1300 131 163, **t** (02) 9882 5997, **agnssales@advantra.com.au, www.attglobal.net.**
- **CompuServe Pacific, t** 1300 555 520, **pacifichelp@compuserve.com, www.compuserve.com.au.**
- **CybaNet Internet Services Pty Ltd, t** (03) 5450 3744, **t** (03) 5450 3747, **brad@cybanet.net.au, www.cybanet.net.au.**
- **Dingo Blue, t** 1300 5510 455, **t** (02) 9775 7098, **inquiries@dingoblue.com.au, www.dingoblue.aom.au.**
- **Down Under Internet Services, t** 1300 888 NET, **t** (08) 8941 4445, **accounts@downunder.net.au, www.downundernet.au.**
- **Escape Online Internet, t** (03) 9820 2258, **t** (03) 9820 8685, **citizen@escapenet.com.au, www.escapenet.**
- **Future Web Pty Ltd, t** 1300 361 355, **t** (07) 5526 2396, **sales@futureweb.com.au, www.futureweb.com.au.**
- **Holo Host, t** (03) 9846 4752, **t** (03) 9846 1502, **sales@holohost.net.**
- **Instant Communications, t** 1300 139 369, **t** (07) 3278 5666, **sales@in.com.au, www.in.com.au.**
- **ION Internet Services, t** 1300 889 991, **t** 1300 889 992, **admin@ion.com.au, www.ion.com.au.**

- **My Access, t** (03) 9878 2611, **t** (03) 9878 2689, **enquiries@myaccess.com.au, www.myaccess.com.au.**
- **Network Technology Pty Ltd, t** 1300 136 266, **t** (03) 5278 3334, **sales@net-tech.com.au, www.net.tech.com.au.**
- **Nobby's Net, t** (02) 4925 3080, **t** (02) 4385 3720, **sales@nobbys.net.au, www.nobbys.net.au.**
- **Octa4, t** 1300 363 935, **t** (08) 8941 0833, **info@octa4.net.au, www.octa4.net.au.**
- **Oz E-mail, t** 132 884, **t** (02) 9437 5888, **sales@ozemail.com.au, www.ozemail.com.au.**
- **Sapphire Planet, t** 9553 1167, **t** 9553 1167, **contact@sapphireplanet.com.au, www.sapphireplanet.com.au.**
- **Spiderweb Access, t** (07) 5483 8888, **t** (07) 5482 5205, **admin@ spiderweb.com.au, www.spiderweb.com.au.**
- **Telstra Big Pond Home, t** 1800 804 282, **info@bigpond.com, www.bigpond.com.**
- **Totalise, t** (02) 9959 1911, **t** (02) 9959 3003, **info@totalise.com.au, www.totalise.com.au.**
- **TPG Internet, t** (02) 9850 0888, **t** (02) 9850 0817, **Internet_sales@tpg.com.au, www.tpg.com.au.**
- **Win Net, t** 1300 139 949, **t** (02) 9906 6445, **sales@winnet.com.au, www.winnet.com.au.**

E-mail

The chances are you already have an e-mail account that can be transferred to Australia. If you don't, there are hundreds, if not thousands, of companies that offer free e-mail addresses. The main ones are Hotmail, Yahoo! and Excite. The problem with these is it is likely that the address you want is taken and you'll end up with an impossible-to-remember alternative. For this reason one of the smaller web-based e-mail providers is usually a more attractive option.

If you are moving around and need to check your e-mail, the options are to take a laptop with you (which can incur high call charges, especially from a hotel room), or use an Internet café. In rural areas, and even smaller towns, Internet access can be difficult, but in tourist regions there will be a lot of choice and usually very competitive rates.

Internet Cafés

If you want to use Internet cafés in Australia, there are some important points to consider. Find out where they are by researching on the Internet before you leave home. A couple of good websites for this are **www.netcaféguide.com** and **www.cybercaptive.com**. However, new cafés and shops are opening (and closing) all the time, so websites list only a fraction of those that exist. Internet access is charged by the minute or in half-hour or hour blocks. Internet cafés will normally allow **faxes** to be sent and received, as will newsagents and photocopy shops. You can also have faxes sent to your e-mail address, depending on whom your account is with. The cost of using Internet cafés varies enormously but is usually A$2–5 per hour. Here is a short list of Internet cafés in Australia in early 2005, but remember that these may change quickly.

New South Wales and Sydney

- **Atlantis Internet Café and Grill**, Shop 20, 74–8 The Corso, Manly NSW 2095.
- **Café Sydney**, 236 Clarence Street, NSW 2000, **www.cafesydney.net**.
- **Terrigal Cake Shop, Café, Internet Café** (24 hrs), 86 The Esplanade, Terrigal NSW 2260, **www.terrigalcakeshop.oomah.com**.

Northern Territory

- **Didjworld**, 60 Smith St, Harry Chan Arcade Shop #6, Darwin, Northern Territory; and 33 Todd Mall / Springs Plaza, Alice Springs, Northern Territory 0870; **www.didjworld.com**.

Queensland

- **Noosanetcafé**, 75 Noosa Drive, Noosa Heads, Queensland 4567, **www.noosanetcafe.com.au**.

South Australia

- **Kisscafé**, corner of Morphett and Hindley Streets, Adelaide, **www.kisscafe.com.au**

Tasmania

- **Bigpond**, Shop 9, 33 Salamanca Place, Hobart, Tasmania 7000, **www.users.bigpond.com/drifterstelstra1**.

Victoria

- **Brighthikers**, 4 Ireland Street, Bright, Victoria, **www.brighthikers.com.au/café**.
- **Internet-café**, 812 Glenferrie Road, Hawthorn, Melbourne, Victoria 3122, **www.internet-cafe.org/cafe**.
- **Rizz**, 633a Rathdowne Street, North Carlton, Victoria, **www.rizz.com**.

International Calls and Payphones

To call Australia from the UK, dial t00 61 (the international code plus Australia country code) then the area code without the first zero (for instance, for Sydney:

2) and the eight-figure number. To call the UK from Australia, dial **t** 00 11 44 and then the number, omitting the first zero.

The number for local and national **directory enquiries** is **t** 1223. Numbers beginning with **t** 1 800 are **toll-free numbers**, while those beginning with **t** 13 are service numbers charged at the **local rate**.

Payphones are generally in working order and are widely available. They accept coins (the minimum cost of a local phone call is A$0.40) of various denominations or phone cards, although some operate on phone cards or credit cards only. International long-distance and local phone cards are all very good value and can be bought at newsagents in various denominations. **Credit phones** use most major cards, such as AMEX, Visa and Diners International, and can be found at international and domestic airports, central city locations and hotels.

Prices of phone calls have fallen considerably in the last five to ten years – particularly for international calls to countries such as the UK and the United States, but it is much more expensive to call abroad using a pay phone.

If you do not have the use of a home phone, consider calling from a 'Call Shop', which are easily found in areas with a high concentration of tourists.

Mobile Phones

It is a good idea to get a mobile phone as soon as you arrive in Australia. You will find one invaluable if you are in temporary accommodation, moving around or if you need to be contacted about potential work. Most adult Australians own a mobile phone and the cost should not be prohibitive. Do limit your international calls, though, as you could find your bill going through the roof. The best way to get in international contact is by using text messages, which are usually a matter of pence rather than pounds, but check with your service provider.

Just as in the UK, there is a bewildering number of providers to choose from, the main ones being Optus, Orange, Telstra, Three and Vodafone. Contact your preferred mobile phone company to find out where your nearest retail outlet is. This list is comprehensive at the time of writing (early 2005):

- **AAPT Cellular One Ltd, www.aapt.com.au.**
- **Austar Mobile, www.austarmobile.com.au.**
- **B Clear and Simple, www.bclearandsimple.com.au.**
- **Boost, www.boost.com.au.**
- **Call Direct, www.calldirect.com.au.**
- **Cellular One, www.cellularone.com.au.**
- **Cellhire Australia Pty Ltd, www.cellhire.com.au.**
- **Communic8, www.communic8.com.au.**

- **Digiplus, www.digiplus.com.au.**
- **Dingo Blue Pty Ltd, www.dingoblue.com.au.**
- **Mobile Innovations, www.mobileinnovations.com.au.**
- **Optus Communications, www.optus.com.au.**
- **Orange, www.orange.net.au.**
- **People Telecom Ltd, www.peopletelecom.com.au.**
- **PowerTel, www.powertel.com.au.**
- **Primus Telecommunications, www.primus.com.au.**
- **RSL COM Mobile Pty Ltd, www.rslcom.com.au.**
- **Southern Cross Mobile, www.scmobile.com.au.**
- **Telecall, www.telecall.com.au.**
- **Telecorp Ltd, www.telecorp.com.au.**
- **Telstra MobileNet, www.telstra.com.au.**
- **3, www.three.com.au.**
- **Virgin Mobile, www.virginmobile.com.au.**
- **Vodafone, www.vodafone.com.au.**

Deciding on a price plan to suit you is not an easy task wherever you are in the world. What makes comparisons complicated is that a range of methods are used to calculate call costs and free call features. Call costs can be calculated in per-second batches or in 30-second batches. If calls are calculated per 30-second lots then you are charged the specified call cost for every block of 30 seconds in each call that you make. You may save money if most of your calls are less than one minute long by choosing a service that charges by the second.

In order to work out which call plan is most economical for you, you need to estimate how many calls you will be making, the length of each call and whether you will be making the calls at peak or off-peak periods. Although this can seem like a laborious process, it is worth taking the time to go through it, especially if you are signing a network service connection agreement, as penalties may apply for changing plans in the middle of the contract term.

A pre-paid plan can be a good option if you are concerned about running up high phone bills. There are a number of mobile phone networks in Australia that offer pre-paid deals, including Optus Communications, Orange, Telstra, Virgin Mobile and Vodafone. Orange calls are usually cheaper, although the network tends to be limited to big cities and the phones don't use the GSM900 standard so they're are not compatible with most GSM phones. Of the other mobile phone companies, Virgin Mobile (which uses the Optus network) is a good option, and Telstra MobileNet has good coverage to other countries and rural areas.

Should you decide that the cost of a mobile phone is prohibitive, you may want to consider a simple voicemail option, such as **YAC** or **jConnect Free**. These are services accessed online which provide you with a free phone or fax number and allow you to get messages sent to your e-mail address. The YAC service provides you with a UK phone number and your voicemail and faxes can be sent to you by e-mail; phone calls can be forwarded to any phone number in one of 22 countries, including Australia.

Thankfully, a tool to help you through the maze of choices is on hand. The Tool Kit (**www.aca.gov.au** or call the Tool Kit hotline on **t** 1800 351135) is an information portal. It is designed to:

- **assist you in understanding the products and services that meet your individual needs.**
- **identify the relevant questions to ask companies before you sign a contract or purchase a product.**
- **help you to understand your consumer rights and the safeguards in place to protect you.**

However, it is not able to recommend the best product at the best price or the company that provides the best service. It will, however, provide you with relevant information so you can make an informed choice.

Your decision of whether or not to choose Global System for Mobile communications (GSM) or Code Division Multiple Access (CDMA) will be based mainly on the coverage you need in Australia, and whether you plan to use your phone abroad. Although the CDMA system is technically superior in many ways, and offers better coverage in rural areas, until now most mobile phone users – as many as 92 per cent – have chosen GSM, which offers greater flexibility in moving between different networks and a greater choice of handsets. It also means that most mobile phones that have been bought in the UK and the rest of Europe will function in Australia, as long as the SIM card is not locked.

Post

Post offices are marked with a red and white 'P' logo; they are open 9am–5pm on weekdays, and some branches are open at the weekend. Check with Australia Post Customer Service on **t** 13 13 18. It costs 45c to send a letter within Australia and A$1.50 to send a letter to the UK and Europe.

There are various speeds at which you can send mail internationally, but delivery times are generally five to 10 days. Domestic mail can be sent first class or express post, for which you have to buy a special yellow and white envelope at the post office.

If you are moving around or staying in temporary accommodation on arriving in Australia, it is a good idea to set up a system for receiving post, which is more complex than sending it. Holders of American Express cards can pick up mail from American Express offices, listed on the American Express website. If you're having mail addressed to an American Express office, make sure it includes your name, client mail, American Express address, city and country.

If you're not an American Express customer, you can have post addressed to any *poste restante* at most major post offices. Depending on how long you are staying, you may be able to have post addressed to a hotel where you are staying, although this is not the safest option.

Money and Banking

Banks

The Commonwealth Bank of Australia is the largest in the country and, conveniently, it has a migrant banking section in London. This means that an account can be set up for you in Australia from London, and money can be transferred to Australia. In Australia, salaries and government benefits are paid directly into a bank account.

You should open a bank account within six weeks of your arrival, as for this period you usually need only your passport as identification. After six weeks you will need extra identification to open an account. Five big banks are ANZ, Commonwealth, the National Australia Bank, St George and Westpac. It is best to join one of these as they have more facilities and branches than smaller banks, and you will be charged if you use a rival ATM. Banks are normally open Mon–Thurs 9.30–4, Fri 9.30–5. Some open until midday on Saturday. Regional banks can usually offer the complete range of services, including Internet banking, which can be used to pay bills instantly online.

It is easy to open a bank account in Australia, compared with the deal that Aussies get in England. It will take only about 10 minutes. But it will cost you: clients are normally charged a monthly fee of around A$5. Credit cards are even worse: there are no interest-free accounts, most charge interest of around 15 per cent, and the majority of them have annual fees of A$25–70. You can open an account at any bank, building society or credit union. All offer similar facilities and services but there are enough differences between them – in fees, types of account and location – to justify shopping around for the best deal.

Think about the services you might need, and then shop around before making your decision. Talk to the staff and see if they have the right type of account for you. Ask to be provided with all fees and charges information in writing (usually a pamphlet), read it closely, and ask how you can minimise these charges.

If you plan to do a lot of travelling around Australia, or to move between states, opening an account with a major national bank might be a sensible option. These banks have branches and ATMs in virtually every town around the country. If you bank with a small bank or local credit union, you may still be able to access cash from your account using the major bank ATMs, but there may be an extra fee for each withdrawal.

If you are going to hold large sums of money in your account, you should consider a high-interest-bearing account or cash management trust, as ordinary accounts usually offer low interest rates. Be aware that banks in Australia usually take 5–6 days to process an overseas bank draft deposited into your account.

Building Societies and Credit Unions

Building societies are 'mutuals' (i.e. they are owned by their members), and offer many similar services to the large banks, particularly savings accounts and mortgages. The **Australian Association of Permanent Building Societies** lists nine member societies. Virtually all building societies have their head office outside state capitals. They are located in key regional cities in Australia.

A **credit union** is another type of mutual organisation with many financial services. The Australian credit unions are very strong and have around 3.6 million members, amounting to about one in every five adults. There are over 170 credit unions across Australia.

EFTPOS and Cashpoints

Payment in shops is usually made by 'electronic funds transfer at point of sale' (EFTPOS), which is similar to the Switch or Delta arrangement in the UK. Funds are transferred immediately from your account when you have keyed a six-digit number into a machine at the check-out. It works in the same way as the chip-and-pin system in the UK, so that no signature is required. It is a system that enables you to pay for goods and services (and take out extra cash at the same time – a good way of avoiding separate transaction fees) at thousands of shops and stores around Australia using your cashcard (often called a key card). You can also bank online and pay bills by phone.

Withdrawing money from a cashpoint is the same as in the UK and often 'cashback' is available from larger shops. As in the USA, cashpoints are known as automatic teller machines (ATMs). They are typically found outside banks and in locations in major high streets, allowing you to make deposits, find out your account balance, and access cash from your account 24 hours a day, all week.

Converting Money to Australian Dollars

On moving to Australia, you will at some stage need to move your money with you and convert it into Australian dollars. This is not necessarily as simple as you might suppose. Especially when transferring large amounts of money, the exchange rate (which can fluctuate a great deal) needs to be considered. If you are bringing over the proceeds of a house sale, for example, the Australian-dollar-to-pound rate you receive can make tens of thousands of dollars' difference. For example, if you had transferred £250,000 into Australian dollars in March 2003 you would have received A$675,000. If you had waited until September 2003, this amount would have fallen to just A$600,000, representing a difference of over 10 per cent in just 6 months.

Even if you went to an office of an Australian bank in London, you would not be able to open an Australian dollar account there. Those with accounts with the large international banks, such as HSBC, may be able to transfer funds directly from the UK. Otherwise, you will need to wait until arriving in Australia.

Getting Credit

Currently there are more than 200 credit cards available in Australia, so you will be spoiled for choice. Like anywhere else, each card has different features designed to entice you. Many offer interest-free periods when you first sign up; there are loyalty schemes (like Nectar in the UK); and cards that give a percentage of your spending to charity. But of course they all charge you interest unless you clear your balance as soon as the bill comes in!

Unless you see a particularly good deal on offer, you'll probably find it easiest to get the credit offered by your bank (or other financial institution). At least they will know something of your financial circumstances, whereas other providers may not be happy with your lack of financial history in Australia.

If you want to look over different alternatives, a very good comparison website can be found on:

- **www.moneymanager.smh.com.au/tools/compare.**

Taxation

Tax is complex in any country and few people enjoy the subject but, boring as it can be, it's an important thing to get right, not only from a financial perspective, but also from a legal one. There are severe penalties for misinformation and non-disclosure, whether deliberate or not. These pages are designed to give you an overview of the issues and key points you need to consider when dealing with your tax affairs. However, they are not a substitute for obtaining professional advice, and it is highly recommended that you seek the assistance of a tax expert.

The Question of Residency

The first and most important factor is to establish whether or not you are resident in Australia for tax purposes, as this affects the source of income subject to tax, the rate of tax to be applied, and the application of other specific tax provisions.

To count as resident for taxation purposes Australians must either:

- 'reside' in Australia (a question of fact to be determined objectively from all circumstances).

- be Australian-'domiciled' – meaning they were either born in Australia or have otherwise developed a strong connection with Australia, unless they have a permanent place of abode overseas.

- have been in the country either continuously or intermittently for 183 days over the income year (unless they usually live abroad and have no intention of living in Australia).

- be a member or the spouse of a member of certain Australian superannuation schemes.

For individuals entering Australia it is not always easy to reach a conclusion about residency, as some of the above tests require a judgment to be made based on all surrounding circumstances. The ATO has released the following guidelines:

- A migrant who comes to Australia intending to reside here permanently is a resident from arrival.

- Where an individual arrives in Australia not intending to reside here permanently, all facts regarding their presence must be considered. The following factors are relevant:

    - intention or purpose of presence.
    - family and business or employment ties.
    - maintenance and location of assets.
    - social and living arrangements.

The period of stay is not itself conclusive, but as a rule of thumb a stay of 6 months is indicative of residency having been established (from the date the individual first arrived in Australia).

Australian tax residents pay tax on worldwide income.

Those who do not specifically satisfy any of the above tests for Australian tax residency are considered a non-resident for tax purposes. Non-residents pay tax only on income sourced in Australia and on capital gains made on assets that have a 'necessary connection' with Australia. The determination of any income's source is complex; two examples include income from personal services carried out in Australia, and rental income from an Australian property.

Non-residents are liable to higher rates of income tax, and are not eligible for some of the exemptions and tax-offsets or rebates that are given to Australian tax residents.

The Double Tax Agreement

Australia has a double tax agreement (DTA) with the UK. The purpose of the agreement is to avoid the double taxation of income, by assigning taxing rights to types of income to one or other of the countries, or by allowing a credit for tax imposed by one country against tax imposed by the other country on the same income. The application of the DTA is dependent on personal circumstances and the type of income in question. The DTA also deals with the situation where an individual is a tax resident of the UK and Australia at the same time – in this situation the DTA provides 'tie-breaker' rules and helps determine in which country the individual will be a sole tax resident.

Tax File Numbers and Tax Filing

In order to be employed in Australia, you need to apply for a **tax file number (TFN)** and complete a tax file number declaration form for your employer. Failure to do this will mean that tax will be deducted from your salary at a rate of 48.5 per cent, rather than at your marginal progressive tax rate. 'Pay-as-you-go withholding tax' means an employer deducts any tax at the income's source.

The Australian Tax Office supplies tax file numbers. To apply, take your passport with work visa and an additional form of identification – such as a bank statement, birth certificate or international driving licence – to your nearest **ATO** location (see the ATO's website, **www.ato.gov.au**). Bear in mind that tax file numbers can be issued for reasons other than employment and the issue of one does not in itself give you the right to work in Australia.

Even when tax is deducted from a salary at source by an employer, you are required to complete an **annual tax return**. There are various ways to file a tax return – either obtain a tax pack from the ATO, post office or newsagent and submit a completed hard copy, complete your tax return online via the ATO website, or employ a professional tax agent to do it for you. The Australian **tax year** is from 1 July to 30 June. The due date for filing is 31 October after the tax year end, unless you register with a tax agent, where the due date for filing can be extended.

Income Tax

In Australia, income tax from all entities (individuals, partnerships, trusts and companies) is collected by the **Australian Taxation Office (ATO)**, **www.ato.gov.au**.

Income tax on individuals is charged at progressive rates based on the level of annual taxable income, which is calculated from total assessable income minus any allowable deductions, such as unreimbursed employment or business expenses, and less any relevant tax-offsets or rebates.

Australia does not have a separate system of taxation for expatriates, although there are specific allowances and benefits that can be provided in terms of tax to expatriates by Australian employers. The tax system distinguishes between resident and non-resident taxpayers, and individuals are taxed on different sources of income and at different rates according to their residency status.

Tax Rates

Australia imposes tax on individuals according to progressive tax rates – the higher the level of taxable income, the higher the average rate of tax. Tax residents are not taxed on the first A$6,000 of income (referred to as to the 'tax-free threshold').

Tax Rates for Residents: 1 July 2004–30 June 2005

Taxable Income	Tax on this income
A$0–6,000	Nil
A$6,001–21,600	17c for each A$1 over A$6,000
A$21,601–58,000	A$2,652 plus 30c for each A$1 over A$21,600
A$58,001–70,000	A$13,572 plus 42c for each A$1 over A$58,000
Over A$70,000	A$18,612 plus 47c for each A$1 over A$70,000

Proposed Tax Rates for Residents: 1 July 2005–30 June 2006

Taxable income	Tax on this income
A$0–6,000	Nil
A$6,001–21,600	17c for each A$1 over A$6,000
A$21,601–63,000	A$2,652 plus 30c for each A$1 over A$21,600
A$63,001–80,000	A$15,072 plus 42c for each A$1 over A$63,000
Over A$80,000	A$22,212 plus 47c for each A$1 over A$80,000

In addition, resident individuals must pay a further amount of tax equal to 1.5 per cent of taxable income called the **Medicare Levy**, which the government uses to fund its public health system. Reduced rates are payable by those who are on low incomes (below A$27,475), those who are paid certain government allowances, and senior citizens.

An additional 1 per cent is added to the Medicare Levy for higher income earners who do not hold an approved Australian health insurance policy (referred to as the 'Medicare levy surcharge'). As an enticement for Australians to take out private health insurance, a 30 per cent rebate or tax-offset is provided on approved health insurance policies.

Tax Rates for Non-residents: 1 July 2004–30 June 2005

Taxable income	Tax on this income
A$0–21,600	29c for each A$1
A$21,601–58,000	A$6,264 plus 30c for each A$1 over A$21,600
A$58,001–70,000	A$17,184 plus 42c for each A$1 over A$58,000
Over A$70,000	A$22,224 plus 47c for each A$1 over A$70,000

Proposed Tax Rates for Non-residents: 1 July 2005–30 June 2006

Taxable income	Tax on this income
A$0–21,600	29c for each A$1
A$21,601–63,000	A$6,264 plus 30c for each A$1 over A$21,600
A$63,001–80,000	A$18,684 plus 42c for each A$1 over A$63,000
Over A$80,000	A$25,824 plus 47c for each A$1 over A$80,000

Non-residents are not required to pay the Medicare Levy surcharge.

The ATO website provides an online calculator to help you work out your taxable income (see resources below).

Capital Gains Tax

Australia also taxes capital gains and includes this in income. Broadly speaking, resident individuals who dispose of property, regardless of where it is in the world, are subject to capital gains tax in Australia on the gain made. Non-resident individuals are subject to capital gains tax on gains for property disposed of that has a 'necessary connection' with Australia.

Taxable capital gains may be reduced by 50 per cent where the property is held by an individual for more than one year. Any resulting capital gain is included in an individual's taxable income. A capital loss made on disposal can be offset against other capital gains in the future, but cannot reduce other taxable income. Special acquisition and disposal rules apply where an individual changes their residency during the year.

Fringe Benefits Tax

Non-cash benefits paid or provided to employees by employers in connection with employment are subject to fringe benefits tax (FBT). FBT is borne by employers but the cost of the tax is often passed on to the employee as lower remuneration. Certain concessions and exemptions exist relating to benefits provided by an employer in connection with the expatriation (whether permanent or temporary) of employees. Subject to meeting specific requirement, some examples of these benefits include the Living Away From Home Allowance, the provision of temporary accommodation, and the reimbursement of relocation costs such as travel and removal expenses.

Goods and Services Tax

Australia does not have any wealth, inheritance or gift taxes; instead there is a consumer tax known as the goods and services tax (GST). Broadly speaking, this is a tax of 10 per cent that is paid by consumers on the supply of goods and services connected with Australia. As the details of the GST system can be difficult to understand, we suggest that you seek advice from a taxation adviser if you intend to establish a business in Australia.

Other Taxes

Other taxes exist at state and territory level that apply in specific circumstances. These include **stamp duty** on certain contracts regarding transfer of property, and **land tax** on the holding of real estate not used as a principal place of residence or for primary production. Australia does not charge any **estate** or **inheritance taxes**.

Resources

- The **Australian Tax Office** website, **www.ato.gov.au**, has a lot of information, including online tax returns and booklets covering subjects such as international tax.
- **Taxpayers Australia, www.taxpayer.com.au**, is a not-for-profit educational institution, which aims to educate taxpayers.

Social Services and Welfare Benefits

The Australian government provides a number of social security payments. These include:

- **Austudy**
- **Disability Support Pension**
- **Newstart Allowance (unemployment benefits)**

Migrants generally have a 2-year waiting period before they can access these types of benefits. Refugees and holders of certain categories of temporary visas may be able to access these benefits immediately.

Centrelink is the government agency that pays social security benefits and provides other forms of assistance. It is advisable to register with Centrelink on arrival in Australia. Further information about Australia's welfare system is available on the 'Centrelink' website, **www.centrelink.gov.au**.

Applications must be accompanied with passport and travel details, your address in Australia and your bank account information. Possession of a tax file number is a requirement before benefits can be given. As in the UK, payments can take a long time to be made.

Family tax benefits may be payable if you have dependent children. Although these payments are usually made fairly quickly they are not large, as they are intended to be only a supplement to other income. To be eligible you must be in possession of an Australian permanent resident visa. For help with applications and advice, there are family assistance offices which have been set up in branches of Centrelink, Medicare and Australian taxation offices (**t** 13 6150).

Resources

For more information, such as translation services for those who do not speak English as their first language, consult the booklet *Welcome to Centrelink* or **t** 13 1202 or visit **www.centrelink.gov.au**.
Specific information is available by calling:

- **Appointments with Centrelink, t 13 1021.**
- **Employment Services, Newstart, Special Benefit, t 13 2850.**
- **Age Pensions and Pensioner Concession Cards, t 13 2300.**
- **Family Assistance Office, t 13 6150.**
- **Youth allowance and Austudy, t 13 2490.**
- **Disability, sickness and carers, t 13 2717.**
- **Centrelink International Services (overseas pensions), t 13 1673.**
- **Customer feedback, t 1800 050 004.**
- **Payment enquiries, t 1800 810 586.**
- **Customer relations, t 1800 000 567.**
- **If calling from abroad, t +613 6222 3455.**

Retirement, Pensions and Investments

Retiring to a place in the sun is a dream for many but, cliché as it sounds, if you don't make proper arrangements for your pension, it could fast turn into a nightmare. Because this is a complex matter and subject to frequent change, you are advised to seek professional advice. What follows is an introduction to the main issues.

Australia's migration scheme is mainly aimed at young people or those with family in Australia, so you should check that you fulfil the residence and entry requirements – in general, if you are over 55, you will only be allowed a permanent residency visa if you can not only support yourself but also invest some money in the country. *See* **Red Tape**, pp.99–110, for more information.

Receiving Your UK Pension in Australia

A UK state pension is normally payable in Australia, but there are some vital caveats. **You will not get annual increases in the benefit** once you have ceased to be normally resident in the UK. This means that your pension will stay at the same rate as when you left the UK, or when you first qualified for the pension if you were already living in Australia at the time. After 20 years, even with minimal inflation, you could be seriously less well off than when you first retired, and than if you had stayed in the UK where the pension is index-linked.

The Inland Revenue can provide retirement pension forecasts for people who are outside the UK or are about to go outside the UK (if the person is not within four months of UK retirement pension age), which will tell you how much state retirement pension you can expect to get based on the UK National Insurance you have already paid.

If you have paid National Insurance contributions in the UK, the Inland Revenue will usually send you a claim form about four months before you reach UK state pension age. This form asks you about any insurance and residence you may have in other countries. You will usually be paid straight into your bank or building society account in the UK or your bank account abroad, if you have one. Or, if you wish, you can choose to have your pension paid by payable orders sent straight to you by post. Whichever you choose, payment is made every four or 13 weeks in arrears. UK widows' benefits or bereavement benefits are also normally payable in Australia. For full details see the Department of Work and Pensions website, **www.thepensionservice.gov.uk**. You can also contact the Pension Service, Tyneview Park, Whitley Rd, Benton, Newcastle upon Tyne NE98 1BA; **TVP-IPC-Customer-Care@thepensionservice.gsi.gov.uk**, **www.inlandrevenue. gov.uk/pensioners/index**. For information if you have already retired, go to **www.thepensionservice.gov.uk/retired/money-tax/index.asp**.

Superannuation

Like just about every other country in the developing world, Australia is facing a pensions crisis due to a falling birth rate coupled with an ageing population. Australia's strategy to combat this problem is a retirement income policy referred to as 'superannuation'. The broad aim of the system is to encourage individuals to provide for themselves upon retirement rather than be dependent on a state pension.

The Australian government seeks to achieve this aim by a number of means including:

• requiring employers to contribute a prescribed minimum amount for each employee into a superannuation fund for their benefit on retirement; at the time of writing, the prescribed amount is 9 per cent of salary and wages paid to the employee (exceptions apply).

• prohibiting the access to funds contributed into superannuation until retirement age (generally age 60, however this may be earlier where an individual has stopped work and does not intend to be employed again).

• providing for concessional tax treatment for income on funds within the superannuation system.

In general terms, the Australian tax rules provide that any transfers of foreign pension amounts into an Australian-complying superannuation fund will be subject to tax if the transfer is not made within 6 months of Australian tax residency commencing. Accordingly, arranging this transfer should be considered by an individual soon after his or her arrival in Australia. Advice should be sought from both UK and Australian tax advisers well in advance, to ensure that your pension entitlements are not eroded.

Individuals who enter Australia on an eligible temporary resident visa and who later permanently leave Australia can claim any superannuation they have accumulated. However, such a withdrawal will be subject to a penalty tax rate of up to 40 per cent (in addition to other taxes previously levied). Withdrawing the funds is voluntary and you may choose to leave the funds in Australian superannuation until you reach retirement age.

Aged Pension

As in the UK, the Australian government provides an aged pension. As a very rough guide, the government pays a weekly pension of up to about A$200 for a single person or about A$350 per week for a couple.

Individuals qualify for the aged pension at age 65, provided that they are living in Australia permanently and are either:

• **an Australian citizen**

• **the holder of a permanent resident visa**

• **the holder of a special category visa**

The individual must also have assets and income below a certain level. UK pensions and assets are taken into account when calculating any Australian aged pension entitlement.

Migrants must generally first live in Australia for a qualifying period of 10 years before they can be entitled to the aged pension; however, certain exemptions exist. (Note that a social security agreement that Australia had in place with the UK was terminated in March 2001, which previously provided for an accelerated qualifying period for migrants from the UK.)

The double tax agreement (*see* 'The Double Tax Agreement', p.134) specifically addresses the taxation of pensions, and the general outcome is that a pension is taxed in the country where the individual is a tax resident.

Resources

Australian organisations that deal with pension information are:

- **ATO Superannuation, www.ato.gov.au/super.**
- **Australian Government Centrelink, www.centrelink.gov.au.**
- **Australian Government Department of Immigration and Multicultural Affairs, www.immi.gov.au.**

Investments

If you are a permanent resident in Australia, or even if you have only applied for residency, and you have an investment in a UK company, trust or life policy, you should seek professional advice. Even if you are perfectly satisfied with your financial adviser in the UK, it is unlikely that he or she will have the necessary knowledge to be able to help you in Australia. Similarly, make sure you find an Australian adviser who has the credentials to assist you with UK investment matters.

The **National Information Centre on Retirement Investments (NICRI), www. nicri.org.au**, is a free, independent, confidential service, which aims to improve the level and quality of investment information provided to people with modest savings who are investing for retirement or facing redundancy.

Inheritance and Death Taxes

Australia does not charge any estate or inheritance taxes when someone dies, but if you have not yet made a will, it is highly recommended that you do so. Without one, your assets may be divided up according to Australian legislation (which differs from state to state). It is possible to make a will very simply by downloading an online form for around £10. However, legal advice can be crucial because of the tax issues involved.

Shopping

Australia lags behind the UK in its range of shops and variety of products for sale. This is mainly because, with a population of just 20 million spread out over a vast area, there is a limited market. If you are big on European goods, you will probably be able to find them somewhere, but you will pay a premium for them. Walk up to the most sophisticated beauty counter and ask for your favourite

French cosmetic and you may find yourself met with a blank stare. Italian and other European labels can be found in the big cities, but the choice will be limited and the prices high. Books are more expensive than in the UK, too, although bargains can be found in secondhand book shops. Shoes are generally of a poorer quality than in the UK and designer footwear is a luxury. Like so many things in this enormous country, standards vary from state to state: Myers in Sydney is a fairly ordinary department store, while in Melbourne it takes on the status of Selfridges, with legendary Christmas window displays; David Jones in Sydney is the Australian equivalent of Harrods and complete with shiny food hall to rival its London counterpart.

Shops are generally open Mon–Fri 9.30am–5.30pm, with shorter hours on Saturday and shorter again on Sundays. Big shopping centres are usually open at weekends and most shops have a late night, usually a Thursday or Friday. Supermarkets are open long hours, some round-the-clock, and many convenience stores have 24-hour opening. January is generally the holiday month. Shops generally stay open during this period, although family-run businesses and restaurants may close for up to a month from Christmas.

There are variations from state to state. When Christmas and Boxing Day fell on Saturday and Sunday in 2004, a New South Wales law was passed so that staff did not have to work on that Sunday and it was made a public holiday, so that the sales started a day later than usual. In Victoria, however, the shops opened as usual for the mayhem on Boxing Day. Language differences may throw you, too. In Australia, a 'milk bar' is a small, local corner shop, which may also include a basic café, while an off-licence is called a 'bottle shop', or more commonly a 'bottle o'. Changing rooms are known simply as 'change rooms'.

Shopping Centres

Shopping centres are much more common than in the UK. As in England prices are cheaper in supermarkets than in smaller speciality shops or convenience stores, and prices can vary dramatically from one supermarket to another. Major supermarket chains include: Coles, Safeway and Bi-Lo. Coles Express is a downmarket equivalent of Tesco Metro. Discount shops such as K-Mart, Target and Big W sell a large range of household items, toiletries, clothes and hardware. Sales at people's private homes are also a good source of secondhand goods. For discount electrical goods, try shops such as Clive Peeters, Harvey Norman and Retravision, which all sell hairdryers, toasters and so on at reasonable prices. British clothing chains are there – Karen Millen, Jigsaw and Benetton – and the popular Spanish chain Zara is arriving in Australia soon. For younger fashion, Sportsgirl is the equivalent of Miss Selfridge.

Shopping centres can be a godsend in the heat when the air-conditioning comes into its own. (In fact, the elderly are advised to make their way to the mall when temperatures soar; just as they are at risk from the cold in severe winters, in Australia the heat is the problem.) Away from the cluster of urban centres, shopping is a different story. In small communities you will be lucky to find a food shop with limited supplies and a pub doubling as an off-licence.

Markets

Markets are big in Australia, whether they are tourist markets selling clothes, crafts and jewellery, or farmers' markets selling local, often organic produce in school grounds at weekends. Farmers' markets were traditionally for people in rural areas who would otherwise be isolated, but they have sprung up all over the country, including in cities, and now provide a community focus for inner-city areas.

Chemists and Other Shops

In Australia, the words 'pharmacy' and 'chemist' are interchangeable. Soul Pattinson is a big chain of chemists. As in the UK, you can buy toiletries, as well as medication for minor ailments, but a doctor's prescription is needed to purchase stronger medicines. In cities most areas have a 24-hour chemist – check on the door of your closest chemist, or telephone the Chemist Emergency Prescription Referral Service on t 9235 0333 for the location of your nearest after-hours chemist.

Second-hand shops are often referred to as Opportunity Shops or **Op Shops**, and may be charity or privately operated. They can be a good source of cheap clothing, furniture and household goods, and bargaining is quite acceptable. Second-hand shops are particularly big in the city of Melbourne. Second-hand furniture can also be found through the *Trading Post* newspaper.

Case Study: World Records

'I've always said I couldn't live without my music,' says Richard Wiles, who moved from London to Sydney two years ago. 'That may sound dramatic, but music has been in my blood for as long as I can remember; it's like breathing to me. From the age of 14, when I worked in a Soho record shop, I have spent around £100 a week on new records.

'Sydney doesn't really have the records I am looking for, but thanks to the Internet I can access all the music I want. All my favourite shops have websites with up-to-date lists of the latest music in stock. I can listen to whatever I want online and then order it. The only thing I can't do is physically flick through vinyl in a shop, but I can do it virtually. I don't pay VAT, which is about the same as the postage from the UK to Australia, so it doesn't even cost me any more this way. And I can listen to all my favourite radio stations from home online so I really don't feel on the other side of the world.'

How To Pay

In Australia there is a variety of methods to pay for goods and services:

- cash
- cheque
- credit card (you will be asked if you want to pay by 'cheque or savings')
- store credit card
- EFTPOS (*see* p.131)
- lay-by (this is a good way to buy goods that you can't afford straight away; you pay a small deposit and service fee and make regular payments until the total amount is paid; the shop keeps the item until the cost is paid)

Online shopping is a boon in Australia, meaning that products from around the world are easily available, so getting presents for people at home is much cheaper. Sites such as **www.xpat-world.com** offer goods like the 'Great British breakfast box' and English goodies from Kendal mint cake to treacle toffee.

Bars and Cafés

Drinkers in Australia range from farm workers downing a 'tinnie' of beer at a basic outback 'hotel' (which double as pubs) to besuited office workers perched on a bar stool sipping the latest cocktail creation. As a rule, bars tend to be less plush than those in the UK, partly because the social life in Australia is more focused on the outdoors, so that décor matters less than a waterfront view. The tradition of al fresco eating and drinking is big here, and even cities like Melbourne with its more temperamental weather have large heaters and tarpaulins in case the climate suddenly changes. Many bars, even in the major cities, remain a male preserve. It is not unusual to walk into a remote pub full of men and cigarette smoke, and with porn on a big screen, as if it were the most normal thing in the world. *See also* 'Food and Drink', pp.23–32.

Open-air cafés, delicatessens and a generally cosmopolitan approach to eating and drinking have been enjoyed by the Australians from as far back as 50 years ago, the European immigrants transforming the traditionally staid ways of the English, bringing a dining culture and café society that was altogether sunnier and relaxed.

Royal Service League (RSL) clubs are similar to the UK's working men's clubs, where drinks and food are considerably cheaper than at other establishments. If you are not a member, you can visit free as a visitor with ID, but if you think you want it as your local, it is worth bargaining for annual membership of around A$20.

Coffee culture is a huge thing in Australia, where people seem to drink coffee at breakfast lunch and dinner. 'Doing coffee' is an important social ritual,

A Café for Sailors, Soldiers, Cabbies, Starlets and Coppers

In Sydney's inner-city suburb Woolloomooloo, a focus for its chic restaurants and apartments, is Harry's Café de Wheels, a late-night pie cart on the pavement. It is a Sydney icon, which has fed the area and the local Naval Dockyard continuously since 1945. A whole string of celebrities has feasted on its legendary pies, peas and 'pie floaters', including Frank Sinatra, Robert Mitchum and Marlene Dietrich. More recently, stars such as Elton John and Pamela Anderson have been seen here.

Pie floaters have a history of 130 years, which has been traced by the South Australian National Trust. They are made up of an upside down pie with a pool of mushy peas and gravy, sometimes topped with mashed potato, a dish that undoubtedly has its roots in English cuisine of the 19th century. Pie floaters can be found in locations other than Harry's Café de Wheels in Sydney and in Newcastle, such as the GPO pie cart in Franklin Street in Adelaide.

especially in Melbourne, and in all the major cities inhabitants scour for the best caffeine fix and then stick with their favourite barista. As well as all the big chains, lattes and cappuccinos are served up in a range of places from traditional coffee houses to slick cafés. 'Babycinos' are on most menus, allowing tots to hang out with their mums and drink from a tiny cup of frothy milk sprinkled with hot chocolate. In Sydney there is even a coffee shop for dogs.

Transport

Private Transport

Most newsagents in Australia sell city maps for less than A$10. Alternatively, the *Yellow Pages* telephone directory in each city features good maps. In tourist areas, less detailed maps are given out free at Australian tourist information centres.

Driving Distances in Australia

	Kilometres	Miles
Sydney to Brisbane	1,022	639
Sydney to Canberra	285	178
Sydney to Melbourne	1,045	653
Sydney to Adelaide	1,568	980
Melbourne to Adelaide	945	591
Adelaide to Perth	3,194	1,996
Adelaide to Alice Springs	1,529	956
Alice Springs to Darwin	1,490	931
Perth to Darwin	4,355	2,722

Distance Conversion (kilometres to miles)

km	=	miles	km	=	miles
100		62	750		466
200		124	1,000		621
300		186	1,500		932
500		311	2,000		1,243

Licensing

To be eligible to drive in Australia for the first three months after arriving, all you need is your British licence, which must be carried with you at all times when driving, along with your passport. After three months you need to obtain a local licence, which usually involves taking a knowledge test, a practical driving test, and an eyesight test. In Australia, drivers' licences are issued by state and territory governments as follows:

- **Western Australia:** Licensing Services, Dept of Planning and Infrastructure
- **Northern Territory:** Driver Licensing, Dept of Infrastructure, Planning and Environment
- **South Australia:** Transport SA
- **Queensland:** Queensland Transport
- **New South Wales:** Licensing Department of the Roads and Traffic Authority
- **ACT:** Road User Services (Overseas Drivers)
- **Victoria:** Overseas Department of Victoria Roads New Residents
- **Tasmania:** Dept of Infrastructure, Energy and Resources.

Rules of the Road

Driving laws and speed limits can differ from state to state. In most cases, the maximum speed limit in cities and towns is 60km/h (35mph) and 100km/h (60mph) on country roads, unless signs indicate otherwise. Police regularly check motorists' speed with radars and cameras.

The use of seat belts is compulsory and all states in Australia have severe fines for speeding. Driving cars (or indeed boats) in Australia while under the effect of alcohol is a serious offence punishable with heavy fines, driving bans and even jail. The limit is only 0.05 mg of alcohol per litre of blood – much lower than a lot of other countries. This amounts to two glasses of beer or one glass of wine. Breath tests can be conducted by police anywhere and at any time. Insurance companies don't pay out if an accident is caused under the influence of *any* quantity of alcohol.

Roadside Assistance

Call the appropriate number from this list if you need roadside assistance:

- **Western Australia: RAC**, 228 Adelaide Terrace, Perth, WA 6000, **t** (08) 9421 4444, **f** (08) 9221 1887.
- **Northern Territory: Automobile Association of the Northern Territory**, 79–81 Smith St, Darwin, NT 0800, **t** (08) 8981 3837, **f** (08) 8941 2965.
- **South Australia: RAA**, 41 Hindmarsh Square, Adelaide, SA 5000, **t** (08) 8202 4600, **f** (08) 8202 4520.
- **Queensland: RACQ**, 300 St Paul's Terrace, Fortitude Valley, QLD 4006, **t** (07) 3361 2444, toll free 131 905.
- **New South Wales: NRMA**, 151 Clarence St, Sydney, NSW 2000, **t** toll free 13 11 22, **f** (02) 9502 7329, **www.nrma.com.au**.
- **Victoria: RACV**, 360 Bourke St, Melbourne, VIC 3000, **t** (03) 9642 5566, **f** (03) 9642 5040.
- **Tasmania: RACT**, corner of Patrick and Murray Sts, Hobart, TAS 7000, **t** (03) 6232 6300, **f** (03) 6234 8784.

Insurance

The Internet is the best bet when searching for the best insurance quote for you and your vehicle. Many of the sites listed below can give online quotes:

- **www.budgetdirect.com.au**.
- **www.nrma.com.au**.
- **www.1stforwomen.com.au**.
- **www.allianz.com.au**.
- **www.cityauto.com.au**.
- **www.onlineinsuranceoffice.com.au**.
- **www.nrma.com.au**.
- **www.justcarinsurance.com.au**.
- **www.motorpoint.com.au**.
- **www.motor.comminsure.com.au**.
- **www.newcarinsure.com**.
- **www.cgu.com.au**.
- **www.racq.com.au**.
- **www.gtaus.com.au**.
- **www.youngandcool.com.au**.
- **www.drive.com.au**.
- **www.carinsurance.com.au**.
- **www.aussiecarinsurance.com.au**.

Driving Safety and Accidents

Because of the long distances travelled in Australia, fatigue causes large numbers of accidents. Take a break from driving at least every two hours; get a good night's sleep before a long trip; share the driving whenever possible; avoid long drives after work; avoid drinking before driving; pull over and stop when drowsiness, discomfort or loss of concentration occurs; find out whether any medicine you are taking may affect your driving. Keep at a safe speed and drive appropriately for the road and weather conditions.

If you are involved in or witness an accident, the procedure is pretty much the same as in the UK. Stop immediately, use hazard lights to warn other drivers, and if necessary send someone to warn oncoming drivers. If anyone is killed or injured or if property damage of more than A$500 has occurred; exchange drivers' names, addresses, registration numbers and names of vehicle owners with others involved in the crash.

Bringing Your Car to Australia

Think seriously before deciding to bring your car over to Australia. Apart from the obvious cost, there are strictly enforced regulations for the importation of vehicles which can make it a frustrating process.

To import a vehicle, you must have owned it for at least 12 months before the date of importation and must obtain an import permit from the Federal Office of Road Safety in advance. You must make a formal application, supplying relevant documents, and pay duty and sales tax if applicable. There are also safety and cleaning requirements. The following documents are required:

- **a temporary permit for all left-hand drive vehicles (obtained from the Department of Road Safety)**
- **a completed B357 customs form**
- **a valid passport (and previous passport if the current passport was issued after purchase of vehicle)**
- **a valid insurance policy, driving licence, service record and log book**
- **an import approved certificate**
- **a receipt**
- **an import permit (not issued to importers travelling on a temporary visa)**
- **an Australian Quarantine Service clearance approval**
- **a steam-cleaning certificate**
- **a Federal Office of Road Safety authorisation**
- **an original purchase receipt and registration document**
- **a vehicle condition report**

Hiring a Car

Most people relocating to Australia will decide to buy a car, but it may be necessary to hire when you first arrive. You can hire a car in Australia if you are over 18 years old and hold a valid international driver's licence or a current local licence. Some car hire companies require the driver to be over the age of 25. Renting with unlimited mileage starts at about A$30 per day. *See* pp.235–7.

A number of rental companies specialise in providing vehicles that are several years old at substantially reduced prices – often known as 'Rent a Wreck'.

Buying a Car

Considerations when buying a car are pretty much the same wherever you are in the world, but there are some that are specific to Australia. Choose a car with a 'kangaroo bar' or 'roobar' if you are going to be driving in rural or remote areas. Avoid buying a car that does not have at least three months of registration remaining. If you are likely to be travelling outside large towns and cities, buy a car that can easily be fixed in the outback or in a small town. Air-conditioning is essential in a country that frequently has searing heat. Contrary to some perceptions, four-wheel-drive vehicles (4WDs) are not necessary for driving around Australia. Conventional two-wheel-drive vehicles are fine for transport between all major capital cities, although for outback or beach driving you will need a 4WD.

It is possible to buy cheap, used cars in Australia in good condition for only a couple of hundred dollars. Before jumping at what appears to be a bargain, do at least make sure that the vehicle is registered and roadworthy, without rust and with decent tyres. Most mechanics will check a car for around A$30. Consider too a check on the Register of Encumbered Vehicles (REVS), which is only A$10 and can be made over the phone if you have a credit card.

Registered car dealers are required by law to provide a warranty for the vehicle for three months after purchase, and provide details of the car for you. The seller must provide a 'roadworthy certificate' and the relevant state department of vehicles has to give you a 'transfer form'. Once the deal is complete, you have 14 days to transfer the vehicle into your name.

Car Broker, www.carbroker.com.au, is an Australian car broker with a highly sophisticated website and offices throughout the country:

Melbourne (head office) A1 Car Broker ABN, **t** 443 6468 2203; PO Box 1366, Box Hill, VIC 3128, 22 Galovac Close, Donvale, VIC 3111, **t** 613 9013 9268, **f** 613 9013 9269. Also Sydney, **t** 612 8215 0516; Brisbane, **t** 617 3305 0012; Canberra, **t** 612 6296 8695; Adelaide, **t** 618 6461 4237; Perth, **t** 618 6461 4237.

Also check out **www.drive.com.au** to search for new and used cars throughout Australia.

Buying a car privately or through the newspapers can be hard work and risky, although you may find yourself a bargain. The best place to look is the *Trading Post* every Thursday. Daily papers, such as the *Daily Telegraph*, the *Age* and *Herald Sun* also carry car ads.

If you decide to buy a car from anyone but a licensed car dealer, get the seller to prove that it is their name on the registration papers. This can be done by comparing their name and photograph on their licence or passport with the name on the papers. If the seller's name is not on the ownership papers, you may find you have bought a vehicle that is stolen, had its registration cancelled or has multiple fines against it.

Every car in Australia must be **registered**. Payment for this includes car tax and requires a minimum of third-party insurance. This type of insurance is called the Green Slip, or compulsory third party (CTP) insurance. Pink Slips are proof that a vehicle has passed an annual roadworthy inspection and are another legal requirement. Be aware that this does not indicate the reliability of a car, only that it has passed a roadworthy test at some point. White Slips are given if the car does not pass the test, listing the faults that need correcting.

You do not need a Pink Slip to buy or sell a car. In fact, it can be to your advantage to buy a car with a White Slip, as long as you are clear about the cost involved to fix any problems, as you will probably get a reduced price. However, if the problems are considered serious, you might not be allowed to drive the car until repairs are made.

Cars are required by law to have their registration sticker glued on the inside left side of the windscreen. This shows the motor and chassis numbers and a large number indicating the month your registration will expire. For example, if the number is 3, it means the registration will expire in March. Payment for registration can be made annually, which is cheaper than the six-month option. With annual registration costing around A$550, it is worth checking how many months of registration are left on any car you are considering purchasing.

Selling a Car

Selling a car in Australia that was bought in another state can be difficult, and transferring registration can be costly. Many people choose to sell at a greatly reduced rate or to return to the state they bought it from to sell. For cars with very little value it is worth choosing free options to advertise, such as putting a card in the vehicle window, or using the Internet or local newspapers.

Car markets are good places to sell cars and cost only a few dollars a day. You must have a Roadworthy Inspection certificate – a Pink Slip, *see* above – to sell at any car market. One of the best and most famous in the country is the Kings Cross Car Market in Sydney (**t** 1800 808 188).

Public Transport: National

By Air

Because of the size of the country, you are likely to find yourself using internal air services much more than you would at home. In the last few years, several budget airlines have been established, cutting the cost of domestic air travel to a fraction of what it previously was. However, the variety of routes can make choice quite complicated, and travel between the more remote airports can be expensive.

Domestic flights are available all along the eastern half of the country, and to major cities elsewhere in the country. Flights to smaller airports can be infrequent, however, and are much more expensive. Perth, Hobart, Darwin and Alice Springs are the largest cities in more remote areas.

The most comprehensive service is offered by the national airline, Qantas, which sells a **Boomerang Pass** to international travellers. This allows travel within Australia and to selected airports in New Zealand and other South Pacific islands. Passes must be purchased before entering the country.

The Main Airlines

• **Qantas Airlines, t** 13 13 13, **www.qantas.com.au**. International flights that are legendary for their service and their safety. If you've ever seen the film *Rain Man* you may remember that the Dustin Hoffman character refuses to fly any other airline than Qantas because of its safety record. But Qantas also operates the biggest network of internal Australian flights, serving some 50 destinations. These range from Perth in the west to Brisbane in the east, and from Hobart in the far south to Horn Island in the remote north – and places you've never heard of in between. Qantas sells passes to international travellers that allow travel within Australia and to selected airports in New Zealand and other South Pacific islands. But check on the current requirements before entering the country, because certain purchases must be made before you arrive. The **Boomerang Pass** is based on a coupon system. You can buy up to 10 coupons, although two must be purchased before arriving in Australia. The **Qantas Backpackers' Pass** also works on coupons. You must buy three coupons initially, and can then buy a further six coupons. There is also a **G'day Pass**, which works on set prices for travel within three zones around Australia and is available for the duration of your International flight ticket.

• Very confusingly, Qantas also owns a number of other airlines within the country. One of these groups is **QantasLink**, which Qantas calls its 'wholly owned regional airline, comprised of three different regional airlines – **Airlink, Eastern Australia Airlines** and **Sunstate Airlines**'. This group operates over 1,900 flights each week to 49 metropolitan and regional destinations across Australia, from bases in Tamworth, Newcastle, Cairns, Mildura, Brisbane, Sydney and Melbourne. Booking through Qantas.

- **Jetstar Airways**, **t** 13 15 38, **www.jetstar.com**. Another Qantas venture, but this is a budget airline, launched in 2004, which makes internal flying more affordable. Operating out of Melbourne Avalon Airport, the airline flies to 14 destinations within the eastern half of the country (Adelaide, Hobart, Melbourne, Sydney, Cairns and between). Jetstar's fares start from A$65 one way Sydney–Melbourne Avalon and A$95 one way Brisbane–Melbourne Avalon. Reservations can be made online, or by phone, but there is a A$10 fee for telephone bookings.

- **Virgin Blue**, **t** 13 67 89, **www.virginblue.com.au**. The other major internal budget operator, from the Virgin stable as the name suggests. It has more destinations than Jetstar. Internally it goes to 22 places around the country, including all the state capitals apart from Canberra. It also goes to New Zealand (three destinations), Nadi (Fiji), Port-Vila (Vanuatu) and Raratonga (Cook Islands).

- **Regional Express**, **t** 13 17 13, **www.regionalexpress.com.au**. The country's largest independent regional airline, connecting some 30 metropolitan and regional centres across New South Wales, Victoria, Tasmania and South Australia. This airline offers some good special deals for unlimited travel. Monthly or two-monthly passes can be bought, during which period you get unlimited flights. You can visit places including Byron Bay, King Island, Coober Pedy, Broken Hill, Mildura and Wagga, making it a great way to explore southeastern Australia. In spring 2005 the passes cost A$499 for one month or A$949 for two months. Also known as Rex.

- **Macair**, **t** 13 13 13, **www.macair.com.au**. A Qantas-owned Queensland airline with its headquarters in Brisbane. It has about 30 destinations, including larger centres like Cairns and Townsville, and also smaller places with indigenous names like Toowoomba and Doomadgee.

- **Skywest**, **t** 1300 66 00 88, **www.skywest.com.au**. Operates, as the name suggests, mainly in Western Australia. It serves 14 destinations, from Perth to places like Albany and Kalgoorlie, but also into the Northern Territory at Darwin.

- **Airnorth**, **t** (08) 8920 4001 or **t** 1800 627 474, **www.airnorth.com.au**. Based in Darwin and flies to eight destinations across the Northern Territory, North Western Australia (throughout the famous Kimberley region) and internationally to Dili in East Timor. Its partners Merpati Airlines also fly to Kupang in Indonesia.

- **Australian Airlines**, **t** 1300 799 798, **www.australianairlines.com.au**. Not really an internal operator like those discussed above, but it deserves a mention because it is a budget airline and has some internal connections.

Yet another Qantas venture, it serves mainly Asian/Pacific destinations. Australian Airlines fly from Melbourne, Perth, Sydney, Gold Coast, Cairns and Darwin to Bali, Singapore, Sabah, Hong Kong and Japan. Online bookings are currently available to Australian residents only. You can get information overseas by phoning your local Qantas office.

By Rail

Travelling by train for long trips can be slow and somewhat dull, although it is often more comfortable than coach travel, especially in sleeping carriages. If you compare the cost with national air travel, though, it may just not make economic sense.

The **Austrail Flexipass** allows you to travel for a wider range of days within a 6-month period, and costs between A$550/£201.65 for any 8 days and A$1439.90/£527.93 for any 29 days. These passes are available only to those carrying a non-Australian passport and must be bought before you arrive in the country. For more information, visit **Rail Australia**'s website (**www.railaustralia.com.au**). Your travel agent can arrange ticket and passes, but if you want to book direct, **Leisurail**, 12 Coningsby Road, Peterborough PE3 8XP; **t** 0870 7500 222, **f** 0870 7500 333, handles reservations in the UK. There's usually a small additional administration fee payable.

Duration and Distance of Rail Routes

- Brisbane–Cairns, 32hrs, 1,681km (**www.pacificislandtravel.com/australia/trains/sunlander.html**)
- Sydney–Adelaide–Perth, 64hrs, 4,352km (**www.pacificislandtravel.com/australia/trains/indianpacific.html**)
- Brisbane–Townsville, Spirit of the Tropics, 31hrs, 1,681km (**www.pacificislandtravel.com/australia/trains/sunlander.html**)
- Brisbane–Longreach, the Spirit of the Outback, 24hrs, 1,326km
- Brisbane–Cunnamulla–Quilpie, the Westlander, 22hrs, 998km
- Adelaide–Alice Springs, 20hrs, 1,559km (**www.pacificislandtravel.com/australia/trains/ghan.html**)
- Townsville–Mount Isa, the Inlander, 19hrs, 977km
- Sydney–Brisbane, 14½hrs, 987km, (**www.pacificislandtravel.com/australia/trains/xpt.html**)
- Adelaide–Melbourne, the Overland, 12hrs, 774km
- Sydney–Melbourne, 10½hrs, 961km (**www.pacificislandtravel.com/australia/trains/xpt.html**)
- Sydney–Canberra, XPLORER, 4½hrs, 326km

Tilting Train

Australia has an innovative train service, which allows you to explore the tropical regions on Queensland's coast. The Tilt Train allows you to travel in comfort between Brisbane and Cairns three times a week, and Brisbane and Rockhampton six times a week in each direction. Passengers travelling business class can enjoy entertainment via personal entertainment screens and make the use of laptop connections. There is also in-seat dining and a club car. For more information, consult **www.railaustralia.com.au/tilt_train**.

Each of the individual states has its own rail system: **Countrylink** in New South Wales, **V/Line** in Victoria, **Queensland Rail** in Queensland, **Westrail** in Western Australia and the **Great Southern Railway** in South Australia and Northern Territory; *see* pp.233–4 for contact details. Coast-to-coast travel is available on the Indian Pacific. Austrail Passes can be bought by international visitors before entering the country, which allows unlimited travel over consecutive days, or there is the Austrail Flexipass, which allows you to purchase a number of days in a set period.

Scenic Train Journeys

Travelling by train through Australia can be a wonderful, even romantic, way to see the country and there are a number of long distance and interstate train routes across different regions of Australia. In addition, within each state there are several shorter commercial and specialist heritage train journeys in operation. They are not only used by tourists, but by locals and to transport goods.

• **The Ghan, www.australian-trains.com/ghan**, is perhaps the most desirable and well-known train journey in Australia. It runs from Adelaide in the south, up to Alice Springs in central Australia, to Darwin in the far north, taking a total of 22 hours. The line gets its name from an abbreviation of 'Afghan', which refers to the camels that were once the only real means of desert transport in Australia, and the Afghans who were responsible for them. The Ghan takes passengers through a number of Australian landscapes – from the relative green around Adelaide through the dry desert land of central Australia, up through to the unique Katherine Northern Territory and on to steamy, tropical Darwin.

• The **Indian Pacific service,www.gsr.com.au/indian**, travels from Sydney on the Pacific Ocean, across the Blue Mountains of New South Wales, through atmospheric outback towns, to Adelaide in the south, and right across to Perth on the Indian Ocean in the west of Australia. It forms one of the world's longest train journeys and travels along the planet's longest straight stretch of railway track, which runs for 478km. It takes three days and nights to complete the full journey from Sydney to Perth, but stops can be made.

• The **Great South Pacific Express, www.pacificislandtravel.com/australia/ trains/greatspexpress**, began service in December 1998 as a partnership with the Orient-Express. The luxury tourist train runs year-round from Sydney up the east coast to Cairns. The entire journey takes four nights or can be done in segments. The 3-day Brisbane to Cairns component includes all meals and sightseeing.

- One of the most unusual train trips is the **Gulflander** – a historic rail journey between Normanton, 700km west of Cairns, and Croydon on Cape York Peninsula in far north Queensland. It is a rocky ride from Normanton, from where the train runs through the bush on a straight piece of track. It has been described as a journey from nowhere to nowhere.

- Other journeys that offer travellers and tourists the opportunity to experience some of Australia's unique and varied scenery by train include the **Overland, www.gsr.com.au/overland**, which runs between Melbourne and Adelaide and has been operating since 1887; the **Sunlander, www.traveltrains.com.au**, from Brisbane to Cairns in the north; and the historic **Bellarine Peninsula Railway, www.bpr.org.au**, a steam train journey between Drysdale and Queenscliff in the state of Victoria.

- The **Queenslander, www.qroti.com/longdistance/queenslander**, is another long-distance train running between Brisbane and Cairns in Queensland.

There are also shorter lines.

- **Puffing Billy, www.puffingbilly.com.au**, is an historic steam train known throughout the country and very popular with tourists. The line still runs on its original mountain track in Victoria's Dandenong Ranges, which lie 40 kilometres east of the city of Melbourne. It was built in the early 1900s as one of four lines in the region and winds along a scenic 24.5-kilometre track, which runs through dense rain forest and pretty mountain villages. There are lunch and dinner specials, and Thomas the Tank engine and Santa Claus days for children. Every year, Puffing Billy hosts a Great Train Race in which runners race against the train up a 13km stretch of the mountain track.

Other short train journeys include:

- **Pichi Richi Railway** in South Australia, just north of Port Augusta (2½hrs)

- **Kuranda Scenic Railway**, a stunning journey through the tropical hill country in the northeast between Cairns and Kuranda, taking in the Atherton Tablelands; although only 34km long, the track reaches 300m as it winds uphill past scenic waterfalls through lush tropical rainforest up the valley of the Barron River and passes deep river gorges and rugged mountain ranges; one of the highlights of the journey is the Stoney Creek Falls.

- **Hotham Valley Railway**, an hour and a half southeast of Perth, an upmarket operation offering rail safaris and dinner trains.

- The **Zig Zag Railway**, in the beautiful Blue Mountains of NSW, is only 200 metres to the bottom of the Lithgow Valley as the crow flies, but the route is so steep that the train has to travel back and forth for 7.5km.

- The **Cockle Train** runs along the coast from Victor Harbour to Goolwa in South Australia; because it is just for tourists, it operates only on weekends and school holidays.

By Coach

The coach network in Australia is comprehensive and cheaper than rail travel, although not as comfortable. As journeys tend to be long, you may find yourself sleeping upright in a seat. Travel passes are available to reduce the cost. For more remote areas, **Greyhound Pioneer** or **McCafferty's Coachline** operators have touring passes that allow you to save money by purchasing in advance or following a designated route. There are also jump-on, jump-off bus services such as **Oz Experience**, which allow for flexibility with tickets valid for up to a year. *See* pp.228–34 for a complete list.

Public Transport: Cities

Most of the country's largest cities have excellent public transport systems that put the UK to shame. That said, the transport systems are obviously less extensive in the smaller towns and in rural areas. Urban public transport is not restricted to trains and buses. For example, there are trams in Melbourne and good ferry services in Sydney, which are both much loved.

Adelaide

This city is served by a very well-organised public bus and train transport system, as well as a free bus service around an Adelaide city loop, with bus stops in central locations such as Victoria Square, King William Street and North Terrace. The city train station is on North Terrace, while interstate trains like the Ghan arrive at the Keswick rail terminal, which is centrally located. National buses arrive at and depart from Franklin Street.

For more information look at the *Metroguide*, which is easy to use and has lots of information. It features a good suburb index with links to all Adelaide Metro bus, train and tram timetables and route maps. If you know the route number of the service you wish to catch, a full list of them is also available at **www.adelaidemetro.com.au**. It has details about Metrotickets, including fare prices, the best ticket available for you and how to use your ticket when you board the bus, train or tram.

Brisbane

This big city (**www.brisbanecitylife.com.au/bcl/trans/public.htm**) has a good system with electric trains, Brisbane City Council buses and private coach companies. There are often traffic jams and car drivers have problems with parking, so public transport is a good option for tourists and commuters alike. For those who want to take to the water there are good transport links (*see* **www.brisbanecitylife.com.au/bcl/trans/water.htm**) on the Brisbane River from Newstead to the university.

Consult **www.transinfo.qld.gov.au** for details of **South East Explorer**. This offers unlimited, all-day travel on trains and certain buses and ferries in the southeast part of Queensland. Use **www.transinfo.qld.gov.au** to find out how to get from one address to another. If you are travelling in Brisbane or southeast Queensland by train at night or at weekends, you need to have plenty of change as you have to use the ticket machines at unstaffed stations before you get on a train; sometimes the machines take only coins.

TransLink is a relatively new public transport network covering southeast Queensland all the way from the north (Noosa) to Coolangatta and west to Helidon. One single TransLink ticket will allow you to go wherever you want by bus, train or ferry.

Canberra

Public transport in the city is generally good but to visit many places – including several tourist sights – a car or taxi is required. **Action** is a bus network based around four town-centre bus interchanges: City, Woden, Tuggeranong and Belconnen. It allows you catch a bus from any bus interchange or stop along the bus route. Just signal the driver. Stops are indicated by a yellow sign on a pole or by a yellow wooden peg with the words 'Signal Bus'. A daily ticket can be purchased from any bus driver as you board the bus, or from any ticket agent that offers unlimited travel on all of Action's bus services for a whole day.

Hobart

The relatively small city of Hobart has a good public transport system, with the main service provided by the state-owned **Metro Tasmania**. Tickets are sold on the basis that the further you travel (defined by sections) the more you pay. There are five ticket prices in total. Section numbers are shown on all bus stops, with number 1 beginning at the city centre. Free transfers are allowed between buses for up to 90 minutes from the time of boarding.

Two types of sectional tickets can be purchased. Single-use tickets are bought from the driver, while Metro 10 tickets offer ten trips in a day, at a 20 per cent discount – these must be purchased from an agent.

Melbourne

Melbourne has a great public transport system, which is made up of trains, trams and buses. It has been massively modernised in recent years, with new vehicles and better customer comfort. Trams are the main form of transport in the main business area – known as the Central Business District (CBD) – and operate along its most important streets. This is a free service known as the **City Circle Tram**. There is a lightrail service to reach popular tourist destinations such as St Kilda and Port Melbourne. For other parts of the city, trains are the most useful form of transport, although there are buses too.

There are two main railway stations in the CBD. Flinders Street Station, at the corner of Swanston and Flinders streets, is the main terminus for Melbourne metropolitan rail services, while Spencer Street Station, at the corner of Bourke and Spencer streets, is the main terminus for out-of-city services. When travelling in the rest of the state, there are rail and bus services, that interconnect major regional centres with smaller rural communities.

Perth

Travelling in this city means choosing from a variety of transport – car, bus, train, ferry, bicycle... Go to **www.perthweb.net.au/transport** and see what is available. Two main roads meet in the city, joining the north (Mitchell freeway) and south part (Kwinana freeway) of Perth. The company **Transperth** manages all public facilities, which is good news for travellers as all trains, buses, ferries, CATS timetables (**www.lookatwa.com.au/transport**) and tickets work together.

In the central city area there is a '**free transit zone**', which means commuters can travel on buses or trains for free. The free transit zone functions every day of the week and reaches from Kings Park to the Causeway, and all the way from Northbridge to the Swan River.

Tickets can be bought at every train station from a machine or directly on the bus from the driver. It is a good idea to work out beforehand how many zones you need to travel through on your journey. Otherwise, ask your bus driver. Tickets can be used across different modes of transport, depending on which zone you are travelling in. If you are changing buses or forms of transport, make sure you finish your trip within two hours of the validity period after purchase (for a journey up to 4 zones), or three hours for trips covering 5–8 zones. There are also prepaid tickets called 'MultiRiders' for zones 1–10, which are available for either 10 or 40 trips. These kinds of tickets must be validated (before boarding a train) at a ticket validating machine – usually found at the train station entrance.

Sydney

Sydney inter-city transport is probably one of the best in the world. The **Sydney Buses** website (**www.sydneybuses.nsw.gov.au/timetable**) provides access to timetable and fare information, and **www.sydneybuses.nsw.gov.au/common-pdfs/sta/bus/map** and **www.sta.nsw.gov.au/regionalmaps.php** show the bus routes. There is a **Sydney pass** (**www.sydneypass.info**) for tourists, available from Sydney Buses.

Ferries are a great way to travel around the city and have been operating in Sydney Harbour for over 135 years. Services run from Circular Quay to over 40 locations. Use the **Sydney Ferries** website (**www.sydneyferries.info**) to check timetables and routes. Less functional routes run around Sydney's harbour day and night, taking in popular tourist attractions such as the zoo and aquarium (check **www.sydneyferries.info/attractions**). More expensive **JetCat** services run between Sydney's Central Business District and Manly during peak travelling periods.

Crime and the Police

National Emergency Services

The national telephone number for all emergency services in Australia – ambulance, fire and police – is **t** ooo. Emergency calls are answered by a Telstra operator who will ask which service you require. The operator will ask relevant questions, and arrange an appropriate response from the local police, ambulance or fire service.

On all mobile phones, **t** ooo calls are free. From analogue phones, **t** ooo will connect callers, although many newer digital phones require the user to dial **t** 112, the international standard emergency number. Consult your carrier if you are uncertain how to access the **t** ooo emergency network.

If you require the assistance of the emergency services for routine matters that are not emergencies then you should call the local number of the required service nearest to you. These numbers and other 24-hour emergency numbers can be found in the local *White Pages* telephone directory, or you can search for them online (**www.whitepages.com.au**). *See* pp.171–2 for police websites.

Crime

Australia is a relatively safe destination, despite the prevalence of news about shark, dingo and outback attacks. It is perhaps ironic that a country that was created by convicts should have one of the world's lowest crime rates. There are

Dial ooo for Emergency Services

The national telephone number for all emergency services in Australia – ambulance, fire and police – is **t** ooo.

The Poisons Information Centre can be contacted on **t** 12 11 26.

Useful Internet addresses are:

- **Australian Federal Police, www.afp.gov.au.**
- **Emergency Management Australia, www.ema.gov.au.**

few slum areas – the nearest to a dangerous area is Redfern in Sydney – and the murder rate is half that of Switzerland's. That said, street crime, burglaries and car thefts are a daily occurrence in the larger cities and weapons may be used. Use your common sense and take obvious precautions.

If you lose your passport, or it is stolen, report the loss immediately to the local police and the nearest British embassy or consulate. If you are a victim of any kind of crime, the embassy or consulate staff can, for example, help you find appropriate medical care, to contact family members or friends and explain how funds could be transferred. Although the investigation and prosecution of the crime is solely the responsibility of local authorities, consular officers can help you to understand the local criminal justice process and to find an attorney.

Crime Statistics

Crime statistics for 2002 show that, of 7.5 million households in Australia, it was estimated that in the previous year:

- **354,000 (4.7 per cent) households were victims of at least one break-in to their home, garage or shed.**

- **254,600 (3.4 per cent) households found signs of at least one attempted break-in.**

- **553,500 (7.4 per cent) households overall were victims of either a break-in or an attempted break-in.**

- **134,300 (1.8 per cent) households had at least one motor vehicle stolen.**

In total, an estimated 8.9 per cent of households experienced at least one of these crimes. The same survey showed that:

- **95,800 (0.6 per cent) people were victims of at least one robbery.**

- **717,900 (4.7 per cent) people were victims of at least one assault.**

- **33,000 (0.2 per cent) people aged 18 years and over were victims of at least one sexual assault.**

The experience of crime varies across the states and territories. Victoria has the lowest crime rate and the Northern Territory has the highest. Car theft was experienced by 2 per cent of people, a rate that tends to remain fairly stable. Robbery stands at around 1 per cent. Again in the same survey, around 80 per cent of people indicated that they felt safe or very safe when at home alone during the day, compared with 69 per cent feeling this way after dark.

Across the states and territories there was some variation in perceptions of safety: 77 per cent of those in New South Wales, compared with 83 per cent of persons in Queensland, said they felt safe or very safe when at home alone during the day; 66 per cent of people in Western Australia, compared with 73 per cent of persons in the Australian Capital Territory, said they felt safe or very safe when at home alone after dark.

Residential Burglary

Much of the advice that can be given about preventing residential burglary applies to the UK, and the chances of it happening to you are much lower than in the UK. For example, the number of home burglaries in Victoria has fallen each year for the past three years and the state now has the lowest burglary rate in Australia. It is a good idea to lock up when you leave your home, even if it is just for a short time. Put strong locks on your doors and windows. Never let people know when your home will be empty and when you're not at home, and make it look as if somebody is there by leaving a radio tuned to a talkback station, keeping some lights on and closing the curtains.

If you have commercial premises, take steps to protect your business. Make sure there is security fencing around your property and that there is adequate lighting – especially at night. Fit all doors with commercial quality deadlocks and ensure that key systems for all commercial premises are restricted.

Car Theft

Sadly, due to the well-publicised abduction of British backpacker Peter Falconio and his girlfriend Joanne Lees in July 2001, the old rule of the road that meant you stopped to help anyone in trouble in the outback has been largely abandoned. It is common sense when visiting remote areas anywhere in the country to travel in daylight and take plenty of water in case you break down.

Car theft is no more common than at home, but take sensible precautions:

- **Don't carry much cash on you.**
- **Don't leave valuables in a vehicle.**
- **Put expensive possessions out of public view.**
- **Close windows when you leave the car.**
- **Lock the doors when you leave the car.**
- **Use an engine immobiliser.**

The Criminal Justice System

There are two criminal justice systems in all Australian states and territories: the federal criminal justice system and the relevant state system. In all states of Australia the courts form a hierarchy. **Courts of summary jurisdiction** are at the bottom of this hierarchy and they deal with both civil and criminal cases – generally hearing matters concerning small debts, small property claims and minor criminal offences. The next courts in the hierarchy are called **district courts** in some states and **county courts** in others. These courts have substantial, though limited, civil and criminal jurisdiction. Above the district courts are the **state and territorial supreme courts** and the **Federal Court of Australia**. The highest court in Australia is the **High Court**.

In addition, each state, territory and the Commonwealth have put in place tribunals and a range of other mechanisms to deal with a number of jurisdictions similar to the courts, which include areas such as licensing, arbitration and trying child crime cases.

Legal Assistance

If you require legal advice or representation in Australia, consult a solicitor. If you need to go to court or an expert legal opinion is needed, the solicitor can advise you. Most solicitors advertise their services in the phone book and appointments can be made over the phone.

Useful Legal Resources

- **Law For You, www.lawforyou.com.au.**
- **Australian Legal Information Institute, www.austlii.edu.au.**
- If you are in immediate danger of domestic violence, call **t** 000. If you are looking for support, information or safe accommodation, the **Women's Domestic Violence Crisis Line** is open 24 hours on **t** 1800 015 188.

Legal Aid Offices

Should you find yourself accused of a crime, you may be eligible for legal aid from one of the regional offices:

- **New South Wales Legal Aid Commission**, Chief Executive Officer, 323 Castlereagh Street, Sydney, NSW 2000 (PO Box K847 Haymarket NSW 2000) DX 5 Sydney, **t** (02) 9219 5000 or helpline **t** 1800 806 913, **f** (02) 9219 5935, **www.legalaid.nsw.gov.au.**

- **Victoria Legal Aid Commission**, Managing Director, 350 Queen Street, Melbourne, VIC 3000, DX 228 Melbourne, **t** (03) 9269 0234 or country callers toll free **t** 1800 677 402, **f** (03) 9269 0440, **www.legalaid.vic.gov.au.**

- **Queensland Legal Aid Commission**, Chief Executive Officer, 44 Herschel Street, Brisbane, QLD 4000 (GPO Box 9898, Brisbane QLD 4001) DX 150 Brisbane, **t** (07) 3238 3444 or local call within Queensland **t** 1300 651 188, **f** (07) 3238 3014, **www.legalaid.qld.gov.au.**

- **South Australia Legal Aid Commission**, Director 82–98 Wakefield Street, Adelaide SA 5000 (GPO Box 1718 Adelaide SA 5001) DX 104 Adelaide, **t** (08) 8463 3555 or advice on **t** 1300 366 424, **f** (08) 8463 3599, **www.lsc.sa.gov.au.**

- **Western Australia Legal Aid Commission**, Director, 55 St George's Terrace, Perth, WA 6000 (GPO Box L916 Perth WA 6001), DX 123 Perth, **t** (08) 9261 6222 or country callers toll free 8.30–12, **t** 1800 809 616, **f** (08) 9325 5430, **www.legalaid.wa.gov.au.**

- **Tasmania Legal Aid Commission**, Director 123 Collins Street, Hobart TAS 7000 (GPO Box 9898 Hobart TAS 7001), DX 123 Hobart, **t** (03) 6233 8383 or local call within Tasmania **t** 1300 366 611, **f** (03) 6233 8555, **www.legalaid.tas.gov.au.**

• **Northern Territory Legal Aid Commission,** Director National Mutual Centre, 9–11 Cavenagh Street, Darwin NT 0800 (Locked Bag 11 Darwin NT 0801), **t** (08) 8999 3000 or country callers toll free **t** 1800 019 343, **f** (08) 8999 3099, **www.ntlac.nt.gov.au.**

• **ACT Legal Aid Commission,** Chief Executive Officer, 4 Mort St, Canberra City, ACT 2600 (GPO Box 512 Canberra ACT 2601), DX 5638 Canberra, **t** (02) 6243 3411, **f** (02) 6247 5446, **www.legalaid.canberra.net.au.**

Health and Emergencies

Medicare

Australia's health care system is Medicare, which provides reciprocal treatment for travellers from the UK and several other countries. This means that for as long as you are in Australia you will get free medical treatment in public hospitals, and essential and unforeseen care from a doctor. It does not mean, however, that you do not need medical insurance, as the agreement does not cover medical evacuations, prescriptions and ambulance transport.

Medicare provides free treatment in public hospitals, and free or subsidised treatment by doctors and certain dental services, but there are a number of types of treatment that are not covered by Medicare, and waiting lists can be long. Medicare is mostly funded through taxation, through the 1.5 per cent **Medicare Levy** payable by most income-earning individuals.

Not everyone is eligible for Medicare. Broadly speaking, if you are a citizen or permanent resident of Australia or if you are a visitor from the UK (which has a reciprocal healthcare agreement with Australia) you can apply for Medicare (**t** 13 20 11 in Australia). It is highly advisable to apply for a Medicare card as soon as you arrive in Australia: take your passport and your visa to the nearest office and fill in an application form. If you go to a doctor who offers what is called 'bulk-billing' then you won't have to pay for any treatment up front. However, if the practitioner you go to doesn't bulk-bill, you will need to pay, and then take your receipt with your passport and visa to a Medicare office; they will then refund you.

For non-emergencies, go first to a family doctor or a medical centre. Unlike in the UK, you can choose your own doctor, and there is no restriction on using doctors outside the area you live. For a list of local doctors, look under 'Medical Practitioners' in the *Yellow Pages*. Your doctor may then refer you to a specialist or give you a prescription to be taken to a chemist.

Unless you have a healthcare card (given by Centrelink to low-income earners), you will have to pay for medicines, but you may be able to get the charges reduced under the Pharmaceutical Benefits Scheme (PBS freephone information line: **t** 1800 020 613), through which the Australian government subsidises the cost of many prescribed medications for everyone. Pensioners may also get further assistance.

Vaccinations and Precautions

Although no specific vaccinations are recommended for a visit to Australia, it is a good idea to make sure you are up to date with all your standard jabs.

Insect repellent is essential all over the country, but particularly in north Queensland and the Northern Territory, where mosquito-borne diseases, such as dengue fever and Murray Valley encephalitis (MVE), are more common. Wear high-factor (30+) sunscreen wherever you go. It is advisable to carry a basic first-aid kit at all times, but particularly in remote areas where the nearest doctor may be miles away. This should include any prescription medicine you require, along with painkillers, antihistamine, Immodium, bandages and plasters.

Water is generally safe to drink wherever you go except in some places in the outback.

Medical Insurance

Many more people in Australia take out private medical insurance than in the UK. If you decide to be treated as a private patient in a public or private hospital Medicare will only pay 75 per cent of what is called the 'Schedule Fee' for the consultant doctor's attendance. It will then bill you for accommodation, nursing care, medicines and certain additional medical services. The government is trying to encourage private healthcare and currently offers those taking out cover a rebate of 30 per cent of the premium. Also, in a drive to get more young people to take out medical insurance, it has introduced 'Lifetime Health Cover'. This means that if you are over 30 and have taken out insurance after July 2000 you will be penalised by having to pay 2 per cent extra each year on top of the premium for each year of your age over 30.

As with any type of insurance cover, you should always take care when choosing the type of health cover, as you need to make sure that it meets your and your family's needs. If you have family and friends already living in Australia, ask them about which fund they have used. If you decide to obtain private health insurance, shop around. Although it is not absolutely essential to take out private health insurance, the cost of it is quite economical by international standards.

When considering private health cover, look for the following:

- **The waiting period – how long you must wait from the time of taking out the policy before being able to claim.**

- The excess amount, whether any contributions to the cost of treatment are necessary and the limit on claims.
- The coverage outside Australia.
- What extra services are covered.

Chemists and Medicines

Chemists in Australia work on the same basis as in the UK. They provide prescriptions and sell sunscreen, cold and 'flu tablets and personal items. On-site pharmacists can usually offer advice on minor ailments. Soul Pattinson is an established and reliable chain of chemists; some outlets are called by their old name, Washington H. Soul Pattinson.

Medicinal products brought into Australia are subject to strict controls and must be declared on arrival by using the red channel exits from baggage halls. You may require an **import permit** for products containing prohibited substances such as narcotics, amphetamines, barbiturates, tranquillisers, hallucinogens, and anabolic and androgenic steroids. Restrictions also apply to medicines of human or animal origin, and traditional medicines containing protected wildlife species. Keep any medicine you do bring over in the containers in which they were supplied. Don't send medications in advance through the post or as unaccompanied goods.

Medicines are categorised in a similar way to the UK: prescription only medicines (POM) and over-the-counter (OTC) medicines. If you are prescribed a relatively expensive brand which you agree to, you must pay the difference between it and the cheaper brand. Payment varies between A$3.50 per prescription for those eligible for concessionary rates and A$23.10 for most other patients.

Medical Emergencies

For emergency treatment, contact medical centres or emergency departments at major hospitals. Many doctors' after-hours phone messages explain where to get emergency medical attention when their surgery is closed. There are some emergency phone numbers inside the front cover of the *White Pages* telephone directory. In an extreme emergency call for an ambulance, police or fire service by phoning **t** 000 (**t** 000 calls are free on all mobile phones). From analogue phones, **t** 000 will connect callers, although many newer digital phones require the user to dial **t** 112, the international standard emergency number. The ambulance service is free only to people on a government pension or who have a health are card. Otherwise, ambulance services are expensive, so you may want to consider joining a private health insurance programme.

Safety

Dangerous Snakes and Spiders

Despite what you may have seen in *Crocodile Dundee*, you are unlikely to be bitten by a deadly **snake**. When bush walking, wear boots, socks and long trousers and take local advice. If you do get bitten, antivenoms are available. The key is to remain calm, seek immediate medical attention, and take along the dead snake for identification if possible (or remember what it looked like). Ignore what you may have seen on television and don't apply tourniquets or try to suck out the poison.

There are thousands of Australian spiders and insects, but surprisingly, only three have bites that alone are capable of causing death – the funnel-web spider (and related atrax species), the red back spider and the paralysis tick. All spiders can and will bite if in danger or if accidentally touched, for instance by shoes or clothing. Any spider bite can cause an adverse reaction, so it is best to be cautious and avoid handling them. In the case of most bites, rest and elevation, local application of ice packs and lotions, simple analgesics and antihistamines are all that is required. In some people, anaphylactic reactions may occur after insect bites, and these may be life-threatening.

The Sydney **funnel-web spider** is a killer. These fierce black spiders have large bodies (up to 5cm) and powerful fangs, which can easily penetrate human skin or fingernails. Funnel-webs are very vulnerable to drying out, so high humidity is more favourable to activity outside the burrow than dry conditions. They are most active at night. Gardeners and people digging in soil might encounter funnel-webs in burrows at any time of the year, but bites mostly occur during summer and autumn when males leave the burrows in search of females.

Accidental encounters with wandering males tend to happen in and around suburban houses, gardens and out-buildings, particularly ground-level dwellings on concrete slabs. During a bite the spider firmly grips its victim and bites repeatedly; in most cases the experience is horrific. The highly toxic venom attacks the nervous system, causing muscle spasms, salivation, vomiting, perspiration and tears. Shock and coma due to brain damage can also occur. An antivenom became available in 1980, and provided the victim reaches hospital before serious illness has developed, he or she has an excellent chance of recovery. The Sydney funnel-web spider is mostly found near Sydney (from Newcastle to Nowra and as far west as Lithgow) but sightings have been reported as far north as Brisbane. Related species are found along the eastern coast of New South Wales.

The **red-back spider**, a close relative of the black widow, is found throughout Australia except in the hottest deserts and on the coldest mountains. Red-backs are very common in summer. The female has a spherical satin-black abdomen with an orange-red stripe. The abdomen is around 1cm wide. The red back is not aggressive and if attacked will usually fall to the ground and play possum. If cornered, the female will bite the intruder with her small but effective fangs. Most bites occur when the spider is trapped against the skin e.g. when clothes are put on that contain a spider, or the spider is picked up in rubbish.

Although this spider injects only a tiny amount of venom, it can cause serious illness, and deaths used to occur before an antivenom became available in 1956. The action of the venom is unique as it can attack all the nerves of the body and in serious cases cause a paralysis that may lead to death. At first the bite is only as painful as a minor insect sting, but after a few minutes it becomes intense and spreads to other parts of the body. Uniquely, the bitten area may sweat profusely while the rest of the skin remains dry. Fortunately the serious effects of the venom take several hours or even days to develop and there is plenty of time for treatment with antivenom.

The Australian **paralysis tick** is distributed in southeastern coastal temperate regions. It secretes a neurotoxin in its saliva that causes a progressive, and occasionally fatal, paralysis. Sometimes a severe hypersensitivity reaction may occur. Often the tick goes unnoticed until weakness or ataxia develop, and is then found during an ensuing search (don't forget to look behind ears). Occasionally localised paralysis of facial muscles occurs, but more commonly there is progressive ascending flaccid paralysis affecting the lower limbs first.

Other **grass ticks** can be a nuisance at times, causing really itchy bites. Prevention is better than cure. If you know you are going into tick areas, wear long, light-coloured trousers and tuck them inside tight socks. If you look out for ticks crawling up the outside of your trouser legs you can brush them off before they get inside.

Information on Australian wildlife may be obtained from the **Australian Institute of Marine Science** (**www.aims.gov.au/dma**), the **Wet Tropics Management Authority** information on marine life (**www.wettropics.gov.au/vi/vi_marine.html**) and the **Wet Tropics Management Authority** information on animals (**www.wettropics.gov.au/vi/vi_animals.html**).

Swimmers should use safety precautions, swim only where a lifeguard is present, and never swim alone. Scuba diving is a dangerous sport and there have been several deaths over the past few years related to diving incidents.

Safety at the Beach

You are advised to follow these safety guidelines when you are at the beach:

- **Only swim or surf at a beach patrolled by lifeguards.**
- **Swim between the red and yellow flags which mark the safest areas to swim.**
- **Read and obey the signs.**
- **If you are unsure of conditions, ask a lifesaver.**
- **Don't swim directly after a meal.**

- Don't swim under the influence of alcohol or drugs.
- Don't run and dive in the water.
- Conditions change frequently, check before you enter the water.
- If you get into trouble in the water, don't panic – signal for help, float and wait for assistance.
- Use at least factor 15 sun screen and wear a shirt and hat.
- Float with a rip current or undertow. Do not swim against it.

Sunshine and the Ozone Layer

With all that sunshine, Aussies love to be outdoors. If they are young, then the chances are it will be with a minimum of covering and baking on the beach. That at least is the image, and to a great extent it still applies. But the fashion may be changing. The medics predict that half of all Australians will get skin cancer, and that is a thought that is making many Aussies think again about their habits.

Exposure to the sun is a complicated matter. Spending time in the sun is actually important. We get valuable vitamin D from sunlight. Problems arise when we spend too much time in the sun without protection. Until less than a hundred years ago, few pale-skinned people willingly spent long hours in the sun. Those who did were usually peasants toiling in the fields, who got brown while working. Fashionable Europeans, particularly women, showed they were not peasants by keeping out of the sun and having pale faces. Things changed as most workers toiled inside factories or offices, and Coco Chanel was one of the first to make a tan fashionable. The way to show you are able to afford to lie around in the sun, and go on holiday, has been to get a tan. But the skin cancer risk is now getting a lot of publicity, which could change things around again.

One of the reasons Aussies are taking the skin cancer issue so seriously is the ozone layer. You probably know that ozone is a naturally occurring molecule containing three atoms of oxygen. Anyway there is (or was) a lot of it in a layer in the upper atmosphere above the surface of the earth. This layer protects life on earth by absorbing ultra-violet (UV) radiation from the sun. UV radiation is linked to skin cancer, genetic damage and immune system suppression in living organisms. There has been a general thinning of the ozone layer over most of the globe, but most dramatically over Antarctica, south of Australia, where an ozone 'hole' has formed. Over Australia the ozone layer has thinned 5–9 per cent since the 1960s, and scientists estimate that one per cent thinning means a 1–2 per cent increase in the radiation that causes skin damage.

So Aussies are among the strongest campaigners against pollutants that put the ozone layer at risk, and they are also increasingly taking measures to reduce personal risks from the sun. One sign of this is the way children are dressed. All school kids wear big floppy hats – in fact they are not allowed near school without them. Sunblocks are the norm, and the macho Aussie cricketers started the fashion for wearing sunblock on the cricket pitch.

Protecting the skin is most important for people with fair skin and blonde or red hair. That does not mean that people with a darker complexion cannot get damaged skin, just that it takes a bit longer. The current advice for all skin types in Australia is summarised under four headings.

Avoid the Sun When Possible

- Try to stay out of the sun between 11am and 3pm. These are the peak times when the sun can do most damage.
- If you are planning a barbecue, have it in the late afternoon.
- Take care on cool sunny days. You don't feel as hot and you may sit in the sun too long. The rays will still do damage.

Cover Up

- Wear long sleeves, collars and long trousers when in the sun. Tight weave is important to block the sun. Some clothes may even have UV information on them. The higher the UVP number, the better the protection.
- Wear a hat. This will protect the common areas for skin cancer: neck, ears, temples, lips, nose and face. Hats with a brim all the way around are best.
- Wear sunglasses. Wrap-arounds give the best protection. Check to see they meet the Australian standards – eye protection factor (EPF) 10.

Use Sunscreen

- Sunscreens do not block out all UV rays, so also cover up. But sunscreens should be used every day as a means of protection. It has been estimated that 80 per cent of sun exposure happens doing everyday things like walking.
- Sun protection factor (SPF) shows how much protection the sunscreen can provide. SPF 15 filters about 93.3 per cent of UVB rays. SPF 30+ filters out 96.3 per cent, so they are not twice as good, but 30+ is the one to use.
- Broad-spectrum sunscreens also filter out UVA rays.
- Lotions and gels can dry out skin and may irritate. Creams moisturise, but this can make acne worse. Try different types to see which is best for your skin.
- Water-resistant sunscreen should be used if you are going swimming and also if you will be doing anything that will make you sweat a lot.
- Put the sunscreen on clean dry skin 20 minutes before going into the sun.
- Use lots of sunscreen, about one teaspoon for each arm and leg and half a teaspoon for the face, ears and neck. Reapply every two hours.

- If you wipe some off, by blowing your nose for example, reapply.
- Sunscreens last about 2 to 3 years in the container. But they become useless if the cap is left off or if they are left in the sun for a long time.

If You Get Sunburnt

- Cool the burnt area for 20 minutes under cold running water.
- Don't pick blisters, as they might become infected.
- See your doctor if you have a bad burn that covers a lot of your body.
- Antiseptic creams should be used only if your doctor tells you to.
- Anaesthetic creams may help a bit, but they can sting and irritate the skin.
- Take some paracetamol to ease the pain.
- Ask your chemist or doctor about anti-inflammatory creams.
- If an area is weeping you may need to use a burn dressing.

Bushfire Hazards

Bushfires are a common feature of the summer in parts of Australia. Remember that to an Aussie 'the bush' is simply an uncultivated area, which may often be forested with large trees. So bushfires can actually mean forest fires. Large areas of Australia have been ravaged by bush fires in recent years. Although a number of the bigger fires were caused by arsonists, many of them could have been prevented by taking care with cigarettes and open fires. During hot weather, there are periodic total fire bans, including wood, gas or electric barbecues. These are announced on the radio and in the press, but you can also telephone the **Country Fire Authority** on t 13 15 99. In addition, the level of fire danger in a particular area is posted along roadsides. All states in the country have experienced catastrophic fires in recent years. The economic costs of these is astronomical and the environmental damage is often permanent. In 1993–4, blazes in New South Wales resulted in the loss of a lot of lives. In 1997, the state of Victoria also suffered severe bushfires.

Bushfires can occur naturally, perhaps caused by lightning. On a small scale and in moderation they can have a rejuvenating effect on the natural habitat. A build-up of brush is removed, so that groundplants can grow. And gum trees, which occupy so much of the bush, have an amazing natural protection which allows them to grow again after a fire. If conditions are right (i.e. it rains) a scorched area can soon burst into green again. But of course if the fire becomes widespread the wildlife cannot escape, so becomes trapped and perishes.

Unfortunately humans, rather than natural events, are the main cause of bushfires. A cigarette butt carelessly thrown from a car, barbecue embers left to ignite, even deliberate arson, are common sources. And when there has been a drought and the bush is as dry as tinder, the results can be devastating. Huge uncontrollable areas erupt into fire, endangering the lives of people, farm animals and wildlife. Nor are the dangers necessarily always confined to sparsely populated areas. There have been occasions in recent years when a big city like Sydney has had fires on its doorstep and charcoal debris floating on the wind into the downtown area.

So it is understandable that Aussies take bushfire precautions very seriously. Roadside indicators maintained by the fire service show the risk level. **Low to moderate** applies for about four days out of five in the danger season, meaning that a fire can be fairly easily put out. **High** applies about one day in ten, and means that houses may be threatened and fires could take a day to put out. **Very high** applies one day in twenty, and means that fires are liable to move rapidly and be more intense. **Extreme risk** occurs around one in a hundred days, and means there is a risk of a severe wildfire which could become uncontrollable very easily. Such fires may burn continuously for up to six hours, with flames reaching as high as 40 metres and sparks driving ahead of the fire.

Wherever you are, if you do light a fire, use a designated area if possible. Otherwise, make a hole in the ground and surround it with stones to stop flames spreading. Afterwards, make sure the fire has been completely extinguished. If you are caught in a bushfire in your car, the standard drill is to stay in your vehicle with all windows and air vents shut, lie on the floor and cover bare flesh. If you are on foot, try to lie face down in a rocky or open area and if possible dig a hole in the ground.

Useful Websites

General
- Australian Federal Police, **www.afp.gov.au**.
- Emergency Management Australia, **www.ema.gov.au**.

Western Australia
- Fire & Emergency Services Authority, **www.fesa.wa.gov.au**.
- Police Service, **www.police.wa.gov.au**.
- St John Ambulance Service, **www.ambulance.net.au**.

Northern Territory
- Bush Fires Council of the Northern Territory, **www.nt.gov.au/bfc**.
- Police, Fire and Emergency Services, **www.nt.gov.au/pfes**.

South Australia
- Ambulance Service, **www.saambulance.com.au**.
- Country Fire Service, **www.cfs.org.au**.
- Metropolitan Fire Service, **www.samfs.sa.gov.au**.
- Police Service, **www.sapolice.sa.gov.au/index.html**.

- St John Ambulance Service, **www.sa.stjohn.org.au**.
- State Emergency Service, **www.sessa.asn.au**.

Queensland

- Ambulance Service, **www.ambulance.qld.gov.au**.
- Department of Emergency Services, **www.emergency.qld.gov.au**.
- Fire & Rescue Authority, **www.fire.qld.gov.au**.
- Police Service, **www.police.qld.gov.au**.

New South Wales

- Ambulance Service, **www.asnsw.health.nsw.gov.au**.
- Fire Brigade, **www.nswfb.nsw.gov.au**.
- Police Service, **www.police.nsw.gov.au**.
- Rural Fire Service, **www.bushfire.nsw.gov.au**.

Australian Capital Territory

- Ambulance Service, **www.ambulance.act.gov.au**.
- Fire Service, **www.firebrigade.act.gov.au**.
- Police Service; **www.afp.gov.au**.

Victoria

- Ambulance Service, **www.ambulance-vic.com.au**.
- Fire Service, **www.mfbb.vic.gov.au**.
- Police Service, **www.police.vic.gov.au**.
- St John Ambulance Service, **www.sjaa.com.au**.
- State Emergency Service, **www.ses.vic.gov.au**.

Tasmania

- Fire Service, **www.fire.tas.gov.au**.
- Police Department, **www.police.tas.gov.au**.
- State Emergency Service, **www.ses.tas.gov.au**.

Education

Again and again, when listening to people's reasons for coming to Australia, you hear that the main factor was their children, along with the outdoor life and a more relaxed lifestyle. The education system in Australia has some similarities with the UK. It is overseen by a national body, although there may be some variations between the states and territories.

Children usually begin primary school at the age of 5 or 6 and go on to secondary school after seven years. Schooling is compulsory until the age of 15, although almost all students continue past that. The school system is provided free, although there is a well-developed private sector.

Childcare in Sydney and Melbourne can cost as much as A$85 a day for a child in long day care. The summer holiday in Australia is from February to December.

The Australian education system is divided broadly into five stages:

- **preschool**
- **primary school**
- **secondary school or college**
- **career and vocational training**
- **university or other tertiary institutions**

Schools

Be aware that the system of schooling, national curriculum and attitude to discipline in Australian schools are very different from those in the UK. As a general rule, less emphasis is put on memorising facts and there is more of a focus on a child's interests.

How you choose a school is obviously a matter of personal preference. There are some rules to follow, however. Try to start looking before you relocate. Gather as much information as you can from the Internet and from the **Australian Government Dept of Education, Science and Training (DEST)**, **www.dest.gov.au**. The selection process can be more complex for older children as you will want to find a school with a compatible school system and know what the provisions are to go on to further education. Just as in the UK, many schools have waiting lists, so it is advisable to get your name down as soon as possible and pay any registration fees immediately so as to secure your place. Before deciding, look at the facilities, size of the classes and the mix of students. The attitude of the head teacher influences almost every element of a school – try to make personal contact with her or him and ask questions.

Children are much more adaptable than adults, but it is still crucial to prepare them for the move. Sit down and go through some of the emotions and problems they might face in a strange country; encourage them to talk about their fears before and after the move, to enable them to make social and academic adjustments. The move will expose them to different experiences, some of which will be challenging. It is generally agreed that relocating a child before the age of 13 should not cause too much of a disruption. After that time, their peer group becomes much more significant, making a move potentially traumatic. There is no perfect time to relocate a child, and each child will react to such a move differently. Some questions to ask yourself might include:

- **How sociable is your child? How easy is it for them to make friends?**
- **Do they have any particular problems or needs at school?**

- Do they have interests that it would be important for them to continue pursuing in Australia?
- In what areas do you think they might need support?
- How disrupting would a move be to their schooling?

You may want to work with an educational consultant to find your way through what can be a difficult and stressful procedure. If you are being relocated by a company, the human resources manager may be able to help you. Although they have a tendency to focus on moving you and your personal effects, they may be able to provide you with a list of other parents from your company who have made the same move, who could be a valuable resource to you.

Choices of state schools will be limited by where you live. The website for the **Commonwealth Department of Education, Training and Youth Affairs** has links to the State and Territory Government School Education Department's sites (*see* p.238), which in turn will enable you to access websites of individual schools. A good source of information for private schools is the website of the **Association of Independent Schools** in the state or territory to which you are moving, which will have links to the websites of individual schools (*see* pp.238–9).

Further Education

In 2004 Australia could no longer afford to market itself as a low-cost study destination to international students. The latest research shows that the country is now the second most expensive place to study – after the UK – in the five main English-speaking destination countries (Australia, Canada, New Zealand, UK and USA). In the last three years alone, the cost of studying in Australia has more than doubled. Experts say the rise in costs is the result of the increased value of the Australian dollar since 2001, combined with increased tuition fees, health costs and living expenses. These factors have pushed up the cost of living and studying in Australia by a far greater level than that seen in the UK or the US.

In addition, China, Hong Kong, India, Malaysia, Singapore and Thailand are posing an increasing threat to Australia as good-value study destinations, because of the region's lower cost of living and studying. Nevertheless, the international student market is still big business in Australia. It contributed 14 per cent to universities' revenues in 2000 and education is the country's ninth largest export.

Another negative factor affecting Australia's international recruitment is the length of its courses. Whereas in the UK a full-time master's course typically lasts for one year, in Australia it is more often 18 months to two years. Although annual fees for the same course can be twice as much in the UK as they are in Australia, because the Australian course lasts for two years, the total cost of living and studying is 50 per cent higher in Australia than in the UK.

Taking Your Pet

If you are considering taking a pet to Australia, consider carefully whether your animal can cope with the 24hr journey and 30 days of quarantine, and whether you are prepared to pay the costs of transportation. Talk to your vet about possible health risks and consider your animal's emotional make-up. You will be required to have a 'fit to fly' document from your vet before the animal will be allowed on any aircraft to Australia. You may decide that a better option would be to find an alternative home for your pet in England.

Be aware that the cost of transporting animals may well work out to be more expensive than your own air fare. Not only is there is the price of the flight, but vets' fees for micro chipping, vaccinations and blood tests, import permits, quarantine (which alone can be £500) and possibly insurance.

Rules about Importation of Animals

There are strict rules about the importation of animals into Australia. Normally dogs, cats and horses can be brought in, but birds, hamsters and guinea pigs cannot. The government agency, the **Australian Quarantine and Inspection Service (AQIS), www.aqis.gov.au**) deals with the legalities of the importation of animals and provides a guide to importing cats and dogs.

In some parts of the country, there is a cat curfew in place. Cats must be kept inside after a certain time in order to protect endangered species; this rule is strictly enforced. Also, some states restrict the number of dogs allowed per square metre of land.

Before your pet is allowed into the country, you will need to obtain:

- **an export certificate from the Animal Health Divisional Office of your nearest UK Department of Environment, Food and Rural Affairs (DEFRA).**
- **an import permit; application forms are available online from the AQIS website (www.aqis.gov.au); applications are valid for six months from application; all animals must be microchipped.**
- **proof of vaccination.**
- **clearance of notifiable diseases certificate (EC618 or 618NDC) from DEFRA, which comes with the Official Export Health Certificate from your vet.**
- **an International Air Transport Association (IATA) approved box that allows the animal to stand up and turn around with enough room.**

Organising the Trip with Airlines

Although you can choose to approach an airline directly, this can prove to be a complicated process given the different rules of each airline. You must make sure that you meet the usually strict regulations of the airline. For example, British Airways allows a dog and a box of less than 40 kilograms to travel if it fits under your seat. There are plenty of horror stories of people being told at check-in that their pet couldn't fly with them because the box was too small or they had the wrong licence. Airlines will not bend these rules because they may be fined and the animal impounded, or even worse.

Animals usually travel in the hold of planes – the part of the aircraft where luggage is stored. It has the same pressurisation and temperature as that in the passenger section; the only difference is that it is dark, which can frighten some animals. The director of Jets4Pets, which specialises in transporting animals, recommends the following if you decide to arrange transportation yourself.

- **Talk to the airline and see if it can transport the pet as excess baggage, which may be possible only if it can fit under the seat. Ask for the size of container necessary.**
- **Find an agent to provide the export licence (definitely) and import licence (maybe).**

If you don't feel looked after either by the airline or the agent on the phone, the chances are your pet won't get to fly as the necessary criteria won't be met.

Specialist Companies

Alternatively, you can use a specialist company. Get several quotes and look at testimonials before making a decision, and remember not necessarily to go for the cheapest option: you want to get the best conditions for your animal. Many companies charge extortionate fees and airlines charge each company the same – there are currently only eight of them in the UK. Some airlines allow animals to be transported only through a company and not with an individual.

Jets4Pets, **t** 0845 408 0298, **www.jets4pets.com**, can arrange all aspects of getting your animal to Australia, except for those elements that must be dealt with by your vet.

Quarantine

There are only three quarantine kennels in Australia, in Melbourne, Perth and Sydney, so animals must enter the country at one of these airports. Quarantine lasts 30 days and costs can be several hundred dollars for just one animal, on top of which are removal, examination and documentation fees.

Transport of Pets within Australia

Once in Australia, it is a much more straightforward (and much cheaper!) procedure to transport your pet by air within the country. Most national airlines will transport small pets for an extra charge, but suitable arrangements must be made first with the airline.

Jetstar, t 13 15 38, **http://jetstar.com/flyingWithUs/airport/pets.html**, is able to take up to two on each of its flights operated by Boeing 717 aircraft, subject to some conditions. Pets are carried in the hold of the aircraft. To reserve a place for your pet on your flight, you must call Jetstar at least 24 hours before your flight departs. Jetstar charges a fee of A$10 per reservation, in addition to the following handling charges:

- small container: A$20 (up to 15kg)
- medium container: A$30 (up to 20kg)
- large container: A$40 (up to 30kg, maximum height 65cm or size 4 crate)

Importing Personal Effects

Any goods for personal use can be brought in free of any duty as long as they have been owned and used for 12 months or more. If this rule does not apply, an original B534 customs form, a complete inventory and receipts must accompany any shipment. If the goods were packed by the owner, the owner must supply a list of contents. Provided all these documents are in order, and there are no dutiable items within the shipment, the goods may be cleared before the owner's arrival. A valid visa and passport (Customs will also ask for a photocopy of each page of the client's passport) is also required to be presented for customs clearance.

Each person over the age of 18 is allowed to bring 1,125ml of alcohol and up to 250 cigarettes or 250g of tobacco products into Australia. Duty or tax-free allowances of A$400 per person aged 18 or over, and A$200 per person under 18 are granted for other goods brought as gifts.

Sports and Recreation

Participating in recreational courses and joining in sports activities are good ways to assimilate yourself into local life, while having fun and keeping fit at the same time. The beach is the focus for much of the recreation in Australia. Beach culture is a massive thing here – on a par with California or Rio de Janeiro. Swimming, beach barbecues and body surfing all loom large in the Australian psyche. Bear in mind, though, that because of a hole in the ozone layer Australia has one of the biggest skin cancer rates in the world and a high-protection sun cream is necessary at all times (*see* 'Sunshine and the Ozone Layer', p.168). Rips can take lives in the ocean, too, so always take note of flags placed by lifeguards, and of swimming restrictions.

Surfboarding, Windsurfing and Kitesurfing

Australians love their surf. Surfers broke a long-term hold on the surf scene by the Americans and Hawaiians, and today there is not one international contest without several Aussies running in top position. Sports events sponsored by companies such as Billabong and Rip Curl have become a symbol of Aussie culture all over the world. Serious surfers claim that surfing is more a culture than a sport. Certainly there are many for whom riding the surf waves is more obsession than pastime. Australia's long beaches offer a wonderful variety of strong waves, from the city beaches of Sydney to remote strands of the north-west coast. All levels of expertise are accommodated, from the simple body surfing of youngsters in gentle wave conditions, to the awesome (a favourite surfie word) mastery of giant rollers. The sport has come a long way since James King (of Captain Cook's *Discovery*) gave the first written account of Hawaiian surfboarding, which he watched in 1799. Despite almost dying out in the 19th century, the sport's revival somehow captured a Polynesian attitude of communion with the sea. Today's Australian surfers clearly relish their encounters with the waves, even when they are in wetsuits against the winter cold.

Windsurfing, or sailboarding as it is usually known in Australia, is a more recent invention of the 1970s, which has gained great popularity. The crucial part of this invention is the universal joint, which allows the mast and sail to be rotated at any angle to the board – if the sailor is nimble enough and can manage to stay upright. A great sport for those who are fit and agile, it combines much of the adventure of surfing with the power of sailing.

A more recent invention still is kitesurfing, which uses a kite to propel the board and sailor, in place of a sail. Again a great experience, but it needs more equipment and much more space to operate. Consequently kitesurfing is less widespread, and is not always popular among other water users.

All water sports are potentially life-threatening, but Australian beaches are generally made safe by a wonderful organisation called **Surf Life Saving Australia**. This has been going for more than a century. It is made up of local life-saving clubs, whose members are trained to provide a beach service for most of the year. They treat injuries, rescue thousands of people, and are well worth giving a donation.

Despite the comfort of the life-savers, anybody who takes up water sports should get proper training first. As with all sports in Australia, there are plenty of places offering tuition in all water activities. Surf clubs are not as widespread as for other sports, but some sailing clubs have sailboarding sections.

Sailing

Sailing is big in Australia, as indeed are the boats. Every shape and size of craft is sailed, though tiny Mirror dinghies tend to be confined to inland waters, such as Canberra's three artificial lakes. At the smaller end of the scale is the Windrush Cat and Sloop class; Lasers of different sizes are popular, and there are clubs that specialise in 1m and 1.5m skiffs. Catamarans come in all sizes, and then there are the yachts, of which the 505s seem to be much loved.

At weekends, and often on weekday evenings, any large stretch of water near a city will have its quota of sails. Mostly these craft are being raced against one another as part of a regular club programme, though family sailing jaunts are also popular at holiday times.

As with all Australian activities, yacht clubs usually avoid the snobbery that comes with some clubs in the Old World, and so they can be a good places to join for both sailing and socialising. However, Aussies always take their sports very seriously, so friendliness doesn't get in the way of competitiveness. And, as anywhere, the bigger the craft you sail, the more you must expect to pay.

A useful website giving useful information on sailing clubs is **www.sailoz.net**. It lists clubs for each state; New South Wales has 24, Victoria has 17, Queensland and West Australia have 10 each, Tasmania and the Northern Territory have 4 each, and even landlocked ACT (Canberra) has 3. More surprising still is a yacht club listed for Alice Springs, which is rather a long way from any sea.

Swimming

Australia's enormous, beautiful coastline and its warm climate make swimming a popular sport, and one that is enjoyed by people of all ages. Many children are taught to swim as early as their first year. As they grow older, they become skilled in different strokes and even life-saving techniques. Every summer, locals and tourists alike flock to one of the many sandy beaches to enjoy the clean water. This is not the only option: swimming pools are found in many communities and backyards, while lakes and rivers provide another alternative.

Swimming has always been a popular Olympic sport in Australia, with its residents regularly scooping medals. They won two gold medals way back at the 1900 Paris Olympics and more recently took home no fewer than five gold, nine silver and four bronze medals at the 2000 Sydney Olympic Games.

Fishing

Recreational fishing is very popular in Australia. In money terms it is the biggest outdoor sport, ahead of all others combined, including horse- and dog-racing. It is even as big as one of the Aussies' favourite 'indoor sports', casino gambling. An estimated 4 million Australians fish at least once a year. Although the sport is more popular among men than women, some 20 per cent of adult women fish regularly, compared with 40 per cent of men. Spending on fishing supports a huge industry worth about A$3 billion a year and provides employment for 42,000 Australians directly, plus about 40,000 indirectly. All this is understandable if you look at a map and see that most towns and cities are near the coast – although people living outside the big cities are generally the ones who fish most often.

There are numerous scenic locations throughout the country offering world-class fishing and a huge variety of species. In every state apart from Queensland a licence is needed, which can be bought from fishing-tackle shops or local convenience stores. There are restrictions on the kinds of fish that can be captured, as well as on size and quantity ('bag limit'), and no female crustaceans can be taken. A free booklet from tackle shops outlines all the rules. A licence is also needed to drive any boat over 6 horsepower.

Like fishing everywhere, there are many different approaches to the sport in Australia. However, recreational fishing is normally done with a rod and reel, rather than nets or other aids used commercially. Broadly, there are four main groupings: heavy tackle game fishing, light tackle sport fishing, lure fishing and fly-fishing:

- **Heavy tackle game fishing**: the macho, high-tech and correspondingly expensive end of the activity. If you have the money, you can readily charter well-equipped craft to take part in this high-adrenaline pursuit. Size is the name of the game, and giant marlin are the most prized quarry. They provide spectacular angling, often leaping into the air to evade capture. The Queensland coast is noted for this type of fishing, with many craft operating near the Barrier Reef from ports such as Cairns.

- **Light tackle sport fishing**: again this needs an equipped craft, but as the name suggests it is a bit more low-tech. The approach favours the 5–10kg range. Barramundi, wahoo, spanish mackerel, yellowfin tuna, dolphin fish, barracuda and scaly mackerel are among those fished in this way.

- **Lure fishing** or **bait fishing** (often called coarse fishing in the UK): takes place from boats in calm waters, or in the traditional manner of an angler sitting on a bank beside a river or the sea. This more patient pastime uses various baits on hooks, with a rod or pole. Fish weighing as much as 10kg may be caught in tidal estuaries by this method. In the right places and seasons the varieties can range through barramundi, flathead, barracuda, queenfish, sooty grunter, tarpon and jungle perch.

- **Fly fishing** – an ancient method of wafting an artificial fly over a salmon or trout that has been adapted to the Australian environment. It has been used in the traditional fresh-water manner in streams and rivers where fish feed on insects. More recently the method has been extended to salt-water fishing, where imitation shrimps, prawns and even crabs have been recruited to entice fish to bite.

Even in Australia there are increasing concerns about over-fishing, and each state has its own laws for conserving stocks. Not only do anglers need licences, but there are limits to the number of certain fish that may be landed or may be in the angler's possession. Check on the local rules before you fish.

Golf

Golf is another popular sport in Australia, with more than 8 per cent of the population playing it. The country's good climate allows golf to be played throughout the year and there are plenty of opportunities to tee-off on a highly rated golf course. The game's popularity has been stimulated by the regular and often spectacular successes of Australian players, such as Greg Norman, Steve Elkington and Robert Allenby.

The two oldest clubs in the country are the Australian Golf Club in Sydney, which was formed in 1882, and the Royal Melbourne Club, formed in 1891. Today there are more than 1,500 courses, ranging from the manicured elegance of Huntingdale in Victoria to the basic nine-hole layouts in the outback, which are made of oiled sand. Courses range from upmarket private resorts to more basic public golf courses, all of which have club facilities. Quality hire equipment is usually available at reasonable rates but caddies are seldom used and motorised carts are usually available only at resort courses.

Tennis

Tennis in Australia dates back to the beginning of the 19th century, when it was something of an élite sport. At that time it was known as 'lawn tennis' and the courts were surfaced with grass. Today it is enjoyed at all levels by players who make year-round use of public tennis courts, private clubs and courts. Children are taught tennis from an early age, both in schools and at private clubs. Many Australian children spend school holidays at tennis camps wtih professional coaches. *See also* **Australia Today**, 'Tennis', p.81.

National Parks and Conservation Areas

There are lots of opportunities for recreational activities in Australia's national parks, whether it is energetic bush-walking or rock-climbing, or simply enjoying a picnic in a scenic environment. Many parks contain elements of Aboriginal culture, such as paintings, burial grounds and ceremonial sites. Most national parks can be easily accessed by car, although public transport links are not always good.

In total, Australia boasts more than 3,000 conservation areas including fauna and flora reserves, conservation and environmental parks, Aboriginal areas and national parks. While in general the state is responsible for creating and managing national parks, there are a small number of parks and reserves that are administered by the federal government.

In addition, there are 145 marine protected areas. These take the form of highly significant Commonwealth Marine Parks, like the Great Barrier Reef Marine Park, right through to fish sanctuaries, aquatic reserves, and marine and coastal parks. The federal government takes responsibility for 19 areas, New South Wales 8, the Northern Territory 3, South Australia 15, Tasmania 3, Victoria 3, Western Australia 13 and Queensland 81.

Most national parks charge visitor fees. Day passes are usually around A$10 per vehicle, but if you are planning to make several visits, a Parks Pass is a good option. It allows unlimited visits to selected parks within a set period. Camping is possible in some parks but a permit may be required.

These are the contact points for information about each state's parks service. Most of them provide free publications on state and national protected areas:

- **www.ea.gov.au/pa/contacts.html** has direct links to individual parks across Australia.

- **www.galactic.net.au/bushwalking** features a list of walks and parks, and gives useful tips as well as links to national parks.

- **New South Wales National Parks Centre**, 102 George St, The Rocks, Sydney, NSW 2000, t (02) 9253 4600, f 9251 8482, **www.npws.nsw.gov.au**.

- **Northern Territory Visitors Centre**, 22 Cavenagh St, Darwin, NT 0800, t (08) 8941 2167, f 8941 2815, **www.northernterritory.com**.

- **Queensland Parks and Wildlife Service**, Dept of Environment, PO Box 155, Brisbane, QLD 4002, t (07) 3227 8185, **www.epa.qld.gov.au**.

- **Nature Foundation South Australia**, PO Box 448, Hindmarsh, SA 5007, t 1300 366 191, f (08) 8340 2506, **www.naturefoundationsa.asn.au**.

- **Tasmania Parks & Wildlife Service**, GPO Box 44, Hobart, TAS 7001, t 1300 368 550, **www.parks.tas.gov.au**.

- **Victoria's Parks**, Level 10, 535 Bourke St, Melbourne, VIC 3000, t (03) 8627 4699, f 9629 5563, **www.parkweb.vic.gov.au**.

- **Conservation and Land Management**, Western Australia Locked Bag 104, Bentley Delivery Ctr. 6983, t (08) 9442 0300 or general enquiries t 9334 0333, f 9334 0466, **www.calm.wa.gov.au**.

Working in Australia

More and more people in the UK are seeking to relocate to Australia to work, perceiving that employment there will generally mean less stress and a better work–life balance. This may not necessarily be the case. Australians work some of the longest hours in the world and the pay they receive can be a third of what it is at home, making the cost of living not the bargain you might expect, but about the same as in the UK. That said, just about everyone who has made the move says it has made their quality of life infinitely better – something that global studies bear out. The standard of living on the other side of the world is much higher when it is measured not just in pounds and pence but in a more healthy approach to work and life.

What work you look for will largely be dictated by your visa. If you are on a 12-month working holiday visa, you are legally allowed to work for only three months at a time, so the employment you get is likely to be more menial and will hardly further your career. Those who have obtained a visa because of skills that are in short supply in Australia will be looking for a job in that area, and shouldn't have too many problems. The key is to sort out your visa first and look for a job second. A lot of professionals make the mistake of trying to get employment without a visa in their hand, and will have their application ignored by potential employees. Even with the best CV and experience on the planet, unless you get a visa, you can waste an awful lot of time (*see* **Red Tape**, 'The Basics', pp.99–110).

Business Etiquette

Most British people are attracted to Australia because of the more relaxed attitude to work that prevails there. Management tends to resist goal-orientation; business is conducted informally; and the work environment is more easygoing than in the UK – although that doesn't mean that Australians have a casual approach to work itself. Australian people are friendly and usually make outsiders feel at ease, but in a working environment it is important to be respectful and particularly not to be arrogant or self-important. Australians hate nothing more than someone who takes him or herself too seriously – they hate pretension and pulling rank. Be very careful of what you ask colleagues to do, particularly if it is a task you could complete yourself.

A suit and tie is standard attire in city offices, although because of the weather business clothing tends to be relatively informal outside office hours. If in doubt, over-dress, and always wear more conservative clothes when meeting government representatives. Guard against characterising people by their appearance or the way they talk. The older generation in Australia, especially, may look aged from the elements and have broad accents, but this does not mean they don't have a senior position within a corporation. Don't be fooled by

Australian friendliness, either. Just because a business contact is warm and calls you 'mate', doesn't mean they are not hard-headed. And, despite their position on the 'other side of the world', most successful Australians are well used to dealing with the overseas market, particularly in the USA, Asia and Europe.

A clear advantage of relocating to Australia from the UK for work is that the two countries have a culture in common, and there is no language barrier. Australia has a long tradition of employing English people, and if you can show you have particular skills, you have a good chance of getting a job. Relationships between Australian and British businessmen have always been strong and often extend to personal and family levels. Australians are, by nature, very hospitable, and tend to be particularly accommodating towards their British counterparts.

Tips for Conversational Topics

Here are a few suggestions for topics to raise when in conversation:

- **Wine**: easy to bring up over lunch or dinner if you familiarise yourself with the main wine regions; see **Getting to Know Australia**, pp.28–30, and also **Profiles of the Regions**.
- **Politics**: if you know the rudiments of the political system and the major players (leaders of the six states are known as premiers, not prime ministers, and the only prime minister is in the capital, Canberra). See **Australia Today**, pp.56–67.
- **Sport**: especially rugby, football and cricket, the three main interests; see **Australia Today**, pp.77–82.
- **TV**: if you have watched some of the popular or topical programmes.

The Working Day and Holidays

Australians generally work a 38-hour week and get 4 weeks annual holiday. As a rule, business-day hours are 9–5, but managers sometimes work longer hours. Colleagues socialise with each other with a drink after work, but are also likely to go to the beach or the gym. The general consensus is that it is fine to take more than an hour at lunchtime if you are doing some kind of sport or exercise, but check before you put this into practice.

Always be punctual for business meetings, though you may find that others aren't, especially the further north you go. As Christmas falls at the peak of summer, the workforce really gets only one long holiday a year (at Christmas), with July and August being busy working months. Those few people who are not on holiday regard January as a time to take things a bit easier, so doing business and making appointments may prove difficult then.

Case Study: From Roses to Riches

When Emily Lilyfield arrived in Perth from Bristol 16 years ago, she was just 18 and struggling to make a living selling roses in nightclubs. Now she runs her own company with a turnover of several thousand dollars, dealing with multi-national, multi-billion-dollar corporations. 'I was pretty young and naïve, and things were really tough at the beginning. I got my business by falling into a series of opportunities that I think is very much the Australian way. England corporate life to me seems much more rigid, especially in my field of financial services. You would need years of experience in this competitive industry before you could set up a company like mine in England, and I don't think I would have managed it there.

'There is good support for small businesses here, too, and I would always recommend contacting the state department for small businesses. Some states have a six-month mentoring programme, which helps women in business and offers a series of courses in subjects such as marketing, and accounting, which are really cheap because they are so heavily subsidised. They still e-mail me about seminars on things like exporting which are usually free. Certain states also have business start-up grants, which pay you a minimal salary instead of being on benefit.'

Emily loves the fact that people in Australia take you as you are. 'At first I wouldn't tell clients it was my own business because I thought they might think I was not capable as a young woman. But here companies are not so focused on how established you are as in the UK, and I haven't ever been asked how long I have been in business. Here, it's more about who you are and what you can offer. No one seemed surprised that I was setting up my own business even though I was young and inexperienced. I felt a great deal of respect, which made the whole process less scary. I think Australians are more relaxed than back home, but it's not a case of them being lazy or less productive, just less showy. In Australia it's all about having a go, and people will give you a go.'

The Labour Market

Bear in mind that just because your application for a visa is approved you are not guaranteed to have a job once you enter Australia, and it may take some time to find work there. The labour market in Australia can be very competitive. Traditionally, because of the long history of migration to the country, Australia has been able to rely on a steady influx of skilled workers (in 1999–2000 24 per cent of the labour force was comprised of employees born in countries other than Australia). The result is that industries have not had to train their workers, and this culture continues, so demand for those with skills continues. But this changes from year to year, even month to month, so check the latest on the government immigration website.

Certain professionals, such as IT technicians, nurses and health workers, seem to be perennially in demand, while the need for people in the building trade is more cyclical. Some estimates say that in 2005 Australia is short of 20,000 tradespeople. The Australian government produces an up-to-date list of the skills currently in demand on its website, but state governments may also produce their own lists. However, these lists are not exhaustive, so it is always worth checking whether there are jobs for which you are qualified. Obviously, those with skills that are in high demand can normally command comparatively higher salaries – in 2005 electricians, boilermakers and plumbers were earning A$100,000 or more each year. Just as in the UK, people in these trades are frequently raking in higher salaries than doctors and architects.

In 2000, Australia was ranked 11th in the world for overall productivity, as measured by GDP per person employed. These days, the economy is largely international, and differences between business in Australia and the UK are minimal. However, changes in the British manufacturing industry, for example, have meant that they are more opportunities for engineers in Australia than in the 'mother country'. That said, the Australian manufacturing sector is relatively small, but those with engineering skills may be able to translate them to the mining industry, which is still strong.

There has been a dramatic shift away from manufacturing and towards the service industries in Australia; today, well over a third of workers are in managerial, professional, technical or administrative jobs.

Your chances of finding work are defined by a number of factors. Where you live in Australia is crucial. The country is huge and very varied and job opportunities can be vastly different depending on where you are located. Some areas have very low populations and others have rocketing unemployment rates. You may be very highly skilled but find there is no demand for people in your particular field in that part of the country.

People moving to Australia from the UK understandably tend to focus on the major cities when looking for work. Sydney, Melbourne and, to a lesser extent, Brisbane, Adelaide and Perth are usually the first port of call when seeking employment. These urban centres are more familiar to us and have a higher concentration of job opportunities. However, by considering the regional centres, you might have more of a chance of securing work. Regional businesses often have problems finding good employees, not least because there is little unemployment (in 2005 it is at a 27-year low of 5.3 per cent).

It is highly advisable to research the labour market thoroughly before considering a move to Australia. There is a wealth of information on this subject on the Internet; **www.myfuture.edu.au** is a good site, with detailed information on occupations, industries and market trends. It lists the top 20 occupations in various areas of the country. In addition, the site provides labour statistics, employment and job vacancies. Links are given to articles of particular interest.

Case Study: Fishing for Work in the Desert

Jade Alliston was not one of those people prepared to work around the clock in a city job she hated in order to save up enough money to see something of a country she had travelled so far to visit. 'I have a pretty haphazard attitude to life and I was lucky to get a once-in-a-lifetime experience. I was sitting by a pool at a backpacker's hostel in Alice Springs with some friends, having just discovered that our funds had almost run out, when a guy walked in and asked, "Does anyone want some work?" We all hauled ourselves out of our horizontal positions and tried to look employable. It was work for a month on a fairground that travelled through the bush. The money was minimal, around A$100 a week, but we would get food and board. And more importantly, the fairground visited only Aboriginal missions dotted throughout the outback, which are not open to tourists or even Australians, so we would experience something that few people get to see.

'We were working for a 25-year-old Australian, Sandra, who had a 5-month-old baby, Daniel, as well as a deadly black Dobermann called Cassius. Sandra knew the seemingly endless miles of desert as if it were her local neighbourhood, but asked me once if Canada was in Europe. We travelled through the desert in a convoy of trucks, following the cloud of red dust from the one in front. Just one of my many jobs was changing Daniel's nappy on the bumpy "road", trying not to stab him or me with a nappy pin, because her husband would get angry if we stopped. When we did take a break from driving, we unloaded everything – baby, budgie, table, chairs – into the middle of the "road" for lunch, as we knew no cars would be coming along.

'To avoid the heat of the day, the men would set up the dodgems overnight, creating a bizarre sight in the middle of the bush. I worked on the fish tank, where Aboriginal children fished with magnetic rods for metal shapes in the bottom of an inky tank. It was sometimes sad to watch the empty exchange in which they handed over paper dollars in return for a toy as a prize, neither of which seemed to have any value for them. Equally, it was hilarious to see the German girl who had insisted on what she thought was the easiest job of selling tickets hopping around the neon-lit booth which was buzzing with enormous insects.

'I remember dusting the coin machines with talcum powder so they wouldn't slide off so easily and seeing a deadly red-back spider on a soap dish in the shower, which I smashed off the wall with a large stone, only to find another one in my towel as I dried myself. At night, we took Cassius with us to the toilets for protection and slept on mattresses on top of the trucks away from the mosquitoes and under the stunning star-filled sky. I feel privileged to have had such an amazing experience, and it's one that I will never forget.'

Job Ideas

Casual Work

In 2003, nearly 40,000 British citizens aged under 30 got working holiday visas – half of all those issued worldwide. A 12-month working visa restricts the holder to working just three months in any one position, so it highly unlikely that with this kind of visa you will find a job that will be part of a career move: the chances are you will pick up casual, unskilled work. The kind of opportunities falling into this category include bar work, seasonal work such as fruit-picking, administration jobs or office temping. You may also get seasonal work in the tourism industry. In Australia, to work in a bar you need a Responsible Service of Alcohol (RSA) certificate, which requires that you pass a 6-hour course covering subjects such as alcohol abuse and drink-driving prevention.

Fruit-picking and Farm Work

For farm work and fruit-picking you usually don't need any experience, although the wages reflect this. Depending on your employer, you may get paid by the hour or by the load, and accommodation and food is normally included. Work can be hard and in the heat of the summer, so early starts are usually necessary. A certain level of physical fitness is clearly required, along with some agility, as you may be asked to climb ladders, kneel for long periods of time, or do a lot of lifting. Most of these kinds of jobs involve working six days each week.

One thing to watch for with both kinds of work is that it can be difficult for the farmers to predict when they are going to need extra hands, as this depends so much on weather and other conditions. With fruit-picking, in particular, the ripeness of the crops cannot always be predicted, so pickers may arrive at an agreed time and find there is no work for them yet.

The kind of farm work you do will ultimately depend on the season, state and region within it, but hay- and silage-making is pretty much a constant. Very few farms in Australia have only crops; the vast majority have cattle or sheep as well. Some of the properties, or 'stations', are in the most remote parts of Australia – so remote that it might take you two days to get to them. They might be hundreds of miles from the nearest pub or shop and as big as 5,000 square miles in size. The usual way to get around is on horse or motorbike. You might find yourself branding, injecting and tagging cattle, or mending fences and clearing fallen trees.

Fruit-picking is a big source of casual work. The main season peaks in the summer months, from December to May, with fruit such as peaches and grapes becoming ready to eat. However, because the weather is so variable within a country the size of Australia, this is only a very rough guide and there is always a crop somewhere that needs to be planted or harvested, whether it's cotton or sunflowers. There are also fruits of the sea that need to be gathered, so you could find yourself collecting local prawns and crayfish, or even lobsters.

Most people who choose to pick fruit do it as a means of combining a small income and travelling around Australia. It is by no means restricted to young backpackers – people of all ages take this option. Depending on the seasons, it may be possible to work your way around the country, experiencing the outdoors in environments ranging from the steamy tropics to the lush green of Tasmania. Some of Australia's most scenic spots are fruit-picking locations.

Come prepared for this sort of work. Bring some old, hard-wearing clothes and shoes that will protect you from the elements. A high level of sun protection is a must, along with a wide-brimmed hat. When out in 'the field', keep your fluid intake up by drinking lots of water, and apply insect repellent.

Other crops, such as vegetables, may require additional harvest workers. Also, general maintenance and trimming might be necessary. The **National Harvest Information Service** (Freecall **t** 1800 062 332) can offer a wealth of information and contacts for harvest work opportunities throughout Australia. This office is open every weekday from 8am to 8pm throughout the year.

Visitoz (Springbrook Farm, MS188, Goomeri, Queensland 4601, Australia; **t** 011 61 7 4168 6106, **www.visitoz.org**) has jobs on its books for tractor and bulldozer drivers, mechanics and engineers, carpenters and joiners, as well as plumbers, electricians and builders. Employment is mostly for periods of 4–10 weeks and initially at least pays the minimum wage. After a short course of 4–5 days, you could find yourself living in very basic accommodation and working 16-hour days. The course takes place on Springbrook Farm and costs A$1,500; it is designed to teach you how to 'stick rake' (remove bush and scrubland) and, if you can drive a tractor, to handle animals and repair fences. Visitoz promises you work with one of around 1,000 employers on their books for the length of your working visa if you book from abroad, or for three months if you book it when already in Australia.

Case Study: Difficulties Finding Work in Sydney

Sally Hampton, from Leeds, was serving chips at the café in the beautiful outdoor swimming pool next to Sydney's Botanic Gardens. She had worked her way from Perth, through the outback and Adelaide to Sydney. 'I had no problems getting work before I got here. I did all sorts of things, even working in a homestead in the middle of nowhere. The owners trained me for two weeks and then left me in charge! I did things I had never done before, like building fires and feeding chickens, but it was a great experience. Coming to Sydney, I got really down because even after three weeks I hadn't found anything. It partly depends on the time of year. I arrived at the end of November when most employers have taken on their Christmas staff and a lot of travellers on working visas arrive in town.'

The website **www.waywardbus.com.au/seaswork** features a directory of hostels offering seasonal work and farms needing fruit-pickers; **www.picking jobs.com** and **www.jobsearch.gov.au/harvesttrail** are two other online sources for fruit-picking work.

If you decide to get work in a city, be aware that the vast majority of British backpackers flock to Sydney as their employment and recreation Mecca. This can cause problems, particularly just before the start of the summer in November or December, and many people interviewed in the course of researching this book reported that they found work most difficult to get in Sydney out of all the places they travelled to in Australia.

Employment

Looking for Work

Ideally, anyone planning to live and work in Australia should have a job already lined up, although this is not always practical and there is no reason why, if you are prepared to take the risk, you shouldn't make the move first and fix up a job later. Obviously, if you have a family, this is something to consider seriously, especially if you have no financial safety net to see you through for a month or two after arrival.

Whether you are seeking long- or short-term employment, the Internet is a great source of information when searching for jobs abroad. Agencies can be registered with online and most will notify you by e-mail if a suitable vacancy comes up. Often websites give advice on finding work, from compiling a successful CV to how to wow potential employers at an interview. Most companies have their own website and accept job applications online. Employment agencies are listed in the *Yellow Pages* telephone directory. It makes sense to register with more than one agency in order to maximise your chances of finding work.

National and local press in Australia are also good resources when looking for work, and many are easily accessible online. Vacancies are usually advertised in the 'Positions Vacant' part of the Classifieds section of newspapers – particularly on Saturday and Wednesday). If you are seeking employment in a particular sector, it is a good idea to subscribe to trade publications. Read any advertisement carefully, paying particular attention to specific instructions on how to apply.Once you arrive, make it known to as many friends, relatives and associates as possible that you are looking for a job. A surprising number come about through word of mouth, especially in the case of smaller businesses. Never underestimate the power of networking. Invest in some business cards and hand them out with abandon. It is much easier to carry them around in your wallet than multiple CVs.

Short-term Employment

As with all the advice in this chapter, before you take action it is highly advisable to target your search according to the visa you have. Those with a 12-month working holiday visa – and therefore limited to being able to work for a maximum of three months – are unlikely to find suitable positions through employment agencies, as the commission gained for these kinds of contracts is minimal. Those seeking short-term work may find it harder to set up work before arriving. Once in the country, any hostel you stay at can be a good source of information about seasonal work. Potential employers know that hostels are a hotbed of young, eager-to-work travellers and often contact them with job offers. Also, ask your fellow backpackers. They may be at the end of a trip and have some good advice, or information about local sources of work. The student unions of universities and colleges can be another good source of employment as they tend to run casual employment services for their students. Ask whether they can give you information about seasonal work, which may be possible only if you are registered with them.

Resources

- **BUNAC** or **Work Australia**, PO Box 430, Southbury, CT 06488; **t** (203) 264 0901, **www.bunac.org**. The American company BUNAC offers short-term work opportunities in Australia for graduates, gap-year students and independent travellers. You need to apply for a working holiday visa (which can be held once only), be aged between 18 and 30, and be a citizen of Canada, Cyprus, Denmark, Finland, Germany, the Hong Kong Special Administrative Region, Ireland, Japan, Republic of Korea, Malta, Netherlands, Norway, Sweden or the UK. You must also be able to provide evidence that you have the required amount of personal funds available. Placement fees are around A$500.

- **My Career**, **www.mycareer.com.au**. Features jobs that appear in the *Sydney Morning Herald* and the *Melbourne Age*.

- **Northern Victoria Fruitgrowers' Association**, PO Box 394, Shepparton, Victoria 3632, Australia; **t** (03) 5821 5844, **www.nvfa.com.au**. Offers work to fruit-pickers between January and March.

- **Rocky Creek Farm**, Isis Hwy, MS 698, Biggenden, Queensland 4621, Australia; **t/f** (07) 4127 1377, **www.isisol.com.au/rockycrkfarmstay**. Offers a 4-day course for around A$500, which includes placement on a Queensland property.

- *TNT* **Magazine**, **www.tntclassifieds.com.au**. Includes a harvest calendar, classified ads and advice for working travellers.

- **Travellers Contact Point**, Level 7, Dymocks Building, 428 George St, Sydney 2000; **t** (02) 9221 8744, **www.travellers.com.au**. This agency, with affiliated offices around Australia, assists those with working holiday visas to find work and provides services such as mail-forwarding for a fee starting from around A$200.

- **Troys Hospitality Staff**, Ste 1, Level 11, 89 York St, Sydney 2000, Australia; **t** (02) 9290 2955, **www.troys.com.au**. Places casual staff in the hospitality industry in Sydney.

Long-term Employment

Resources

Employment agencies are listed in the *Yellow Pages* telephone directory – look under 'Employment Services' and 'Employment – Labour Hire Contractors'. These may be either placement agencies, which charge the employer a fee, or labour-hire agencies, which pay you and provide your services to another company or organisation which they then bill. Most of these agencies have websites that advertise vacancies. It's a good idea to register with several agencies to maximise your chances of finding work.

The following sites are just a sample to get you started, and are all nationwide, but it is also worth looking at state- or even city-specific companies:

- The **Department of Employment and Workplace Relations (DEWR)**, **www.workplace.gov.au**. Information on a number of websites that can help people in Australia to find work. They provide details of jobs, training and government.

- **Australia's Careers OnLine, www.careersonline.com.au**. Features self-help tools with the aim of making your job hunting and career search more successful.

- **Affinity Nursing, www.affinitynursing.com.au**. An agency that provides contract and permanent nursing jobs throughout Australia.

- **Affordable Au Pairs & Nannies Australia, t** (07) 5530 1123, **www.nanny.net.au**. Has offices in Sydney, Melbourne and Brisbane to place au pairs and nannies. There is a registration fee of A$120 plus a placement fee of A$330.

- **Career One, www.careerone.com.au**. An online employment service that advertises details of vacancies in a range of Australian newspapers. Jobs can be searched by industry, job type or location.

- **Jobrepublic, www.jobrepublic.com.au**. Run by expatriates for expatriates and set up so you don't have to search for a job every day. After entering your skill details, the site promotes you to would-be employers and e-mails you with details.

- **Worldwide Workers Sydney**, 234 Sussex St, Sydney, NSW 2000; **t** (02) 8268 6001, **www.worldwideclub.com**. Membership costs A$30 for one month and entitles members to personal assistance in finding work, including fruit-picking, plus free Internet access and other benefits.

Other online employment agencies include:

- **www.employment.com.au.**
- **www.jobsguide.com.au.**
- **www.jobsearch.gov.au.**
- **www.monsterboard.com.au.**
- **www.seek.com.au.**

Qualifications and Skills

Some occupations have special requirements, such as registration or licensing with a government authority or membership of a professional or industry association. Make sure you establish if this is the case before leaving the UK, which is a fairly straightforward procedure. Further, you may find that your particular skills of qualifications are not recognised in Australia. If so, you may find that if you complete a bridging course you will be considered qualified to meet necessary requirements.

- **National Office of Overseas Skills Recognition (NOOSR), t** 1800 020 086, **www.dest.gov.au/noosr/brgcourses.htm.** Can supply information about skills and qualification recognition, as well as bridging courses (available to professionals who have Australian citizenship or permanent residence).
- **Trades Recognition Australia (TRA)**, GPO Box 9879, Sydney, NSW 2001, **t** (02) 9246 0760; from overseas GPO Box 9879, Canberra, ACT 2601, **t** (06) 12 6121 745 627. Provides information on recognition of trade qualifications such as engineering, catering, electrical and construction.

Applying for a Job

The procedure for applying for a job is pretty much the same the world over. It is often worth amending your CV according to the job you are applying for. That way, your potential employer gets a sense of not only why you are particularly suitable for the post in question, but why you want to work for that particular employer. When applying for positions in Australia, try to point out in your covering letter why you have chosen to move to the country and specify any work visas you have.

It is now standard practice to apply for jobs via e-mail, which can dramatically reduce costs incurred through postage, as well as taking a fraction of the time. The Internet is a boon when it comes to registering with employment agencies and for accessing resources. Online web pages can advise you about specific

ESI

ESI is an Australian company that arranges international health and travel insurance for expatriates in Australia. ESI also helps companies manage their obligations relating to business visas and medical expenses.

For further information, contact: GPO Box 3162, Sydney NSW 2001; **t** +61 1300 365 385, **info@esiexpat.com, www.esiexpat.com.**

interview techniques, provide templates for CVs for your particular field and even give information about the company you are applying for.

If you know of a particular company or organisation you would like to work for, there is nothing to stop you contacting them directly. In fact, it is a much better approach than waiting for jobs to be advertised, when you will then have to compete with other candidates. In addition, it often impresses employers, as it demonstrates initiative and that you have selected their particular company as a place you want to work. Contact can be made by telephone, e-mail or even in person.

A good strategy is to telephone to get the name and contact details of the person who deals with job applications. It is no good sending a dazzling CV and an impressive, tailored covering letter to the wrong person. Send a covering letter saying what you are looking for, and outlining your experience, why you have picked that organisation, what you have to offer, and so on, with your CV attached, and saying at the end that you will make a follow-up call in a week. When you do telephone, ask if it would be possible to come in to the office and meet face to face, even if a relevant position isn't currently available. One woman got a well-paid job as a researcher at the Sydney offices of the international publishing company *Reader's Digest* by using this approach.

Resources

• **The Job Network** (employment services information line **t** 13 62 68, **www.workplace.gov.au**). If you have residency, once you are in Australia the Job Network can be contacted through the Job Seeker Hotline (**t** 13 62 68) for the cost of a local call (or mobile rates from a mobile phone). The Job Network is a network of private, community and government organisations, contracted by the Commonwealth government to help people find employment with offices throughout the country. It provides a range of services, including training advice, assistance with developing interviewing skills and tips on presentation to potential employers. Information can be given on how to improve your CV, job search and networking. Personal one-on-one advice can also be given for those who require it. Those seeking to run their own business may be able to get help under the New Enterprise Incentive Scheme (NEIS), which offers training and general advice for the first year.

Sample CV

NAME

Address:	number, street name city, postcode, Australia *Or English address if not yet moved to Australia*
Home Phone Number:	Area code, e.g. 03 for Melbourne, plus number *Give code for England if not yet moved to Australia*
Work Phone Number:	If applicable
Mobile Phone Number:	Full number including code for England if necessary
Fax Number:	If applicable, with full code
E-mail:	A private, rather than work, address if possible
Website Homepage:	If applicable
Date of Birth:	English format: day, month, year
Nationality:	Dual nationality, if relevant, can be included here, along with visa details
Career Objective:	It can be a good idea to include reasons why you want to spend time in Australia
Languages:	This is less relevant in Australia than in other countries

EDUCATION

University Qualifications   if relevant, with full address and explanation of any details that might not be clear to someone in Australia

Dates (month/year)   Level and subject
Full/Part Time

College Qualifications

Dates (month/year)   Level and subject
Full/Part Time

EMPLOYMENT HISTORY

Dates   Company name

Position: Job title

Company Description: Main business; explain any terms that might not be clear to an Australian employer

Duties: Succinctly outline responsibilities/ achievements

QUALIFICATIONS

Dates   Details of qualification

SKILLS/INTERESTS

This section is optional; it is advisable to only include relevant information here.

REFEREES

Name and relationship   Position and address and, if possible,
(e.g. employer/teacher)   e-mail

• **Centrelink, t** 13 10 21, or **t** 13 12 02 for help in other languages. The government service Centrelink registers job-seekers for job-matching or for full Job Network services. All job-seekers can use the free Job Network Access self-help facilities in Centrelink offices throughout the country, such as telephones, photocopiers, fax machines, computers and daily newspapers. You can locate them using the *White Pages* telephone directory or on their website. In the first instance, telephone to make an appointment with Centrelink. In addition, your nearest Migrant Resource Centre (MRC) or Migrant Service Agency (MSA) can provide advice on finding work. Some MRCs or MSAs may also have specialist placement officers to assist you in your hunt.

Job Interviews

Although most of the same rules apply as in the UK when writing a CV or attending an interview, if you need advice look at **www.mycareer.com.au**, which has information on how to write a covering letter, commonly asked interview questions, and interview dos and don'ts.

Interviews are usually one-on-one, but for more senior positions you will probably have to face a panel of interviewees and at least two, if not three, interviews. As is the case anywhere in the world, punctuality and presentation are highly important. Arrive early, especially as the chances are you will not be familiar with the address you are going to. Dress smartly and conservatively and bring any relevant documentation with you. Research is key. You may find you need to spend more time than you would at home to find out about a particular company, which may well be literally foreign to you. If you get through the first interview, the next stage is likely to involve psychological or psychometric tests.

Employment Contracts and Work Rights

Every employee in Australia should have a contract of employment. They come in various forms and may even be given different names, such as 'Agreements' or 'Australian Workplace Agreements'. Contracts may differ from state to state, but there are some general rules to follow. Always read your contract thoroughly and if necessary get a professional to look over it. Never sign anything you are not 100 per cent sure about, and always make a copy.

Provided they have the correct visa that allows them to work, anybody who goes to live in Australia as a migrant is entitled to the same work rights as an Australian permanent resident. Under the Workplace Relations Act 1996, Australian employees are guaranteed by law the right to join a trade union or any other organisation. For more information, ring the **Australian Council of Trade Unions** (ACTU; **t** 1300 362 223).

Working conditions, rates of pay, working hours, sick pay and holidays are covered either by federal or by state laws or individual workplace agreements. For example, compensation given to employees in the event of injury or illness varies in every state and territory, so it is advisable to check. If compensation is not provided, an individual is covered by common law and it may, if necessary, be possible to claim against an employer through the courts.

The law applying to the majority of jobs and working conditions is outlined by state awards, except in Victoria, where Commonwealth awards apply. In some cases, certified agreements apply. These are agreements about wages and conditions of employment that are made directly between an employer and a group of employees or relevant unions. There are also Australian Workplace Agreements (AWAs), which are an individual agreement between an employer and an employee. Further information is provided by the **Office of the Employment Advocate, t** 1300 366 632.

Pay

The average wage in Australia in 2005 was A$50,000, about £20,000, compared with a national average of £26,000 in the UK. Various factors affect your rate of pay: whether you work full- or part-time, whether you are a trainee, and what qualifications and experience you have. To find out what you should be paid, look at **www.wagenet.gov.au**, or call wageline in Australia on **t** 1300 363 264. You can search by state for wage rates on **www.wages.com.au**. You could also contact ACTU Worklink (**t** 1300 362 223, **www.actu.asn.au**) to get details of your union.

Sample Wages

Trades

- **Aircraft maintenance engineer: A$51,636**
- **Electrician: A$43,420**
- **Mechanic: A$32,864**
- **Plumber: A$45,240**

University graduates

- **Architect: A$28,000**
- **Dentist: A$55,000**
- **Lawyer: A$39,480**
- **Nurse: A$35,000**

Source: *What Jobs Pay 2004–2005*, **www.gradlink.edu.au**.

Tax File and Australian Business Numbers

A tax file number is needed in order to receive wages. This is issued by the **Australian Taxation Office (ATO)** and can be applied for online by giving your passport details and address in Australia. A response is usually given within 10 days by post. Those not wishing to apply online should visit their local Centrelink office, but this method takes 28 days. On starting work, employers are required to provide you with a TFN declaration form. Those running their own business need an **Australian business number**.

For more information on tax file numbers, ring the Australian Taxation Office on **t** 13 2861 option 3 for the helpline; **t** 13 2866 for business enquiries; **t** 13 2861 for other enquiries, or go to **www.ato.gov.au/individuals**.

Benefits

Centrelink, www.centrelink.gov.au, is the government agency responsible for social security benefits such as unemployment payments, student allowance and sickness payments in Australia. Bear in mind that your eligibility will depend on the class of your visa and that you must have been an Australian resident for two years to qualify for any benefits, unless you are a refugee or humanitarian entrant. Those seeking pensions or disability benefits usually have to be resident in the country for 10 years. An exception is if you are covered by an international social security agreement.

See **Living in Australia**, pp.137–8.

A Flexible Approach

As many as 37 per cent of workers in Australia are employed part-time or casually, laying ground for the claim that the country is fast becoming a 'free agent nation'. Australia has adopted more of America's working practices than Britain, so that **flexitime** is more common there than in the UK, with employees increasingly able to work the times they choose. In fact, 39 per cent of workers, a total of more than 3 million people, have flexible working hours according to a study conducted in November 2000 by the Australian Bureau of Statistics.

Flexitime usually involves still working a full week, but some employees may be offered the chance to reduce their total hours. **Flexi-workers**, also sometimes called supplementaries, are another category again, and different from casual or part-time workers. They work full-time but only when called in at busy periods, usually in large corporations and often in call centres. This is the case at Australia Pty Ltd, which has tried to take into account the needs of its employees when asking them to work particular shifts. The company will first ask for volunteers to work a particular time slot, and call them only in emergency situations, such as illness.

More and more companies recognise the benefits of **career breaks** as a chance to take on new challenges and develop new skills, but career breaks are much more common in Australia than in the UK. The normal arrangement is that after an extended period of leave the employee returns to work at the same job as previously.

A ruling in 2004 stated that **casual workers** can now dispute unlawful dismissals, as long as they have been employed for over 12 months, as opposed to full-time workers who can take the same action after just three months. Around one million Australian workers do shift work, while nearly 2.5 million do night shifts. Casual workers are meant to be employed on a temporary basis, but many employers use them as a way of avoiding having to pay out holiday and sick pay. **Part-time workers** are employed permanently or part-time. Unlike in the UK, most of their entitlements are the same as permanent workers, but pro-rata. For example, part-time workers in Australia receive pension contributions from their employers.

In recent years, an increasing number of employees have been asked to sign **'fixed term' employment contracts**. Although they may be permanent workers, it is a way of getting them to 're-negotiate' pay and conditions. The problem with this arrangement is that it takes away some of the employees' crucial rights. Those on fixed-term contracts not only lose protection from unfair dismissal and any redundancy rights, but they forgo any right they had to employment after the fixed term expires.

Students and Work

Those arriving in Australia with a student visa allowing full-time education are not automatically permitted to work in the country. They must apply for work rights after entering the country and starting their registered course. Even if a student visa with work rights is granted, only a maximum of 20 hours' work a week is allowed.

Applications for student visas with work rights can be made online on the Australian government website, which clearly outlines the procedure and states that online payment can be made only with a credit card. The application must include proof of commencing the course from the relevant educational establishment, which can be supplied via e-mail. Visa approval is then given the next working day and must be collected from the nearest immigration office.

Those who prefer to make the application in person need to visit their local immigration office, where payment can be made with the Australian equivalent of Switch, a credit card or a cheque. Approval takes considerably longer than with online applications.

Teaching

In 2005 there is a dearth of teachers in Australia and, if industry experts are to be believed, demand is increasing. That said, it is advisable to arrange teaching work before leaving the UK, as it makes registration easier. Teaching qualifications need to be assessed by **AEI–NOOSR**, part of the Australian government's Department of Education, Science and Training, as part of your visa application. Teacher registration and recruitment practices vary from state to state. For more details, look at the **Department of Education, Science and Training** website **www.dest.gov.au**.

Jobs in the teaching profession are much more widely available in regional centres rather than in the major cities. The chances are you won't have your experience taken into account, although if you can prove you have more than seven years in the job, wages should be higher.

Australia has three types of school, broadly speaking – state, Catholic and independent. You stand a better chance of getting a job in the Catholic and independent sector than in a state school. Contracts vary depending on the school you are working with, and can be anything from an agreement to work one morning to a year. Most follow the academic year, so, while you get long holidays, there are long periods in the year when you are not being paid.

Teaching English

Even though Australia is an English-speaking country, there are still a number of opportunities for those seeking work teaching English, as a lot of people head to the country with the aim of learning English. Trained teachers from the UK have a good chance of finding work because their accent is seen as desirable. The three-month limit on work for people with working holiday visas need not pose too much of an obstacle for those who want to teach English as a foreign language; many schools have seasonal needs, often doubling in size over the Australian summer – from December to February.

Just a few years ago the Australian government categorised teaching English as a foreign language (TEFL) as a profession that was needed by the country, but this is no longer the case. The rise of the racist One Nation Party has discouraged some Asian students from studying in the country and the current economic crisis in that part of the world has only worsened the situation.

Private language schools are a good source of work; they tend to have a mix of Asian and European students, along with some other nationalities, all hoping to improve their English-speaking skills. Get hold of a list of language schools in the area where you want to work and send them your covering letter with CV and proof of qualification. A state-by-state list of accredited language schools can be found at **www.neasaustralia.com**.

Teaching English as a second language (TESL), in countries where English is the first language, describes teaching immigrants or students on a study holiday. The term 'teaching English to speakers of other languages' (TESOL) is used to cover TEFL and TESL. The CELTA and Certificate IV in TESOL courses prepare you to be able to teach in any of these situations.

In Australia, private language schools and universities that are NEAS-accredited normally require teachers to have a degree, as well as the CELTA or Certificate IV in TESOL and some experience. The NEAS website at **www.neasaustralia.com** has further information. University language centres usually require teachers to have a degree and some experience teaching EFL in addition to the CELTA or Certificate IV in TESOL. The website **www.teachers.on.net** claims to have Australia's largest range of teaching and education positions.

One of the advantages of teaching English is that you can supplement your income by taking private classes for which you can be paid in cash. You may be lucky enough to find private students through the language school you work with; otherwise you will need to advertise in libraries, local papers and shops – preferably locally to where you live or just in one area, or could find yourself travelling a lot and paying out not insignificant amounts for transport.

Freelancing

Freelancing is becoming more common all over the world, but there are still certain professions that are more suited to freelance work than others. These include writers, designers and photographers; nurses and healthcare workers; IT specialists; those working in hospitality and tourism; teachers; and musicians and singers. The main advantage of freelancing is the freedom it provides, and it can be a good way to get your foot in the door. But there are downsides too, such as no holiday or sick pay and no pension. You may find yourself out of work for several months of the year and have to wait for months to be paid even when you do find work.

Anyone embarking on freelance work should protect themselves by making sure they have a signed contract with their client. You can draw up a basic template yourself, which can be adapted for each assignment you undertake. It should include delivery date, brief details of the work involved and how payment is to be made. It's a good idea to set up a meeting with an accountant before you embark on your freelance career. That way, you will know in advance what kind of things you can claim for and save receipts accordingly. For example, if you work from home you may be able to claim a proportion of household bills. The website **www.freelancing.com.au** has a directory of freelance jobs throughout Australia.

Case Study: Worker of the World

One of the amazing things about the Internet is that it allows people to do their job equally efficiently whether they are sitting on a beach in Thailand or shivering in the mountains in Switzerland. Global networks, mobile phones and e-mail allow individuals to be contacted cheaply and easily wherever they are on the planet and not dependent on working for clients in the country in which they are resident. In the case of living in Australia and working for English clients, the main benefit is financial. You can be earning English pounds but your Australian costs in dollars are much lower than at home.

William Makepeace moved from London to Melbourne with his young family just a few months ago. His wife, an architect, was sponsored by an international company, while, as a web designer, William simply brought his clients with him. 'All of them were perfectly happy with the arrangement. I would rarely meet them face to face anyway and nearly all our communication is by e-mail, although I do speak to them on the phone every so often. Yesterday I had a conversation with one of my clients who happened to be in Cambodia. The only contract I lost by moving out here was with a woman who had a lot of one-to-one consultations with me – too many of them for which she didn't pay me, so I was happy to let her go.'

William's experience is very different from Simon Chance's. Simon is also a web designer, but one who works for very large corporations. Last year he moved out to Perth, where his wife grew up, but, despite his high level of experience, he found it almost impossible to get work. 'The old boy network in Perth is alive and well and I just couldn't break through it. I was unemployed for eight months which was very stressful as we have a young son. I loved Perth but in the end we had to move to Sydney, where I got work almost immediately. I couldn't have brought my clients from home as they like to meet me face to face in the office. Even telephoning would be difficult because we are usually around 10 hours ahead.'

Starting Your Own Business

Migrating to Australia appeals because of the freedom it offers; combine that with starting up your own successful business and you have some kind of utopia for many people. Obviously, if you have no experience in this field already, you might want to think twice about it. Most businesses do not get off the ground for a year or two, and the vast majority fail well before that. To set yourself up, you need not only a good idea, but commitment, cash and patience, and you must be prepared to work long hours away from your family and handle the stress and responsibility of your 'new baby'.

That said, the rewards when they happen are great and Australia can offer vast opportunities for hard-working entrepreneurs who have done their homework. Unlike many other foreign countries you might choose to settle in, you will not have a language problem in Australia, and being English can be a positive advantage both because of the vast number of expatriates from the UK, and because of the continuing high numbers of British tourists, who provide a market for a potential business. There is also a common basis for commercial law, a similar business culture, a generally positive attitude towards the UK, and the presence of many established UK companies.

It could be a chic Melbourne coffee shop, a basic beach bar in Queensland or even a rambling sheep farm in the outback, but the key to any successful business is establishing a market. Thanks to the Internet, much of your research can be done online before you ever get to Australia, but it also makes sense to make as many local contacts as possible to get the human angle. Be aware that laws regarding the running of a business may vary from state to state. And look at the competition. Can you do it better?

Paperwork

Whether or not you need funding, it is a good idea, if not essential, to draw up a **business plan**. Depending on the type of business, and whether you can initially work from home, probably the first thing you are going to need is premises, which you may want to rent or buy. Other factors to consider are business permits, health and safety regulations, completing necessary paperwork, tax obligations and registering your company.

You need to keep records of all business expenditure. Just as in the UK, you will be able to claim expenses against tax only if you have detailed, ordered and relevant receipts. You will probably want to employ an accountant (*see* **Living in Australia**, 'Taxation', pp.132–7, for more information). Regulations about these matters vary between states, so you may need to take professional advice, which is advisable in any case.

Employing Staff

Before making the decision to employ any staff, calculate the costs very carefully. You will need to at least pay the minimum wage, which is known as the Ward Wage in Australia. You may be tempted to flout employment regulations, but apart from any moral issues, you could easily be ejected from the country if you were ever discovered.

Bear in mind there may be differences from English law – for example, part-time workers have more rights in Australia than in the UK, and as an employer you have more responsibilities towards them, such as having to pay pension (superannuation or simply 'super') contributions. Under superannuation guarantee legislation, contributions made for staff are a percentage of their

Not So Innocent

It's a success story to make most would-be entrepreneurs green with envy. In less than two years, Australia's 'Nudie' brand of natural fruit juices, which promise to contain 'a day's fruit in every bottle', has reached annual sales of A$12 million. Beginning as the archetypal kitchen-table operation, the founder of Nudie quickly set up distribution to 24 shops, increasing the number to over 4,000 in just 18 months. The cuddly logo and the slogan 'emergency nudie delivery' in the corporate colour of lilac adorn the sweet little vans that can be seen whizzing around Australian cities.

But there is nothing fluffy or cute about founder Tim Pethick's business sense. He has a background in management consultancy and saw that a similar product was a great success in London and the US, with nothing comparable in Australia. 'Innocent' drinks were launched in the UK in 1999 by three college friends and now more than 250,000 are sold each week, with the company boasting an annual turnover of £16 million. Pethick maintains that a lot of people have good business ideas but very few put them into practice. The first buzz at an initial business idea can rapidly disappear amongst the daily grind of setting up a business, and even then you cannot sit back and relax; you always have to look at ways of improving and expanding.

The company recently secured export contracts to Singapore, Hong Kong and New Zealand by teaming up with Australia's government-run Austrade, which provides funding and assistance for businesses that want to break into the export market. This is all from a company that indulges in only a small marketing budget, preferring to rely on word of mouth and product sampling to promote brand awareness. Pethick can be seen wearing his Nudie T-shirt with the slogan 'strip down to the bare essentials', which is intended to describe the purity and freshness of his product, but which also quite neatly sums up the marketing success of his business.

earnings. Those employers who don't pay enough contributions will have to pay the Superannuation Guarantee Charge. For all employers, conditions of employment, workplace safety and dismissal are important legal issues to familiarise yourself with.

Registering a Business

The federal, state and territory governments can advise you about registering your business for taxation purposes; before you can begin operating your new small business you'll need to know what you must do to comply with government taxation legislation. Apart from applying for an Australian business number (ABN) and tax file number (TFN) and paying goods and services tax (GST) and fringe benefits tax (FBT), you may also need to pay state and territory land tax, payroll tax and other taxes. It is a legal requirement that you register your business name in the state or territory in which it operates. New companies must also register with the **Australian Securities and Investments Commission (ASIC)**. Business licences and permits may also be required to run your business legally.

Other Government Requirements

If you are running a home-based business there is a range of government requirements that might apply to you. Things to consider when running a small business from home include taxation, employment, council approval and licensing. Grants, funding programmes and industry assistance are available from the federal and state and territory governments. If your business is going to involve either the importing of exporting of goods, there are laws and government policies to take into consideration. All goods must be cleared by Customs; duty may be payable and import and export permits may be necessary. You will also need to make sure that wherever you are planning to trade, you are complying with the rules and regulations of all three levels of government – Australian, state and local.

Registering a Business Name

Registration of a name that a business trades under is compulsory in every state and territory in which your business operates, and it must be completed before the start of trading in order to identify the legal owners. However, this procedure does not offer any legal protection to that name; a trademark must be applied for if that is needed. Obviously, you will want to give a great deal of thought to which name to choose and to make sure it doesn't already exist. ASIC's Identical Names Check is a register of all company names that have been registered in Australia, which can be searched free of charge to see if the intended name for your business has already been used.

By law, a business and company name must be displayed at every location where the business is carried out and open to the public, and the Business Registration Certification must be clearly displayed in the principal place of business. When using your business name on any kind of stationery, it must be in exactly the same form as the one in which it was registered.

Advice and Support

Small businesses can take advantage of a broad range of advice and support offered by the federal, state and territory and local governments. These services include information and advice on starting and expanding a business, obtaining funding and training. The federal government provides information for business people who want to migrate to Australia to start a small business, or employers who wish to employ migrants. Advice and assistance is also available for foreign investors who want to invest in Australia, and for foreign companies wishing to register in Australia.

The federal, state and territory governments can also advise about franchise procedures and disputes, as well as 'e-commerce', including online trading, which can dramatically reduce the overheads of small businesses as well as providing inroads to new markets. Other areas they can help with are tenancy regulations and unfair trading. They can also provide important statistical information and market analysis for start-up and development assistance.

Financial assistance is available to people from the UK who wish to set up business in Australia, but the amount differs from state to state. In the first instance, contact the relevant state Department of Regional Development, as the federal government does not offer any assistance of this kind.

Small-business owners can take advantage of a number of training services and programmes available to them when employing trainees and apprentices. Incentives and subsidies are available from the federal and state and territory governments to help reduce the cost of training employees. Government laws and industry self-regulation for fair trading help small businesses to ensure that they are competitive and do not abuse their market power.

For information on available financial assistance, market analysis and statistics, see **www.business.gov.au**.

Taxation

Goods and services tax (GST) is comparable to UK VAT. In 2005 it was 10 per cent on the sale of most goods and services in Australia. All businesses must register for GST if their annual turnover is at or above the registration turnover threshold of A$50,000 (or A$100,000 for non-profit organisations).

The Tax Office for GST defines your residency status using different criteria from the Department of Immigration and Multicultural and Indigenous Affairs (DIMIA). Usually, it considers you to be an Australian resident for tax purposes if you have always lived in Australia, live in Australia permanently or have physically been in Australia for over half of the financial year (unless your usual home is overseas and you do not intend to live in Australia).

This is a complicated area, and you are advised to seek advice from a qualified professional, especially as laws can vary from state to state. Each state government also has a separate section on their website relating to business migration. Other useful websites include:

- **Australian Bureau of Statistics, www.abs.gov.au.**
- **Australian Chamber of Commerce and Industry, www.acci.asn.au.**

- **Business Entry Point, www.bep.gov.au.**
- **IBIS World, www.ibisworld.com.au.**
- **Invest Australia, www.investaustralia.gov.au.**

There are also state, country and regional chambers of commerce and industry around Australia, for instance, the **Victorian Employers' Chamber of Commerce and Industry (VECCI), www.vecci.org.au**, with additional resources, links and services for potential entrepreneurs.

Each local government council can provide a 'starting a business' kit, which provides a range of information including local networks to join, demographic information and available resources, which are normally all free.

Local councils are listed on the **Australian Local Government Association** website, **www.alga.asn.au/links**.

The Australian Market

Although many of the same considerations for starting a business in the UK apply equally to Australia, there are some other factors to take into account. First, because it is such a huge country, the market can be somewhat fragmented. Around three-quarters of the population live in urban areas, in communities of 20,000 people or more, which makes the market reasonably identifiable. And the principal cities of Sydney and Melbourne have around 3 or 4 million inhabitants, making them significant even by world standards. That said, because the total population is only around 20 million, many businesses need to rely on exports. Australia is closer to Asia and the Pacific countries, so business relationships may need to be developed in that area. As part of the Asia Pacific Rim, it belongs to a vast area of hundreds of millions of people who are potential consumers.

You may have an established business and want to move into Australia. How you do this will largely depend on the nature of your company and your aims. Larger firms from the UK have established subsidiaries, while others have chosen to create a product specifically for this regional market. Others enter into a joint venture with an Australian company, so that the British arm provides expertise, while the Antipodean element brings local knowledge and contacts.

Useful websites include:

- **Australian Institute of Company Directors, www.companydirectors.com.au.**
- **Australian Institute of Management, www.aim.com.au.**
- **Business Council of Australia, www.bca.com.au.**

Networking

University websites can be a good source of information about your particular industry or expertise. A list of all universities in Australia is provided at **www.dest.gov.au/highered/ausunis.htm**. There are also many associations and networks that can support your business, with the most significant ones (usually 'not for profit') listed on the state government websites. These groups can be invaluable for sourcing contacts and developing your business. Some other sites that may be useful include:

- **Australian Business Number, www.abr.business.gov.au.**
- **Australian Competition and Consumer Commission, www.accc.gov.au.**
- **Australian Securities and Investment Commission, www.asic.gov.au.**
- **Australian Taxation Office, www.ato.gov.au.**
- **Commonwealth Ombudsman**, Australia, **www.ombudsman.gov.au.**
- **IP Australia** – Patents, Trade Marks, Designs, **www.ipaustralia.gov.au.**

Volunteering

There are all kinds of reasons for volunteering in Australia. It is a great way to acquire skills, not only in your desired profession, but in many other areas. Many people choose to volunteer not only as a way of giving something back, but to develop professional and personal skills. It is a way of enjoying and challenging yourself, meeting new people as well as getting a reference and experience to add to your CV. It is also a great way to experience the country at a deeper level.

Even those without a working visa can volunteer as long as tourism is the main purpose of their visit.

Before leaving home, it is a good idea to decide exactly where you would like to visit. Then, you can contact a volunteering state centre:

- **Volunteering Australia**, Darwin Office (Northern Territory), **www.volunteeringaustralia.org.**
- **Volunteering Western Australia, www.volunteer.org.au.**
- **Volunteering South Australia, www.volunteeringsa.com.au.**
- **Volunteering Queensland, www.volunteeringqueensland.org.au.**
- **Volunteering New South Wales, www.volunteering.com.au.**
- **Volunteering ACT** (Australian Capital Territory), **www.volunteeract.com.au.**
- **Volunteering Victoria, www.volunteeringvictoria.com.au.**
- **Volunteering Tasmania, www.voltasinc.com.**

Volunteering Australia has informationabout volunteering throughout the country. Alternatively, search the **GoVolunteer** website (**www.govolunteer.com. au**) for an idea of the positions available.

In 2000, nearly 4.5 million Australians over the age of 18 years volunteered in Australia, excluding Sydney Olympic volunteers. The most active age group of volunteers is 35–44 years (40 per cent). On average, people volunteer for around an hour and a half each week. The most common volunteering activities are fund-raising, management, teaching and administration. People tend to choose volunteer activity that reflects their paid employment. Professionals teach (65 per cent), and tradespeople choose maintenance, repairs and gardening work (47 per cent).

A growing trend is for families to volunteer together. This can be particularly beneficial when a family has just relocated, as it can forge links with other individuals and families, and strengthen the family unit. It allows parents, children and other family members to spend time together while contributing to the community and causes they care about.

Involvement Volunteers Association Inc., PO Box 218, Port Melbourne, Victoria 3207, **t** (03) 9646 9392/5504, **ivworldwide@volunteering.org.au**, **www. volunteering.org.au**, runs a programme in which participants pay a fee of A$600 and are placed within a network of voluntary projects around Australia for up to a year. Past placements have included assisting zoology research in Queensland, working at a reptile park in South Australia, and social service work with disabled people.

Big Brothers Big Sisters, **www.bbbsa.org.au**, began in the USA as a way of mentoring children who were coming through the criminal courts and encouraging them into education and the workforce, and it has been operating in Australia for 20 years. It is a preventative programme, which provides vulnerable young people aged between 7 and 17 years with a volunteer adult who can be a role model and a supportive friend.

The main conservation organisation in Australia is the **Australian Trust for Conservation Volunteers**, which accepts large numbers of volunteers to help on its 1,500 projects around the country. Work may involve tree planting, seed collection, track maintenance, surveying endangered flora and fauna, and preserving the national heritage. A fee of A$20 a day covers transportation, food and accommodation in caravans, hostels, huts or tents. Further details are available from the ATCV National Office, Box 423, Ballarat, Victoria 3353, **t** (03) 5333 1483, **www.conservationvolunteers.com.au**.

Willing Workers on Organic Farms, WWOOF; Mount Murrindal Cooperative, Buchan, Victoria 3885; **t** (03) 5155 0218, **www.wwoof.org**, is a worldwide organisation that links travellers with organic farmers. If you are travelling alone on a limited budget, it can be a great way to see the country to work with WWOOF. Membership costs A$50 or A$60 for two people travelling together. WWOOF publishes the 'Organic Farm & Cultural Experience List', with the addresses of more than 1,500 member farmers in Australia who are looking for short- or long-term voluntary help. Opportunities are not restricted to farming, so you might get to muck out at a horse-riding business in Tasmania, carry out some admin at a yoga centre in Sydney, or lend a hand at an artists' retreat in Queensland.

WWOOFing in Australia is restricted to those who are at least 17 years old, but many hosts are happy to have children to stay. To find something to suit you, read all entries in the WWOOF book carefully before making a selection and then call with any questions. The *WWOOF Australia* book makes a good point, which applies to any kind of volunteering: 'If you see your host as free food and accommodation, your host will see you as cheap labour.'

Below are some other contacts for interesting volunteer work:

- **Australian Tropical Research Foundation**, PMB 5, Cape Tribulation, Queensland 4873, **t** (07) 4098 0063, **austrop@austrop.org.au**, **www.austrop.org.au**. Volunteers must be over the age of 23 and able to contribute about A$15 per day in return for lodging.

- **CALM** (Conservation and Land Management), Department of Western Australia, Locked Bag 104, Bentley Delivery Centre, WA 6983, **t** (08) 9334 0333, **www.calm.wa.gov.au**. Offers a volunteer programme open to anyone, although accommodation is not necessarily provided.

- **CCUSA/Work Experience Downunder**, 2330 Marinship Way, Suite 250, Sausalito, CA 94965, USA, **t** (415) 339 2740 or **t** 888 449 3872, **downunder@ ccusa.com**, **www.campcounselors.com**. Work-experience programmes in Australia for up to four months.

- **Conservation Volunteers Australia** (CVA), PO Box 423, Ballarat, Victoria 3353, **t** (03) 5333 1483, **www.conservationvolunteers.com.au**. Short- and long-term voluntary conservation projects in Australia. Overseas volunteers participate in a 4- or 6-week package costing A$790–1,175.

- **HELP Exchange, www.helpx.net**. Provides a free information exchange for people who want to work for free accommodation and meals in Australia.

- **International Student Exchange Pty Ltd**, Unit 16, 172 Redland Bay Road, Capalaba, Queensland 4157, **t** (07) 3390 3838, **ise@i-s-e.com.au**, **www.i-s-e.com.au**. A voluntary work-experience programme allowing people to spend between 3 and 12 months working in a field of their interest, such as animal welfare or theatre without pay. Accommodation is arranged with a host family for SA$55 per night plus a SA$100 application fee.

- **Internship Programs Australia**, 4361 Eastwood Dr., Santa Maria, CA 93455, USA, **t/f** 800 704 4880 or **t/f** 805 937 4880, **www.advc.com/internships**. Arranges unpaid internships in career-related field in Australia. Fees typically are A$4,120 for a 12-week internship. Partner organisation is Global Education Designs in Brisbane.

• The **Office of Multicultural Affairs, t** 6207 6199, has a work-experience programme for long-term unemployed people. This is made up of four weeks of training in office skills, along with a work placement that lasts 8 weeks.

Community Work

Community Work is voluntary work undertaken by job-seekers who register with and are monitored by Community Work co-ordinators (CWCs). The Community Work scheme offers people on income support the opportunity to be part of something worthwhile and get recognition for their contribution. It is also intended to provide the opportunity to gain improved work skills and expe-rience, and to be more involved with their local community. Visit **www. workplace.gov.au/workplace/Category/SchemesInitiatives**.

The Community Work scheme is an 'Australians Working Together' initiative of the Commonwealth Government. It allows people to work in an approved volunteer organisation and earn a training credit to help them find paid work.

Community Work is voluntary work undertaken by job-seekers and income support recipients who are registered with and monitored by a community Work co-ordinator.

The criteria of community work is that it must:

• **be of benefit to the community and the Community Work participant.**

• **not result in any financial payment to participants over and above their income support.**

• **occur only in designated volunteer positions.**

People volunteer for Community Work as a way of gaining work experience. Normally people seek Community Work placements within organisations that they have a genuine interest in. In addition, they may also be interested in the work experience that is provided and how it might improve their chances of gaining ongoing paid employment.

Apart from providing a worthwhile service to their community and an organ-isation, such work is a way of gaining valuable work experience and developing new networks. Credits can be earned in values of A$500, A$650 and A$800, depending on the number of hours a participant works. Mutual obligation is based on the principle that participants supported financially by the commu-nity should actively improve their work skills and give something back to the community that supports them. There are more than ten options a jobseeker can choose from to meet their mutual obligation and Community Work is one of them.

A volunteer organisation arranging Community Work placements must be a not-for-profit organisation, such as a charity, church or religious group, local community association or service organisation, and have public liability insurance cover of at least A$5 million.

The Commonwealth covers participants for personal and medical expenses not covered by Medicare, and participants' public and/or private liability.

It is a good idea to register on the **VolunteerSearch** website (**www.volunteer search.gov.au**) or the **GoVolunteer** website (**www.govolunteer.com.au**). Placements registered on these websites or with a volunteer resource centre are automatically approved for Community Work.

References

08

Australia at a Glance

Capital city: Canberra

Official name of country: Commonwealth of Australia

Type of government: Democratic, federal-state system recognising the British monarch as sovereign

Head of government: Prime Minister John Howard

Constitution: 9 July 1900, effective 1 January 1901

Independence: 1 January 1901 (federation of UK colonies)

Area: 7,686,850 sq km

Coastline: 25,760 km

Geographic highlights: Great Barrier Reef off the east coast, the largest reef in the world; Fraser Island off the coast of Queensland, the planet's largest sand island; the vast expanse of the outback; the natural beauty of Sydney Harbour in the south; lush green tablelands in the north; enormous coast with some of the best beaches in the world; great swaths of rainforest; Blue Mountains in New South Wales coloured by eucalyptus trees; Victoria's Snowy Mountains where skiing is possible; World Heritage Site of the Tasmanian Wilderness

Languages and dialects: English; decreasing number of indigenous languages

Dependent areas: Ashmore and Cartier Islands, Christmas Island, Cocos (Keeling) Islands, Coral Sea Islands, Heard Island and McDonald Islands, Norfolk Island

Neighbouring countries: New Zealand, Papa New Guinea, Indonesia

Surrounding seas: Tasman, Pacific, Coral, Arafura, Timor, Indian Ocean

Population: 19,913,144

Ethnic groups: Caucasian 92 per cent, Asian 7 per cent, Aboriginal and other 1 per cent

Religion: Anglican 26.1 per cent; Roman Catholic 26 per cent; other Christian 24.3 per cent; non-Christian 11 per cent; other 12.6 per cent

GDP purchasing power parity: A$571.4 billion

GDP growth rate: 3 per cent

GDP per capita: A$28,900

Unemployment: 5.3 per cent

Further Reading

Fiction

Oscar and Lucinda, Peter Carey. About a couple on board an ocean liner going to Australia in the 19th century. Critically acclaimed but hard going at times.

True History of the Kelly Gang, Peter Carey. Skilful and authentic story of the infamous outlaw Ned Kelly and his gang, told in the form of a journey.

The Potato Factory Trilogy, Bryce Courtenay. Dense tales set in Australia's difficult past.

A Town Like Alice, Nevil Shute. Story of a Second World War survivor who goes back to Malaya after being taken a prisoner of war.

Non-fiction

Songlines, Bruce Chatwin. Classic by one of the world's great travel writers. Beautiful, erudite and comic account of following the invisible pathways known as songlines used by the Aborigines.

Australia: True Stories of Life Down Under, ed. Larry Habegger (Travelers' Tales). A wonderful collection of tales from the likes of such bright lights as Paul Theroux and Jan Morris.

In a Sunburned Country, Bill Bryson. Typical Bryson offering, but thorough and entertaining.

One for the Road, Tony Horwitz. Pulitzer Prize-winning author's account of his 7,000-mile adventure around Australia.

History

A Concise History of Australia, Stuart Macintyre. Tells the story of the last 200 years, charting the transformation from penal colony to free nation.

The Floating Brothel: The Extraordinary True Story of an 18th-century Ship and Its Cargo of Female Convicts, Sian Rees. Compelling, true account of 200 female convicts who in 1788 sailed from England to New South Wales, each one taken as a 'wife' their male counterparts.

The Fatal Shore, Robert Hughes. Compassionate description of the early history of Australia, which reads like a novel.

At Home in Australia, Peter Conrad. Evocative descriptions of Australia past and present, documenting the making and the remaking of this vast country from the dry frontier to the hedonistic urban centres, with 200 illustrations.

Food and Wine

The Cook's Companion. Revised edition of this kitchen bible, which has sold over 300,000 copies. Over 1,000 pages about more than 100 ingredients.

Australian Food: In Celebration of the New Australian Cuisine, Alan Saunders. A comprehensive look at modern Australian cooking.

Food of Australia, Stephanie Alexander. Recipes from top Australian restaurants collected by the acclaimed Melbourne chef.

Off the Shelf: Cooking from the Pantry, Donna Hay. Nearly 200 recipes from Australia's most popular food writer.

Australian Wine Companion, James Halliday. Comprehensive guide to Australian wines and wineries that many regard as definitive.

Major Films

Gillian Amstrong, *My Brilliant Career*: a well-loved film and rewarding story of a young woman's quest for a better life.

Oscar and Lucinda, beautiful cinematic adaptation of Peter Carey's novel in which two compulsive gamblers decide to build a glass cathedral and transport it to Australia.

The Last Days of Chez Nous, a massive hit in the 1990s – on the surface, about an everyday suburb in Sydney one summer, but the underlying tensions are revealed with devastating effect.

Jane Campion, *Holy Smoke*. Harvey Keitel and Kate Winslet star in this human tale about a young woman who feels lost in the modern world.

Finding Nemo. Not an Australian film but spectacularly showcases Sydney; Barry Humphries did one of the voiceovers.

Andrew Dominik, *Chopper*. Highly successful film from an erstwhile pop-video director that portrays a savage killer with chilling realism.

Stephan Elliott, *The Adventures Of Priscilla, Queen Of The Desert*. Feel-good road movie about three Australian drag queens.

Peter Faiman, *Crocodile Dundee*. Although past its best, this film about Australian bushman-(Paul Hogan)-meets-city living still has some charm.

Scott Hicks, *Shine*. Widely acclaimed story of a piano prodigy's struggle to master Rachmaninov's difficult 3rd Concerto and his psychological decline.

P.J. Hogan, *Muriel's Wedding*. Frumpy Muriel is wasting away in an Abba-fuelled dream world until her friend masterminds her escape. Fast-paced and funny.

Ray Lawrence, *Lantana*. Slick murder mystery in which various members of a Sydney suburb become inexplicably entangled. Suspenseful and superbly acted.

Baz Luhrmann, *Strictly Ballroom*. A world box office success, this film tells the tale of a maverick ballroom dancer with a wonderful lightness of touch.

George Miller, *Mad Max*. Max is a policeman who patrols an apocalyptic landscape ruled by brutal motorcycle gangs.

Chris Noonan, *Babe*. Oscar-winning tale of a little pig who acts as sheepdog. A real treat from 'down under' that is great fun.

Phillip Noyce, *Rabbit-Proof Fence*. Poignant and beautifully photographed film about three small Aboriginal girls taken from their families as part of a government programme to assimilate them into white culture.

Peter Weir, *Gallipoli*. Acclaimed Australian drama that won nine AFI awards about two young men in the deadly battle for Gallipoli during the Second World War; *Picnic at Hanging Rock*. Haunting modern classic based on a true story in which some schoolgirls mysteriously went missing in 1900.

Public Holidays

1 January New Year's Day
Nearest Monday to 26 January Australia Day
Good Friday
Easter Saturday
Easter Monday
25 April Anzac Day
10 June Queen's Birthday
25 December Christmas Day
26 December Boxing Day

Most Australian states and territories observe the public and national holidays. Some also have additional public holidays during the year such as Labor Day and the Queen's birthday. Offices and banks are usually closed on public holidays. In larger cities, most shops, restaurants and public transport continue to operate. In smaller towns, most businesses including shops and restaurants are closed. Additionally, each state generally has two or three bank holidays a year – check with the local tourist office.

Festivals and Celebrations

January	**Sydney Festival**, a range of events that take place throughout the whole month, from theatre and music to street perfomance and boat racing.
mid-Jan to mid-Feb	**Midsummer Festival**, Melbourne's annual gay and lesbian festival.

Mon before 26 January	**Nude Surfing** at Sydney's Bondi beach.
26 January	**Australia Day** marks the founding of the first European settlement in Australia. The day is marked by flag-raising and citizenship ceremonies. Some members of the Indigenous communities mark the day as a day of mourning, or of the survival of Indigenous culture.
26 January	**Great Ferry boat race**, when Sydney's ferries are colourfully decorated for a race from Sydney harbour bridge to Manly and back.
26 January	**Survival Day concert**, an important celebration of Aboriginal and Torres Strait Islander Survival. Day-long festival in La Perouse, a suburb of Sydney.
January or February	**Chinese New Year** (date depends on the phase of the moon, for more information go to **www.sydneychinesenewyear.com.au**), celebrates the Lunar New Year in Chinatown with fireworks and dragon boat races.
Throughout February	**Festival of Perth**, the country's oldest arts festival.
March, biennial	**Adelaide Arts Festival** (biennial in even years); innovative arts festival.
First weekend March	**Australia Formula One Grand Prix**
April, biennial	**Barossa Valley Vintage Festival** (biennial in odd years); Germanic festival set in the heart of wine country.
Week before Easter	**Royal Easter Show**, agricultural show with displays and funfair in Sydney.
Five days over Easter	**International Flower and Garden Show**, in Melbourne.
25 April	**Anzac Day**, remembrance services throughout the country.
March and April	**Gay and Lesbian Mardi Gras** (**www.mardigras.org.au**), world-famous festival, which occurs over a month; street and theatre performances, film festival and parties; parade and Mardi Gras party takes place first Sat in March.
Late March/early April	**Golden Slipper Festival**, major Sydney horse race at Rosehill.
Late March/early April	**Royal Easter Show**, 12-day event at the Sydney showground with parade and various events with an agricultural theme.

17 March	**St Patrick's Day**, Melbourne International Comedy Festival (opens on April Fool's Day).
21 March	**Harmony Day**, celebrates Australia's commitment to racial respect and community harmony. The date coincides with the United Nation's International Day for the Elimination of Racial Discrimination. Events are held throughout Australia to celebrate and foster harmony within communities.
April	**Sydney Cup**, second only to the Melbourne cup in importance in Australia, this horse race takes place at Royal Randwick in Sydney (**www.ajc.org.au**).
25 April	**Anzac Day**, commemorates the day the Australian and New Zealand Army Corps landed at Gallipoli in Turkey in 1915. The day is a public holiday and is marked by remembrance, wreath-laying and military parades. The day is also remembered as part of the beginning of Australia's nationhood.
April	**State of Origin Series**, three rugby league games between Queensland and New South Wales teams taking place in Sydney or Brisbane, depending on the winner in the previous year (**www.nrl.com.au**).
April	**Sydney Biennale** (every even-numbered year) this international arts festival takes place at the Art Gallery of New South Wales and other venues in Sydney (**www.biennaleofsydney.com.au**).
Two weeks in June	**Sydney Film Festival**, national and international films.
July	**Camel Cup**, camel racing on Alice Springs' dry Todd River.
First weekend July	**Darwin Beer Can Regatta**.
First weekend July	**Queensland's Brass Monkey Festival**
From 2nd Sun July	**NAIDOC Week** (commences on the second Sunday in July). A day of remembrance of Aboriginal and Torres Strait Islander peoples and heritage. NAIDOC Week is the outcome of a long history of Aboriginal and Torres Strait Islander efforts to bring issues of concern to the attention of governments and the general public. NAIDOC – National Aboriginal and Islanders' Day Observance Committee – is now used widely to refer to all the events and celebrations that go on during National Aboriginal and Torres Strait Islander Week.

July and August	**Carnivale**, a celebration of multiculturalism with food and folk dancing at various venues throughout Sydney (**www.carnivale.com.au**).
2nd Sun in August	**City to Surf Run**, over 50,000 participants race from Park Street in Sydney to Bondi beach (**wwwcity2surf.sunherald.com.au**).
Last weekend August	**Mount Isa Rodeo**, Australia's largest rodeo – held in Queensland
September	**Rugby League Grand Final** (**www.nrl.com.au**), when two national rugby league teams compete for title of 'team of the year'.
17 September	**Australian Citizenship Day** celebrates the importance of Australian Citizenship. First marked in 2001, this annual event is celebrated with special citizenship and affirmation ceremonies.
Early October	**Sleaze Ball** (**www.mardigras.org.au**), a different Sydney venue hosts a huge party for gays, lesbians, transsexuals and others.
First 3 weeks October	**Floriade**, huge flower festival in Canberra.
First Tues November	**Melbourne Cup**, world-famous, 130-year-old horse race. Most Australians whether at work, school or home, stop and watch the race on television. It is a public holiday in metropolitan Melbourne. Elsewhere in Australia many people have a lunch to celebrate the occasion.
24 December	**Carols by Candlelight** in Melbourne and Sydney.
26 December	**Sydney to Hobart Race**, when Sydney Harbour fills with boats seeing off the competitors in this annual race.
26 December	**Cricket Test Match** in Melbourne.
31 December	**New Year's Eve**, fireworks, Sydney Harbour. No, it's not the same as seeing them on television and still manages to make life-long Sydney residents cry with emotion. Locals and tourists alike find themselves a vantage point around the harbour. One display at 9pm for children and another at midnight, both lasting around 20 minutes.

Climate Charts

25 millimetres is approximately equal to 1 inch. A rainy day is counted if rainfall exceeds 0.2mm.

Celsius to Farenheit Conversion

C	0°	5°	10°	15°	20°	25°	30°	35°	40°	45°	50°	55°
F	32°	41°	50°	59°	68°	77°	86°	95°	104°	113°	122°	131°

Historical Rainfall (mm) and Temperature Averages (°C)

Season	Summer			Autumn			Winter			Spring		
Month	Dec	Jan	Feb	Mar	Apr	May	Jun	Jul	Aug	Sep	Oct	Nov
Adelaide												
Maximum Temperature	26°	28°	28°	25°	22°	18°	16°	15°	16°	18°	21°	24°
Minimum Temperature	14°	16°	16°	14°	12°	10°	7°	7°	8°	9°	10°	12°
Average Rainfall	23	17	19	22	38	59	52	65	50	43	38	24
Rainy Days	7	5	4	6	9	14	13	17	16	13	11	8
Alice Springs												
Maximum Temperature	36°	36°	35°	32°	28°	23°	20°	19°	22°	26°	31°	34°
Minimum Temperature	20°	21°	21°	17°	13°	8°	5°	4°	6°	10°	15°	18°
Average Rainfall	37	36	42	38	14	19	14	16	11	9	21	26
Rainy Days	5	5	5	3	2	3	3	3	2	2	5	5
Brisbane												
Maximum Temperature	29°	29°	29°	28°	26°	23°	21°	20°	22°	24°	26°	28°
Minimum Temperature	20°	21°	21°	19°	17°	13°	11°	10°	10°	13°	16°	18°
Average Rainfall	134	160	158	141	94	74	68	57	47	46	76	97
Rainy Days	12	13	13	15	11	10	8	7	7	7	9	10
Broome												
Maximum Temperature	34°	33°	33°	34°	34°	31°	29°	28°	30°	32°	33°	33
Minimum Temperature	26°	26°	26°	25°	22°	18°	15°	13°	15°	18°	22°	25°
Average Rainfall	42	178	162	94	26	31	20	5	2	2	2	9
Rainy Days	5	12	11	8	3	3	2	1	1	1	1	1
Cairns												
Maximum Temperature	32°	31°	31°	30°	29°	27°	26°	26°	27°	28°	29°	31°
Minimum Temperature	23°	24°	24°	23°	22°	20°	18°	17°	17°	19°	20°	22°
Average Rainfall	179	407	422	447	200	98	50	27	25	36	38	94
Rainy Days	13	18	19	20	17	14	9	9	8	8	8	10
Canberra												
Maximum Temperature	26°	28°	27°	24°	20°	15°	12°	11°	13°	16°	19°	23°
Minimum Temperature	11°	13°	13°	11°	7°	3°	1°	0°	1°	3°	6°	9°
Average Rainfall	53	58	57	56	53	49	37	40	47	50	67	63
Rainy Days	8	7	7	7	8	9	9	10	12	10	11	10

Season	Summer			Autumn			Winter			Spring		
Month	Dec	Jan	Feb	Mar	Apr	May	Jun	Jul	Aug	Sep	Oct	Nov
Darwin												
Maximum Temperature	33°	32°	32°	33°	33°	33°	31°	31°	32°	33°	**34°**	**34°**
Minimum Temperature	26°	25°	25°	25°	24°	23°	21°	**20°**	21°	23°	25°	26°
Average Rainfall	242	393	330	258	103	14	3	1	2	13	52	124
Rainy Days	14	19	18	16	7	1	1	1	1	2	5	10
Hobart												
Maximum Temperature	20°	**22°**	21°	20°	17°	14°	12°	12°	13°	15°	17°	18°
Minimum Temperature	11°	12°	12°	11°	9°	7°	5°	**4°**	5°	6°	8°	9°
Average Rainfall	57	48	40	47	52	49	56	54	52	52	64	55
Rainy Days	13	11	10	11	12	14	14	15	15	15	16	14
Melbourne												
Maximum Temperature	24°	**26°**	**26°**	24°	20°	17°	14°	13°	15°	17°	20°	22°
Minimum Temperature	13°	14°	14°	13°	11°	8°	7°	**6°**	7°	8°	9°	11°
Average Rainfall	59	48	48	52	58	58	50	49	51	59	68	60
Rainy Days	11	8	7	9	12	14	14	15	16	15	14	12
Perth												
Maximum Temperature	27°	**30°**	**30°**	29°	25°	21°	19°	18°	18°	20°	22°	25°
Minimum Temperature	16°	18°	19°	17°	14°	12°	10°	**9°**	**9°**	10°	12°	14°
Average Rainfall	14	9	12	19	46	123	182	173	135	80	55	21
Rainy Days	4	3	3	4	8	14	17	18	17	14	11	6
Sydney												
Maximum Temperature	25°	**26°**	**26°**	25°	22°	19°	17°	16°	18°	20°	22°	24°
Minimum Temperature	17°	18°	19°	17°	15°	11°	9°	**8°**	9°	11°	13°	16°
Average Rainfall	78	104	117	135	129	121	131	100	81	69	79	82
Rainy Days	12	12	12	13	12	12	12	10	10	10	11	11

Time Zones

	Australian Summer Time (hours ahead of GMT)	Australian Winter Time (hours ahead of GMT)
Adelaide	+10.5	+8.5
Brisbane	+10	+9
Canberra	+11	+9
Darwin	+10.5	+8.5
Hobart	+11	+9
Melbourne	+11	+9
Perth	+8	+7
Sydney	+11	+9

World Time and Dialling Codes

Using the **www.whitepages.com.au** site, you can enter any two countries and determine the current local time in each country, together with dialling information that helps you call each country.

Telephone Codes and Postcodes

Telephones

Regional calling codes: 500.
To call Australia from abroad, dial +61 before the number and drop the first 0.

Telephone Area Codes by Region and State

Central East Region (NSW, ACT, parts of northern Victoria)	02
South East Region (Tasmania, most of Victoria and parts of southern NSW)	03
Digital GSM mobile phones (all states)	04
North East Region (Queensland)	07
Central and West Region (South Australia, Northern Territory and WA)	08

Postcodes

For those used to the American postal system, Australian postcodes are the equivalent of American zip codes. They identify and refer to localised mail delivery areas throughout the country.

Comprising four digits, the first digit identifies the Australian state or territory:

0 – Northern Territory
2 – New South Wales and the Australian Capital Territory
3 – Victoria
4 – Queensland
5 – South Australia
6 – Western Australia
7 – Tasmania

As an example, the postcode for the Sydney city centre is 2000. Occasionally you will find postcodes starting with 1. These are specific postcodes that direct mail to particular organisations, such as the Australian Taxation Office, which may have offices in two or more states or territories.

Postcode Search for Australia

On **www.whitepages.com.au** you can search for any Australian postcode and be provided with the suburb name and state or, alternatively, enter a suburb name and be provided with all the matching postcodes across all of Australia.

Resources

- **www.about-australia.com**: highly eclectic site with a personalised directory and interesting features.
- **www.australia.com**: the Australian Tourism Commission site.
- **www.australia-online.com**: useful links, and a guide to Australian slang.
- **www.domain.com.au**: if property is the new porn, this should excite users with its details of homes around Australia, including auctions, agent information and holiday rentals.
- **www.goinglobal.com/countries/australia/australia_work**: directory of resources with useful articles.
- **www.immi.gov.au/allforms/working.htm**: Australian government site, with comprehensive information about immigrating to Australia, including a range of booklets for potential settlers.
- **www.kidslife.com.au**: about life for the little ones down under.
- **www.liveinvictoria.vic.gov.au**: dedicated information about living in the state of Victoria.
- **www.nationwide.com.au**: a directory of businesses across Australia.
- **www.newcomersnetwork.com/mel/home/index.php**: 'Australia's first network for newcomers'.
- **www.surfinglife.net**: for those who love to take to the waves.
- **www.workingin-australia.com**: up-to-date information about job opportunities and information about living in and getting to Australia; lists top occupations and offers a CV service.

Tourist Offices

- **Australian Tourism Commission**, Level 4, 80 William Street, Woolloomooloo NSW 2011, **t** (02) 9360 1111, **f** (02) 9331 6469.

Australian Capital Territory

- **Canberra Tourism and Events Corporation**, Locked Bag 2001, Civic Square ACT 2608, (visiting address: Level 13, SAP House, Cnr Bunda and Akuna Streets), **t** (02) 6205 0044 or **t** 1800 100 660, accommodation and booking, **f** (02) 6205 0776, **canberra_tourism@dpa.act.gov.au**, **www.canberratourism.com.au**.

New South Wales

- **Tourism New South Wales**, 55 Harrington Street, Sydney NSW 2000, **t** (02) 9931 1434, **f** (02) 9931 1424, **visitor.callcentre@tourism.nsw.gov.au**,

www.tourism.nsw.gov.au; for sport and recreation information visit **www.dsr.nsw.gov.au**.

Northern Territory

- **Northern Territory Tourist Commission**, GPO Box 1155, Darwin, Northern Territory 0801, **t** 1800 808 666 freecall in Australia, **t** (08) 8951 8471, **f** (08) 8951 8550, **nttc@nt.gov.au**, **www.australiasoutback.com**, **www.ntholidays.com www.nttc.com.au**.

Queensland

- **Gulf Savannah**, main office, Tourism Gulf Savannah, 74 Abbott Street, PO Box 2312, Cairns Qld 4870, **t** (07) 4031 163, **f** (07) 4031 3340, **www.gulf-savannah.com.au**.

- **Moreton Bay Coast & Country Tourism**, PO Box 538, Redcliffe Qld 4020, **t** (07) 3889 5218, **f** (07) 3883 1723, **info@mbcc.com.au**, **www.mbcc.com.au**.

- **Tourism Noosa**, PO Box 581, Noosa Heads QLD 4567, **t** 1800 44 88 33, **info@tourismnoosa.com.au**, **www.tourismnoosa.com.au**.

- **Tourism Pine Rivers Association Inc (Brisbane Hinterland)**, PO Box 561, Strathpine Qld 4500, **info@brisbanehinterland.com.au**, **www.brisbanehinterland.com.au**.

- **Tropical Tableland Promotion Bureau**, Atherton Tableland Information Centre, Corner of Main & Silo Roads, Atherton, Qld 4883, **t** (07) 4091 4222, **f** (07) 4091 5828, **infocen@athertonsc.qld.gov.au**, **www.athertontableland.com**.

Tasmania

- **Tourism Tasmania**, GPO Box 399, Hobart Tasmania 7001, **t** (03) 6230 8352, **f** (03) 6230 8353, **tasinfo@discovertasmania.com**, **www.discovertasmania.com**.

Victoria

- **Tourism Victoria**, GPO 2219T, Melbourne, Victoria 3000, **t** (03) 9653 9777, **f** (03) 9653 9744, **international@tourism.vic.gov.au**, **www.visitmelbourne.com**.

- **Yarrawonga Mulwala Tourism Inc**, Irvine Parade, Yarrawonga, Victoria 3730, **t** (03) 5744 1989, **f** (03) 5744 3149, **tourism@yarrawongamulwala. com.au**, **www.yarrawongamulwala.com.au**.

Western Australia

- **Western Australian Tourism Commission**, Western Australian Visitor Centre, GPO Box W2081, Perth, WA 6846, **t** 1300 361 351, **t** (08) 9483 1111, **f** (08) 9481 0190, **www.westernaustralia.net**, **www.csu.edu.au.australia/wa.html**, **www.perthtouristcentre.com**.

Transport

State Buses

Australian Capital Territory

- **Australian Capital Territory Internal Omnibus Network (ACTION),** t (02) 6207 7611, **www.action.act.gov.au.**
- **Murray's, t** 13 2251.
- **Transborder Express, t** (02) 6241 0033.
- **Wayward Bus, t** 1800 882 823.

New South Wales

- **Ando's Outback Adventure, t** (02) 9559 2901.
- **Bathurst Coaches, www.bathurstcoaches.com.au.**
- **Berrima Coaches, www.berrimacoaches.com.au.**
- **Blanch's, t** (02) 6686 2144.
- **Black and White Bus Company, www.blackandwhitebus.com.**
- **Blue Mountains Bus Company, t** (02) 4782 4213.
- **Blue Mountains Explorer Bus, t** (02) 4782 4807 .
- **Blue Ribbon Coaches, www.blue-ribbon.com.au.**
- **Busways, www.busways.com.au.**
- **Cavanaugh's, t** (02) 6562 7800, **www.cavanaghs.com.au.**
- **Cockatoo Run, t** 1800 643 801.
- **Coffs Harbour Coaches, t** (02) 6652 2877, **www.holidaycoast.net.au. coffsharbour/bus.html.**
- **Countrylink, t** 13 2232, **www.countrylink.nsw.gov.au.**
- **Deane's Bus Lines, www.deanesbuslines.com.au.**
- **Dions Bus Service, www.dions.com.au.**
- **Dubbo Bus Station, t** (02) 6884 2411.
- **Dubbo Coaches, www.dubbocoaches.com.au.**
- **Firefly Express, t** (02) 9211 1644, **www.pixeltech.com.au/firefly.**
- **Golden Gateway Travel, t** (02) 5536 6600.
- **Great Lakes Coaches, t** 1800 043 263.
- **Jessup's, t** (02) 6653 4552.
- **Joyce's, t** (02) 6655 6330.

- **Keans Travel Express Coaches, t** 1800 043 339.
- **Kiama Coachlines, www.pixeltech.com.au/firefly**.
- **Kingsford Smith Transport, t** (02) 9667 0663.
- **Kirklands, t** (02) 6622 1499, **www.kirklands.com.au**.
- **Lord Howe Island Nature, t** 1800 806 820.
- **Manly Coaches, www.manlycoach.com.au**.
- **Marsh's Bus Service, t** (02) 6686 7324.
- **Metrolink, www.manlycoach.com.au**.
- **Mountainlink, www.manlycoach.com.au**.
- **Newcastle Travel Information Centre, t** (02) 4961 8933.
- **Newmans, t** (02) 6568 1296.
- **Nimbin Shuttle Bus, t** (02) 6680 9189.
- **Orange Coaches, www.orangecoaches.com.au**.
- **Oz Experience, t** (02) 9368 1766, **www.ozexperience.com**.
- **Pioneering Spirit, t** 1800 672 422.
- **Port Macquarie Bus Service, t** (02) 6583 2161.
- **Port Stephens Buses, t** (02) 4982 2940, **www.psbuses.nelsonbay.com**.
- **Premier Motor Service, t** 13 3410.
- **Rendell's Coaches, t** 1800 023 328.
- **Ryan's Buses, t** (02) 6652 3201.
- **Sawtell Coaches, t** (02) 6653 3344.
- **Sid Fogg's, t** 1800 045 952.
- **Surfside, t** 13 1230.
- **Sydney Airporter, t** (02) 9667 3800.

Northern Territory

- **Alice Mini Bus, t** (08) 8955 1222.
- **Alice Springs Airport Shuttle Bus, t** (08) 8953 0310.
- **Alice Wanderer Bus, t** 1800 669 111.
- **Blue Banana Tour Bus, t** (08) 8945 6800, **www.octa4.net.au/banana**.
- **Darwin Airport Shuttle Bus, t** 1800 358 945.
- **Darwin Bus Terminal, t** (08) 8924 7666.
- **Darwin City Shuttle Service, t** (08) 8985 3666.
- **Darwinbus, t** (08) 8981 5233.

Queensland

- **Airporter, t** (07) 5588 8777.
- **Allstate Scenic Tours, t** (07) 3285 1777.
- **Australia Coach Shuttle Bus, t** (07) 4031 3555.
- **Barbours Bus and Coach, t** (07) 4974 9030.
- **Brisbane Bus Lines** (Brisbane), **www.brisbanebuslines.com.au.**
- **Buslink, www.buslinkqld.com.au.**
- **Caboolture Bus Lines, www.caboolturebuslines.com.au.**
- **Cairns Explorer, t** (07) 4033 5244.
- **Coachtrans, t** (07) 5506 9777, **www.buslines.com.au/coachtrans.**
- **Coral Coaches, t** (07) 4031 3555,
www.greatbarrierreef.aus.net/coralcoaches.
- **Gold Coast Air Bus, t** (07) 5527 4144.
- **Kirklands, t** (02) 6622 1499.
- **Kynoch Coaches, www.kynoch.com.au.**
- **Mackay Transit, www.mackaytransit.com.au.**
- **Magenetic Island Bus Service, www.mbtravel.com.au/ferrybus.**
- **Maryborough-Hervey Bay Coaches, t** (07) 4121 3719.
- **Mission Beach Bus Service, t** (07) 4068 7400.
- **Mountain Coach Company, t** (07) 5524 4249.
- **North Stradbroke Island Bus Service, t** (07) 3409 7151.
- **Premier Pioneer Motor Services, t** 1300 368 100.
- **Rothery's Coaches, t** (07) 4922 3813.
- **Ruby Charters Coaches, t** (07) 4743 0576.
- **Stagecoach Queensland, www.stagecoach.qld.com.au.**
- **Sunair, www.sunair.com.au.**
- **Sunbus, t** 13 1230, **www.sunbus.com.au.**
- **Suncoast Pacific, t** (07) 3236 1901, **www.noosanet.com.au/
suncoastpacific.**
- **Suncoast Pacific Bus Terminal, t** (07) 5443 1011.
- **Sunshine Coast Coaches, t** (07) 5443 4555.
- **Tewantin Bus Services, t** (07) 5449 7422.
- **Townsville Airport Shuttle Bus, t** (07) 4775 5544.
- **Trans-Info Service, t** 13 1230, **www.transinfo.qld.gov.au.**
- **Whitecar Coaches, t** (07) 4091 1855.

- **Wide-Bay Transit Coaches, t** (07) 4121 3719.
- **Young's Coaches, t** (07) 4922 3813.

South Australia

- **ABM Coachlines, t** (08) 8347 3336.
- **Adelaide Airport Bus Service, t** (08) 8381 5311.
- **Adelaide Coachlines, www.adelaidecoachlines.com.au.**
- **Adelaide Metro, www.adelaidemetro.com.au.**
- **Adelaide Sighseeing, t** (08) 8231 4144.
- **Barossa Adelaide Passenger Service, t** (08) 8564 3022.
- **BusSA, www.bussa.com.au.**
- **Firefly Express, t** (08) 8231 1488 **/t** 1800 631 164.
- **Hills Transit, t** (08) 8339 1191.
- **Mid North Passenger Service, t** (08) 8826 2346.
- **Murray Bridge Passenger Service, t** (08) 8532 6660.
- **Premier Stateliner, t** (08) 8415 5555, **www.premierstateliner.com.au.**
- **Sealink Shuttle, t** 13 1301.
- **Serco Bus, www.sercobus.com.au.**
- **Smart Car, t** (08) 8554 3788.
- **Southlink, www.southlink.com.au.**
- **TransAdelaide, t** (08) 8210 1000, **www.transadelaide.sa.gov.au.**
- **Transitplus, www.transitplus.com.au.**
- **Victorian V/Line Bus Service, t** (08) 8231 7620 or **t** 1800 817 037.
- **Whyalla City Transport, www.whyalla.sa.gov.au.**
- **Yorke Peninsula Passenger Service, t** (08) 8391 2977.

Tasmania

- **Broadby's, t** (03) 6376 3488.
- **Tamar Valley Coaches, t** (03) 6330 1119.
- **Tasmanian Redline, www.tasredline.com.au.**
- **Tasmaniam Tours and Tigerline, t** (03) 6271 7333 or **t** 1300 653 633, **www.tigerline.com.au.**
- **The Metro, t** 13 2201, **www.metrotas.com.au.**
- **TRC, t** 1300 360 000.
- **TWT, t** 1300 300 520, **www.tassie.net.au/wildtour/mainmenu.htm.**

Victoria

- **Ballarat Transit Centre, t** (03) 5331 7777.
- **Christian's Buslines, t** (03) 5447 2222.
- **Countrylink, t** 13 2232.
- **Gull Airport Service, t** (03) 5222 4966.
- **Martyrs Bus Service, t** (03) 5966 2035.
- **McHarry's Bus Lines, t** (03) 5223 2111.
- **McKenzie's Bus Lines, t** (03) 5962 5088.
- **Met Information Centre, t** 13 1638.
- **Omeo Bus Lines, t** (03) 5159 4231.
- **Portsea Passenger Buses, t** (03) 5986 5666.
- **Pyle's Coaches, t** (03) 5754 4024.
- **Skybus, t** (03) 9662 9275.
- **Trekset Snow Services, t** (03) 9370 9055.
- **Tullamarine Bus Lines, t** (03) 9338 3817.
- **V/Line, t** 13 6196.
- **Walkers Buslines, t** (03) 5443 9333.
- **Wayward Bus Touring Company, t** 1800 882 823.
- **Wild-Life Tours, t** (03) 9747 1882.

Western Australia

- **Airport Shuttle Bus, t** (08) 9479 4131.
- **Bunbury City Transport, t** (08) 9791 1955, **www.bct.com.au.**
- **Catch-a-Bus, t** 019 378 987.
- **Connex WA, www.connexwa.com.au.**
- **Easyrider Backpackers, t** (08) 9226 0307.
- **Fremantle Airport Shuttle, t** (08) 9838 4115.
- **Hedlands Bus Lines Service, t** (08) 9172 1394.
- **Integrity Coach Lines, t** (08) 9226 1339.
- **Kalgoorlie Adventure Bus, t** (08) 9091 1958.
- **Majestic Tours, t** (08) 9948 1640.
- **Path Transit, www.path.com.au.**
- **Perth Goldfields Express, t** 1800 620440.
- **Perth Tram Company, www.perthtram.com.au.**
- **Pinnacle Tours, www.pinnacletours.com.au.**

- **South-West Coachlines, t** (08) 9324 2333.
- **Southern Coast Transit, www.sctransit.com.au.**
- **Swan Gold Charter Tours, www.ca.com.au.swangold.**
- **Swan Transit, www.swantransit.com.au.**
- **Town Bus, t** (08) 9193 6585.
- **Transperth, www.transperth.wa.gov.au.**
- **Westrail, t** 13 1053.

Trains

National train information is available from:

- **CityRail, www.cityrail.nsw.gov.au.**
- **Citytrain (Queensland Rail), t** (07) 3606 5555, **www.citytrain.com.au.**
- **Countrylink, www.countrylink.nsw.gov.au.**
- **Great Northern Railway, www.greatnorthernrail.com.au.**
- **Great South Pacific Express, www.gspe.com.au.**
- **Great Southern Railways, t** 132147, **www.gsr.com.au.**
- **TransAdelaide, www.transadelaide.sa.gov.au.**
- **TransPerth, www.transperth.wa.gov.au.**
- **Traveltrain (Queensland Rail), t** 1300 131 722, **www.traveltrain.com.au.**
- **V/Line, www.vline.vic.gov.au.**
- **West Coast Railway, www.wcr.com.au.**

Australian Capital Territory

- **Countrylink Travel Centre, t** (02) 6257 1576, Kingston Train Station, **t** 13 2232.

New South Wales

- **Coffs Harbour Train Station, t** (02) 6651 2757.
- **Skitube (Snowy Mountain), www.perisherblue.com.au/skitube.**
- **Sydney Airport Link, www.airportlink.com.au.**
- **Sydney Light Rail, t** (02) 9660 5288, **www.metrolightrail.com.au.**
- **Sydney Monorail, t** (02) 9552 2288, **www.metromonorail.com.au** .
- **STA, t** 13 1500, **www.131500.com.au.**

Queensland

- **Airtrain** (airports), **www.airtrain.com.au.**
- **City Train** (suburban), **www.qr.com.au.**

- **Queensland Rail, t** 13 2232, **www.qr.com.au.**
- **Queensland Rail Travel Centre (RTC), t** (07) 3235 1331.
- **Skyrail Rainforest Cableway, t** (07) 4038 1555.
- **Trans-Info Service, t** 13 1230, **www.transinfoservice.qld.gov.au.**
- **Traveltrain Holidays, t** 1800 627 655, **www.traveltrain.qr.com.au.**

South Australia

- **Adelaide Metro, www.adelaidemetro.com.au.**
- **Bluebird Tourist Train, t** (08) 8212 7888.
- **Great Southern Railway, t** 13 2147.
- **Steam Ranger, t** (08) 8391 1223.
- **Transadelaide, t** (08) 8210 1000, **www.transadelaide.sa.gov.au.**

Victoria

- **Met Information Centre, t** 13 1638.

Western Australia

- **Australian Railroad Group, www.arg.net.au.**
- **Great Southern Railways, t** 13 2147, **www.gsr.com.au.**
- **Transperth, www.transperth.wa.gov.au, t** 13 6213.
- **Western Australia Government Railways, www.wagr.wa.gov.au.**
- **Westrail, www.westrail.wa.gov.au.**

Airlines

- **Skywest Airlines Pty Ltd**, Domestic Airport, Perth, WA 6105 (PO Box 176, Cloverdale, WA. 6985), **t** 1300 66 00 88 (call centre) or **t** (08) 9478 9999, **f** (08) 9478 9928, **www.skywest.com.au.** Office open Mon–Fri 8.30am–5pm (AWST); call centre daily 7am–7pm. Book flights using the reservation system on the home page or contact your local travel agent.

- **Qantas**, Qantas Centre, 203 Coward Street, Mascot, NSW 2020, **t** (02) 9691 3636, **t** 13 13 13 (flights and hotels), **t** (02) 9304 7020 (hotels), **www.qantas.com.au.**

- **Jetstar**, PO Box 23, Mendana Avenue, Honiara, Solomon Islands (GPO Box 4713, Melbourne, VIC 3001), **t** (677) 20031, **t** (03) 8341 4901 (enquiries), **t** (03) 8341 4902 (travel agent support), **www.jetstar.com.**

- **Solomon Airlines, www.solomonairlines.com.au.**

- **Virgin Blue, www.virginblue.com.au/.** Contact centre open 24 hours a day, 7 days a week. To speak with a guest contact centre consultant call **t** 13

6789 (calls from Australia), **t** +61 7 3295 2296 (calls from elsewhere).

- **Pacific Blue, www.virginblue.com.au/, t** 13 1645 (calls from Australia), **t** 0800 67 0000 (calls from New Zealand), **t** +61 7 3295 2284 (calls from elsewhere).

- **Australian Airlines**, SYDAPC5, 203 Coward St, Mascot 2020, **t** 13 13 13 (reservations), **t** 1300 799 798, **www.australianairlines.com.au**. For customers outside Australia, contact your local Qantas office.

- **United Airlines**, PO Box 3755, Sydney 2001, **t** toll free 131 777, **www.unitedairlines.com.au**. Offices open Mon–Fri 8am–6pm EST (NZ 9am–5pm), Sat 8am–4pm EST (NZ 10am–6pm).

- **Macair, t** 13 13 13 (reservations), **www.macair.com.au**. Also **t** (07) 4729 9444, **f** (07) 4729 9499 (Townsville); **t** (07) 4775 5076, **f** (07) 4775 6964 (Townsville Airport); **t** (07) 4035 9505 (Cairns); **t** (07) 3274 3663, **f** (07) 3274 5884 (Brisbane).

- **Alliance Airlines**, PO Box 1126, Eagle Farm, Brisbane, Queensland 4009, **t** (07) 3212 1212, **f** (07) 3212 1297, **www.allianceairlines.com.au**. Offices open Mon–Fri 9am–5pm AEST.

- **Golden Eagle Airlines**, PO Box 819, Port Hedland, WA 6721, **t** (08) 9140 1181, **f** (08) 9140 2341, **m** 0428 910 124 or 0428 910 124 (after hours); PO Box 61, Derby, WA 6728, **t** (08) 9191 1132; callers outside Australia call **t** +61 8 9140 1181, **f** +61 8 9140 2341, **m** +61 428 910 124 or +61 428 910 124 (after hours); **www.goldeneagleairlines.com**. Regional airline services in the northwest of western Australia.

Car Rental Companies

- **Avis Rent A Car, www.avis.com.au**. Make your booking online, earn frequent-flyer points and choose from a range of cars. Cars are available from depots located in Adelaide, Brisbane, Cairns, Darwin, Melbourne and Sydney. One-way hires are possible between all depots.

- **Nova Rent a Car, www.novao2.rentacar-worldwide.com**, has offices at airports and cities all around Australia including Adelaide, Alice Springs, Belmont, Brisbane, Cairns, Canberra, Coffs Harbour, Coolangatta, Darwin, Devonport, Fremantle, Geelong, Gold Coast, Hobart, Katherine, Launceston, Maroochydore, Melbourne, Noosa, Perth, Surfers Paradise and Sydney.

- **Value Rent A Car**, Canberra Ave. Forrest, ACT 2603, **t** 1800 629 561 or **t** (02) 6295 6155, **f** (02) 6295 6845, **www.value-cars.com**.

- **Apex Rent A Car, www.apexrentacar.com.au**. The company has small, medium and large cars available from depots located in Adelaide, Brisbane, Cairns, Darwin, Melbourne and Sydney. One-way hires are possible between all depots.

- **Aussie Campervans, www.australiancampervans.com**. Vehicles are available for pick up and drop off in Adelaide, Alice Springs, Broome, Brisbane, Cairns, Darwin, Hobart, Melbourne, Perth and Sydney. The company can arrange a rental vehicle by email.

- **Advance Car Rentals, www.advancecars.com.au**. Tasmania's largest independent car rental operator.

- **Auto Rentals Australia Wide, www.autorentals.com.au**. A nationwide rental service that can provide campervan, motorhome, 4WD campers and car hire to and from all major holiday destinations. Cars, vans and minibuses are available as well as 4WD campers and 4WD wagons. Tasmania and New Zealand rentals also available

- **KEA Campers Australia, www.keacampers.com/australia**. New campervans, motorhomes and 4WDs are available for independent travel. Experienced multilingual staff and an extensive network of rental depots at Adelaide, Alice Springs, Broome, Brisbane, Cairns, Darwin, Melbourne, Perth and Sydney.

- **NQ Rentals, www.campervansaust.com.au/index**. Many different types of camper vans and motorhomes in which to tour Australia.

- **Traveller's Mate, www.travellersmate.com.au**. A family-run business dedicated to supplying budget travellers with an affordable and reliable means in which to explore Australia. A range of cars includes campervans, 4WDs, panelvans, vans and semi-campervans.

- **Wheelabout, www.wheelabout.com**. An Australian-based service providing wheelchair-accessible van rentals for long- or short-term hire. The company caters for the individual needs of travellers with a disability, and for older people.

- **Wicked Campers, www.wickedcampers.com.au**. All Wicked Campers are fitted to the company's own design, allowing for maximum space and comfort. Vehicles are also painted in a wide variety of styles and colours, guaranteed to get attention on your travels.

- **Australian Campervans, www.australiancampervans.com**. Motorhomes, camper vans, cars and 4WDs for your travel all over Australia at competitive prices.

- **KEA Campers Australia, www.keacampers.com/australia**. Specialises in budget car hire, 4x4 campers and 4WD vehicles in the Northern Territory. Offices located in Alice Springs, Darwin and Katherine. One-way rentals to major cities, camping equipment for hire, airport pickup.

- **Ace Tourist Rentals Pty Ltd, www.acerentals.com.au**. A small, family-owned, car rental company specialising in rental car hire to visitors to Queensland arriving and departing through Brisbane.

- **Motorcycle and Car Rentals, www.globalcars.com.au.** Choose from a heavy-duty Harley-Davidson with power to spare on the highway to a nippy 250cc trail bike with enough power to shift two people around town.

- **Rolo Rent a Car, www.rolorentacar.com.au.** From small economy cars to large luxury saloons and minibuses.

- **Skippy Winnebago Motorhomes, www.skippy.com.au.** Head office in Adelaide, with agents in Alice Springs, Brisbane, Cairns, Darwin, Melbourne, Perth and Sydney.

- **Hertz, www.autorent.com.au.** All needs are catered for, whether it's a short business trip or a touring holiday. Choose from a small manual hatchback through to a full-size automatic or an eight-seater people mover for the larger family or group.

- **Rent a Bug, www.view.com.au/bug.** The latest-model Beetles that are clean, well presented and ready for travel for unlimited mileage. Other vehicles available at a price to suit different budgets include early and recent model Mazdas, Holdens, Fords, Nissans and Toyotas in sedans, wagons and minibuses.

Education

State Departments of Education

Australian Capital Territory

- **ACT Department of Education and Community Services**, decs.webmaster@act.gov.au, **www.decs.act.gov.au**.

New South Wales

- **NSW Department of Education and Training**, 35 Bridge Street, Sydney, **www.schools.nsw.edu.au**.

Northern Territory

- **NT Department of Education**, GPO Box 4821, 69 Smith Street, Darwin, NT 0800, **www.nt.gov.au/nted**.

Queensland

- **Education Queensland**, PO Box 33, Brisbane Albert Street, Queensland 4002, **http://education.qld.gov.au**.

South Australia

- **Department of Education, Training and Employment**, GPO Box 1152, Adelaide, 5001, **t** (08) 8226 1527, **f** (08) 8226 1234, **infodesk@learnsa.net**, **www.learnsa.net/learnsa/Default.htm**.

Tasmania

- **Department of Education**, Deputy Secretary (Schools and Colleges), 5th Floor, 116 Bathurst St, Hobart 7000, **www.tased.edu.gov.au**.

Victoria

- **Department of Employment, Education and Training**, 2 Treasury Place, East Melbourne, 3002, **t** (03) 9637 2000, **www.eduvic.vic.gov.au**, **www.sofweb.vic.edu.au**.

Western Australia

- **Education Department of Western Australia**, 151 Royal Street, East Perth, WA 6004, **t** (08) 9264 4111, **f** (08) 9264 5005, **www.eddept.edu.au**.

Association of Independent Schools

Australian Capital Territory

- **Association of Independent Schools of the ACT Inc.**, 42 Tyrrell Circuit, Kaleen, ACT 2617, **t** (02) 6241 2429, **f** (02) 6241 5923, **aisact@ais.act.edu.au**, **www.ais.act.edu.au**.

New South Wales

- **Association of Independent Schools New South Wales**, StudentNet Limited, Level 4, 99 York Street, Sydney, NSW 2000, **t** (02) 9299 2845, **f** (02) 9290 2274, **manager@studentnet.edu.au, www.studentnet.edu.au** or **www.aisnsw.edu.au**.

Queensland

- **Association of Independent Schools of Queensland Inc.**, First Floor, 96 Warren Street, Spring Hill, QLD 4000 (PO Box 957, Spring Hill QLD 4004, Australia), **t** (07) 3228 1515, **f** (07) 3228 1575, **office@aisq.qld.edu.au, www.aisq.qld.edu.au**.

South Australia

- **Association of Independent Schools of SA**, 301 Unley Road, Malvern SA 5061, **t** (08) 8179 1400, **f** (08) 8373 1116, **office@ais.sa.edu.au, www.ais.sa.edu.au**.

Tasmania

- **Association of Independent Schools of Tasmania**, PO Box 616, Sany Bay, TAS 7006, **t** (03) 6224 01 25, **aist@tassie.net.au, www.aist.tas.edu.au**.

Victoria

- **Association of Independent Schools of Victoria Inc.**, 20 Garden Street, South Yarra, VIC 3141, **t** (03) 9825 7200, **moreinfo@ais.vic.edu.au, www.ais.vic.edu.au**.

Western Australia

- **Association of Independent Schools of Western Australia**, Suite 3, 41 Walters Drive, Osborne Park, WA 6017, **t** (08) 9244 2788, **f** (08) 9244 2786, **aiswa@ais.wa.edu.au, www.ais.wa.edu.au**.

Index